Romantic Cities Series

ROMANTIC

DAYS AND NIGHTS IN

CHICAGO

INTIMATE ESCAPES IN THE WINDY CITY

by Susan Figliulo

The Globe Pequot Press

OLD SAYBROOK, CONNECTICUT

Cover design, text design, and illustrations by Mullen & Katz

Library of Congress Cataloging-in-Publication Data

Figliulo, Susan.
    Romantic days and nights in Chicago : intimate escapes in the windy city /
        Susan Figliulo.—1st ed.
        p.   cm. — (Romantic cities series)
    "A Voyager book."
    Includes index.
    ISBN 1-56440-972-4
    1. Chicago (Ill.)—Guidebooks.   I. Title.   II. Series.
F548.18.F54   1996
917.73'110443—dc20   96-44136
                                                          CIP

Manufactured in the United States of America
First Edition/First Printing

With thanks to all my teachers
and love to my guys

ACKNOWLEDGMENTS

From the bottom of my heart, I thank the many people who helped with this book. Anne Basye started the ball rolling; my excellent editors, particularly the fabulous Doe Boyle and the equally fabulous Laura Strom kept it going with patience, humor, and the occasional nudge. I received all kinds of help, all of it greatly appreciated, from Grace Faustino, Jeff Felshman, Anne Gregory, Diane Hightower, Nicole Hollander, Patsy and David Oser, Mary Shaw, Sue Telingator, Shannon Thor, Hedy Weiss, and the writers. My family was wonderful, especially Stan and Barbara, Carly, Jeanne Bean, my mother, and my sisters. Finally, thanks to Steve Rosswurm for doing whatever he could, even at the last minute.

CHICAGO AND ENVIRONS

Northwestern University
Evanston
Andersonville
CHICAGO
Museum of Science & Industry
Hyde Park
Highland Park
Oak Park
Lake Shore Dr.
John F. Kennedy Expressway
Eisenhower Expressway
Chicago-O'Hare International Airport

94 90 41 55 290 57 25

21 1 3 10 13 26 25

Waveland Avenue Golf Course
Bird Sanctuary
Belmont Harbor
LAKE SHORE DRIVE
Lincoln Park Conservatory
Lincoln Park Zoo
Farm In The Zoo
Chicago Historical Society
STATE PARKWAY
Oak Street
900 North Michigan
Shops
Hancock Center
Water Tower Place

41

Live Bait Theater
WRIGLEYVILLE
Wrigley Field
Theatre Building
Briar Street Theatre
Ivanhoe Theater
Touchstone Theater
LAKE VIEW
Apollo Theater
Victory Gardens Theaters
LINCOLN PARK
Steppenwolf Theatre
Royal George Theatre
OLD TOWN
Newberry Library
4th Presbyterian
CLARK STREET
WELLS STREET

BROADWAY STREET
HALSTED STREET
CLARK STREET
BELMONT AVENUE
SOUTHPORT AVENUE
LINCOLN AVENUE
ADDISON STREET
DIVERSEY PARKWAY
DIVERSEY AVENUE
ASHLAND AVENUE
DAMEN AVENUE
FULLERTON AVENUE
WEBSTER AVENUE
ARMITAGE AVENUE
NORTH AVENUE
CLARK STREET
HALSTED STREET
DIVISION STREET
CHICAGO AVENUE
NORTH AVENUE
MILWAUKEE AVENUE

Chicago River
WICKER PARK/BUCKTOWN
Wicker Park

90 94

22 9 10 12 20 18 5 7 19 2 29

9

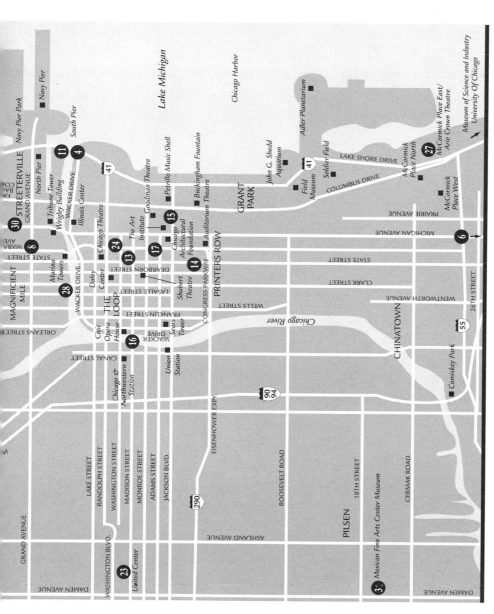

Numbers on map correspond to itinerary numbers (see table of contents).

CONTENTS

INTRODUCTION   viii

HEART OF THE CITY   1

1. SWEET HOME CHICAGO:
   A WEEKEND IN ANDERSONVILLE   3

2. THE GOOD LIFE ON ARMITAGE   13

3. HYDE PARK HONEYMOON   25

4. FIREWORKS FOR TWO:
   A FOURTH OF JULY WEEKEND   33

5. LET IT SNOW:
   A COZY WINTER WEEKEND FOR TWO   43

6. A ROMANCE WITH HISTORY:
   AFRICAN-AMERICAN CHICAGO   49

7. CHICAGO CHRISTMAS À DEUX   57

5. AMORE!
   CHICAGO ROMANCE ITALIAN STYLE   67

NATURAL WONDERS   73

9. ADVENTURES IN LOVE:
   AN OUTDOOR AFFAIR   75

10. LOVE IN BLOOM:
    A GARDEN LOVERS' WEEKEND   81

11. SWEPT AWAY:

ROMANTIC LAKEFRONT CRUISES   89

12. THE ZOO FOR TWO   99

ARTS AND HEARTS   107

13. LOVE BUILT ON BEAUTY:
    ARCHITECTURE IN CHICAGO   109

14. WORDS OF LOVE:
    A LITERARY GETAWAY FOR LOVERS   121

15. ART AND SOUL:
    THE ART INSTITUTE AND MORE   133

16. OPERA LOVERS' TRYST   139

17. THE FOOD OF LOVE:
    MUSIC IN CHICAGO   147

18. SHALL WE DANCE?   155

19. STAGES OF ROMANCE:
    A THEATER LOVERS' WEEKEND   163

20. SMALL PLEASURES   173

THE SPORTING LIFE   179

21. FOOTBALL FANTASIES   181

22. WRIGLEYVILLE WEEKEND   189

23. HOOP LOVERS' HOLIDAY   199

24. ROMANTIC HOLIDAY ON ICE   207

[*Contents*]

OUT OF THIS WORLD **213**

25. STEALING AWAY AT
    STARVED ROCK   215

26. ROMANCE AND THE BUSINESS
    TRAVELER: HOW TO SAVOR THE
    O'HARE AREA   223

27. *UN*-CONVENTIONAL:
    A CHANCE FOR ROMANCE AT
    MCCORMICK PLACE   229

28. ASIAN APPRECIATION WEEKEND   235

29. LOVE IN THE HOT ZONE:
    A TROPICS-INSPIRED WEEKEND   245

30. CITY SLICKERS'
    WESTERN WEEKEND   253

31. HAUNTINGLY ROMANTIC:
    HALLOWEEN WITH YOUR HONEY   261

INDEXES

GENERAL INDEX   268

ROMANTIC RESTAURANTS   272

ROMANTIC LODGINGS   275

NIGHTLIFE   275

The prices and rates listed in this guidebook were confirmed at press time.
We recommend, however, that you call establishments before traveling
to obtain current information.

*A*ny city with a Great Lake in its front yard has a head start on romance. Chicagoans practically live on the lakefront, especially when they're in love. Even the city's legendary winters don't keep sweethearts from strolling and smooching along Lake Michigan's stretch of up-close natural beauty—miles of it within city limits, and nearly all of it couple-friendly, with walking and biking paths, beaches, boating, and much more.

Along the downtown lakefront, Buckingham Fountain is a favorite spot for lovers to linger in its grand presence. If you're here in spring, summer, or autumn, a visit to the fountain is a must when evening falls and colorful lights enhance the play of water in a magnificently choreographed display.

Let it be noted, too, that scarcely a Chicagoan old enough to neck has missed doing so while parked at Montrose Harbor. We were startled when the city announced plans to return that venerable blacktop to grassy parkland, but Chicago sweethearts are nothing if not resourceful, and excellent necking spots can be found all over town—many of them are mentioned right here in these pages, so you won't have to go looking on your own.

Of course, there's much more to Chicago than water and grass and necking! The City of the Big Shoulders makes you want to lean on a soft shoulder yourself as you take in its wealth of world-class art, architecture, music, museums, theater, and opera. It's also a great sports town, with year-round pro action in basketball, football, ice hockey, and, of course, baseball. (And isn't the Cub fans perrenial cry of "Wait till next year!" just as appropriate when one is disappointed in love?)

Chicago's hotels are cosmopolitan but cozy, its restaurants and clubs sophisticated yet friendly. And because Chicago is known—accurately—as a city of neighborhoods, there are many wonderful ways to get off the tourist path and visit real life in an ethnic enclave, an ivy-covered college "town," or a residential area with something special for the cognoscenti. Sharing your exploration with someone you love will give you memories to share forever.

Just a word about the people here: Well, the word is "terrific." Whether they're lifelong South Side Irish or just in from Central America, Chicagoans find their way here because it's an easy city to love. And a great one to be in love in.

Come and see for yourselves!

THE ITINERARIES

As I was writing this book, I described its romantic weekends and activities to a friend whose life included a newborn, a two-year-old, chaos at work, and a recent move. (Her marriage, at least, is great!) Listening, she sighed and said, "Oh, what fantasies!"

I kept that in mind as I worked, and I offer it to you as you read. As you plan your Chicago interlude, browse through different itineraries and let your fantasies develop, mixing your own interests with the suggestions here to make a getaway that's all your own.

And do remember that when you're in love, money is no object—even if you don't have much. After all, Lake Michigan is the city's single biggest attraction, figuring prominently in itineraries from winter's "Holiday on Ice" to summer's "Fireworks for Two." And it's free! So is a leisurely ramble through a neighborhood or a just-looking swoop through a posh department store. For every deluxe hotel or four-star restaurant, there's a charming bed and breakfast or inexpensive bistro that will be every bit as unforgettable because you've shared it.

USING THIS BOOK

All the itineraries here can be used as is, as a sort of romantic road map to an interlude that's intimate, adventurous, challenging, relaxing—whatever you need it to be. At the same time, *please* consider the entire book to be food for your own fantasies.

On the practical side, always call the suggested attractions and establishments to check on dates, prices, and other important information. Every effort has been made to provide accurate information here, but as we all know, things change. Keep in mind that the metro Chicago area telephone system has multiple area codes. Check the telephone directory or dial 411 for directory assistance to obtain complete information. If you're among the huge number of visitors to Chicago who come on business, surprise! This book has two itineraries just for you, performing the seemingly impossible feat of wresting romance from O'Hare International Airport and McCormick Place. Should you find yourselves with a bit of time away from the business, these and other itineraries offer a zillion ways to enjoy.

If yours is a pleasure trip, note how many itineraries are near each other and think about blending. "Hyde Park Honeymoon," for example, is quite near the locations in "Romance with History," while the gardens of Lincoln Park detailed in "Love in Bloom" are only yards from the delightful day in "The Zoo for Two" and a few blocks from the charming shops in "The Good Life on Armitage" and the Midwest Buddhist Temple in "Asian Appreciation Weekend."

Even some far-flung itineraries can be combined: The Oak Park landmarks in "Love Built on Beauty" aren't far from Brookfield Zoo, in "The Zoo for Two."

Finally: Don't *ever* give up on a place you'd love to visit because it seems beyond your means. Hotels are always offering discounts and special rates. (As my friend, fashion writer, and woman-about-town Lisbeth Levine, sniffs: "*Nobody* pays rack rate!") Half-price tickets for practically everything in town are available on the day of the show at Hot Tix booths. (See "Stages of Romance" for details.) And many restaurants offer special early dinner menus with lower prices. Even at an expensive restaurant, a dinner of appetizers may be affordable, and the bill could be downright moderate if you go for lunch instead of dinner. And speaking of restaurant prices: When you see "inexpensive," "moderate," or "expensive" here, it indicates an approximate price range for appetizer, entree, and dessert, but excludes drinks, tax, and tip. "Inexpensive" means less than $20 per person, "moderate" between $20 and $40 per, and "expensive" more than $40.

Remember, then, always to ask about special arrangements. There's no one more special than you and your sweetheart.

GETTING HERE AND GETTING AROUND

The gigantic O'Hare International Airport brings thousands of travelers to Chicago daily—and leaving can be easier than arriving. Domestic and international terminals are linked to the Chicago Transit Authority (CTA) rapid transit train that reaches downtown in about thirty-five minutes for just $1.50 per person. Maps are abundant and clearly marked if you need to make connections (free!) from there.

To go directly to a hotel downtown or in the North Shore or Oak Brook suburbs, consider the Continental Airport Express van service. One way downtown is $14.75 (round-trip, $25.50). If you prefer a taxi, the ride downtown takes about thirty minutes (or much longer in rush hour) and costs about $30. The two of you can take advantage of the shared-ride program, which allows a flat rate of $13 per passenger.

Midway Airport (5700 South Cicero Avenue, 773–767–0500) is a smaller airport whose three terminals meet in a central lobby. Here, too, CTA rapid-transit trains can get you downtown in about half an hour for $1.50. Continental Air Transport van service is $10.50 to downtown, $19.00 round-trip; trip length, again, varies with traffic, but twenty minutes to downtown is possible.

Chicago also is Amtrak's hub, with about fifty trains arriving and departing daily from Union Station (210 South Canal Street, 312–655–2385). Cabs are readily available at both the upper- and lower-level exits from the station.

Public transportation in the city is easy via CTA rapid-transit, subway, and elevated trains— all of which are commonly and collectively referred to as "the El." Bus service honeycombs the city and reaches anywhere the El doesn't. Bus or El rides cost $1.50, transfers get you from bus to train or vice versa, and from bus to bus, for an extra $.25, and there are few surcharges for going into the suburbs. The system is reasonably well-kept and reasonably safe, especially if you're traveling during the day and other people are around. The CTA, for my money, is the best bargain in town.

HEART OF THE CITY

ITINERARY 1

Three days and two nights

SWEET HOME CHICAGO

A WEEKEND IN ANDERSONVILLE

*C*hicago has always been known as the city of neighborhoods, and this little gem is one of the sweetest. It's in the northern part of the Edgewater area, and though it's less than a mile in from Lake Michigan's shore, Andersonville has escaped the high-rent hustle of many lakefront areas. This is a genuine neighborhood, friendly and unassuming, not a bit snobbish or suspicious about strangers.

Andersonville was first settled by Swedes, and you'll find a distinctly Scandinavian flavor along its main avenue, North Clark Street. But don't be fooled by this blue-eyed blond exterior; Andersonville's heart is vibrantly multiethnic and proudly tolerant, which helps explain how, through more than a century of change and growth, Andersonville has kept a homey, down-to-earth feeling that's as cozy and romantic as snuggling by the fireplace.

Practical notes: This three-day itinerary assumes a long weekend, but feel free to tailor it to your availability. Any time of year is pleasant in Andersonville, although obviously a day at the beach works only during the summer. That's when the local bed and breakfast fills weeks in advance, so be sure to call well before your visit.

Getting around in Andersonville mostly consists of walking, though we've noted the places where you'll want to grab a cab. In general, the neighborhood is safe and cabs are needed only at night, for distances too long to walk.

DAY ONE: MORNING/AFTERNOON

Begin your Andersonville visit by settling in at the local bed and breakfast, an exquisitely restored, antiques-filled Victorian home so quiet, you could hear an antimacassar drop. (For the B&B's name and contact information, call or write **Bed & Breakfast/Chicago, Inc.,** a reservation service agency, 312–951–0085; P.O. Box 14088, Chicago, 60614.) "People tell us it's very serene and peaceful here, and that's what they enjoy most," says the hostess, who might offer breakfast eggs in a silver double egg cup. Of her three double-bedded rooms, many guests prefer the third-floor one whose windows resemble portholes. Notice the small, ornate tin chest on this room's wall; it came with the house and holds antique clothing brushes. If the weather cooperates, you'll enjoy breakfast in the backyard garden near a tinkling fountain. And if you're celebrating an occasion, your hostess will be happy to have flowers and champagne waiting for you.

Romance at a Glance

♥ *Stay at a local bed and breakfast.*

♥ *Stroll through Lincoln Park; golf, fish, swim, and sunbathe at the lake.*

♥ *Dine at Ann Sather, Julie Mai, or Cousins.*

♥ *Visit the Swedish American Museum; browse along Clark Street; linger at Kopi; roller-skate at Rainbo.*

♥ *Visit the past at Rosehill Cemetery and Reva's Place.*

Breakfast

Some guests choose to start their Andersonville day the way many residents do: with a serious breakfast at **Ann Sather** (5207 North Clark Street; 773–271–6677), a charming restaurant that only looks as if it has been a neighborhood fixture for years. Its upper story is quieter than the bustling ground floor, but both offer window tables that are fun for people-watching. When ordering, heed the one inviolable rule at Ann's, which is never to skip the cinnamon rolls. These sweet, yeasty favorites are the sort of thing a Chicagoan might bring a homesick friend stuck out of town. And try the Scandinavian specialties, such as a lingonberry pancakes or mild, meaty potato sausage (think boudin blanc). The kitchen can work up a carry-out lunch, too; or choose your own from **Wikstrom's** deli (5247 North Clark Street; 773–878–0601).

Summer weekends in Andersonville mean taking time to stretch out at **Kathy Osterman Beach,** a sandy slice of heaven that, inexplicably, is crowded only on the hottest days. Arrive early nonetheless to stake out your spot. The beach is east and north of Andersonville, starting at Hollywood Avenue, where Lake Shore Drive turns into Sheridan Road. Smart beachgoers beat the parking squeeze by taking a cab.

Not a beach day? Then stroll through the northern stretch of **Lincoln Park,** from around Foster Avenue as far south as your legs care to go. Joggers, bicyclists, Tai Chi practitioners, and other pleasure seekers will be there, too, enjoying this quiet area that's truly open to all and considered not a bit dangerous. As you walk south, keep an eye out for a small hill topped by shrubbery and small trees. This is a federally protected bird sanctuary, and if you've brought the binoculars, you can sit and watch carefully for any rara avis.

A bit farther south is Montrose Harbor, complete with a bait shop to service the pier's fishing enthusiasts. These could include you, of course, so plan accordingly if you or your sweetheart might feel the urge to cast a line. You can even arrange your own fishing expedition, including everything from boat to bait, through the shop; call (773) 742–7527 for information.

Golfers adore the lakeside challenge of the nine-hole, par-36 of **Sidney Marovitz Golf Course,** a little south of Montrose Harbor at Waveland Avenue. It's one of the Chicago Park District's toughest courses, but if you and your partner are up to snuff, get tee-time reservations by calling (312) 245–0909.

EVENING

Dinner

After a day outdoors, head south on Clark Street to **Julie Mai's Le Bistro** (5025 North Clark Street; 773–784–6000), where intimate booths offer individual lighting. The food ranges from spicy Vietnamese to Gallic steak frites, and Julie herself is likely to stop by your table to make sure you're happy. Farther north, there's a dimly lit hideaway at **Madrigal's Cafe** (5316 North Clark Street; 773–334–3033), where the garden is pretty and the menu eclectic. Both are moderate in price.

Two Italian restaurants represent the old and new in Andersonville. The chic **La Donna** (5142 North Clark Street; 773–561–9400) offers a sophisticated menu with attractively spare decor (get a table in back). Or go retro at **Calo** (5343 North Clark Street; 773–271–7725), a culinary time capsule that looks like a set for a Martin Scorsese movie. But don't watch for "goodfellas"; these are just neighborhood people who want noodles, not nouvelle. There's pizza, too, and fish on Friday. Ask for a booth where you can linger over an after-dinner drink.

Andersonville being a residential area, later nightlife in the neighborhood tends to be quiet. North of the area, in Rogers Park, is the famous blues club **Biddy Mulligan's** (7644 North Sheridan Road; 773–761–6532), where nationally known artists generally are booked for weekends. (*Hint:* Cab or drive there; the bus means a long wait at night.) For a more adventurous atmosphere, the two of you can check out the scene to the south of Andersonville at **Big Chicks** (5024 North Sheridan Road; 773–728–5511). Weekends are packed with an incredibly eclectic clientele of gays, artists, and other people who appreciate a *lot* of diversity.

DAY TWO: MORNING

After sampling the goodies from the **Swedish Bakery** (5348 North Clark Street; 773–561–8919), stroll a block south to visit the small but proud **Swedish American Museum**

(5211 North Clark Street; 773–728–8111), which hosts traveling exhibits and is a treasury of anecdotal information about the neighborhood's early days. The gift shop boasts a good supply of Scandinavian-themed books and souvenirs.

Browsing along Clark Street, you'll find plenty of little shops with unique identities and merchandise to match. At **Okee-Chee's Wild Horse Gallery** (5337 North Clark Street; 773–271–5883), the owner's Native American heritage and connections are evident thoughout the store's wide selection of handicrafts. Be sure to look in back, where unique items often are on display (and sometimes on sale). Either of these sections is a great place to scout a man's taste for future gift selection.

Book lovers lose hours at **Women & Children First** (5233 North Clark Street; 773–769–9299), where the staff of guy-friendly feminists stock fascinating books, periodicals, music, and literary paraphernalia. A large area is devoted to books and music for kids, and any staffer can offer educated suggestions on an age-appropriate gift for your favorite small fry. (Don't miss the countertop baskets of lapel buttons for the latest politically correct messages!) Next door, the tiny **Woman Wild** gallery (773–878–0300) offers jewelry and objets d'art by local artists; other one-of-a-kind finds are at **American Hands** (5311 North Clark Street; 773–728–4227).

Also chock-full of beautiful things is the three-level **Landmark of Andersonville** (5301 North Clark Street; 773–728–5301). This corner building holds several little shops with everything from delicate linens to picture frames, as well as **One Touch of Nature,** a haven for environmentally conscientious, quite beautiful gifts. (Don't be surprised by a distinct tilt toward bird-watching; the owner is a stalwart of the city's Audubon Society.)

Lunch

If a day of slow-paced browsing isn't *everyone's* idea of an excellent time, take a lunch break at **Kopi, a Travelers' Cafe** (5317 North Clark Street; 773–989–5674). From the wall of postcards at its entrance to the tiny boutique in back, Kopi is a coffeehouse with a personality—one that likes globe-trotting and dropping a line to the folks back home. *Kopi* is an Indonesian word for "coffee," and behind the counter's upper walls, a neat lineup of clocks tells the time in various parts of the world.

Kopi has plenty of tables for two, but the best place to linger is right in front. Remove your shoes, step up to the elevated area at your right, and snuggle in among the pillows at these near-the-floor tables. This hangout for the neighborhood's artistic types is one of those places where you'll fall silent while eavesdropping on the next table's fascinating discussion. Coffee is the menu's most serious subject—and the barrels in front are full of take-out beans—but the salad and focaccia entrees are good, and the rich desserts are made for sharing.

AFTERNOON

As you explore Clark Street, ramble toward the neighborhood's north end, with its sudden stretch of green at **Gethsemane Garden Center** (5801 North Clark Street; 773–878–5915). This sprawling gardeners' haven offers everything from herbs in tiny pots to ready-to-plant

When the weather's friendly, wander with your sweetheart through the residential neighborhood just east of Clark Street. It's called Lakewood-Balmoral and is one of the city's hottest real estate areas, with blocks of turn-of-the-century homes and two- or three-flats. Many are beautifully restored and home to members of the very tony Saddle & Cycle Club, which lies just west of the lake on Foster Avenue and is one of the city's most exclusive private clubs. But you don't have to be a member to stroll arm in arm along Lakewood-Balmoral's well-tended blocks and dream of the day when you and your honey might move into one of these Victorian jewels.

trees, and browsing together is fun even if you don't buy. Watch out for puddles underfoot, and be prepared for a crowd if the weather is at all nice. Chicago's motto may be *urbs in horto*—"city in a garden"—but weather-dependent gardeners go by *carpe diem*—"seize the day."

Back south on Clark Street, check out performance times at the **Griffin Theatre** (5404 North Clark Street; 773–769–2228). This is one of the newer companies in Chicago's famed theater community, and its productions of *The Second Assassin, And Neither Have I Wings to Fly,* and others have won critical acclaim. Its humble home is nothing to brag about, but nothing to apologize for, either; such makeshift origins preceded glory for Steppenwolf and other local companies.

A more off-beat production is at the **Neo-Futurarium** (5149 North Ashland Avenue; 773–878–4557), just west of Clark along Foster Avenue. In its home above the venerable old Nelson Funeral Home, this company has made a late-night cult hit of *Too Much Light Makes the Baby Go Blind,* a constantly evolving collection of short pieces. It's the kind of eccentric show that Chicagoans love to discover and support with word of mouth, so if you and your beloved are at all interested in the theater, give it a whirl.

And speaking of giving a whirl, consider a different form of amusement farther south on Andersonville's main strip. A plain exterior and dingy interior disguise the colorful history of **Rainbo Roller Rink** (4836 North Clark Street; 773–271–6200). Rainbo has been just about everything a big old barn of a building could be, from old-time movie palace to ice rink to psychedelic haven (where Led Zeppelin performed on its first American tour) to speakeasy— complete with underground escape tunnels exiting in the cemetery across the street! Today Rainbo is a favorite for skating and blading alike, offering open skating on weekends both early in the day (which is the least crowded but more family-oriented time) and late at night after the children have gone to bed; call to check on open-skating times.

No skates? No problem: Strap on rental in-lines or traditional roller skates and glide away with your good sport of a sweetheart. Listen for couples-only songs; the music is loud, but the atmosphere's undeniable—although the noisy, overlit arcade in the rear is best avoided. When you're ready to rest, choose a booth just beyond the skating area. Snacks are strictly of the hot-dogs-and-nachos variety, but this *is* a roller rink.

EVENING

Dinner

After a workout on wheels, you'll probably be ready to think about dinner—and there's nothing better than Middle Eastern for healthful, slightly exotic fare. Several Middle Eastern restaurants are among the neighbrhood's best for dinner. The largest is **Reza's** (5255 North Clark Street; 773–561–1898), where the decor is loftish, the menu is Mediterranean, and kebabs are a familiar choice of entree. A table for two along one of the sandblasted-brick walls will let you linger over tea long after the baklava's finished. Turkish fare is on the menu at the upscale **Cousins** (5203 North Clark Street; 773–334–4553), where a window table is the nicest. At **Kan Zaman** (5204 North Clark Street; 773–506–0191), ask for the front area where seating is on comfy floor pillows, which will let you relax while enjoying a mix-and-match menu offering specialties prepared with your choice of fish, seafood, or meat. All three restaurants are located an easy stroll from the Griffin and the Neo-Futurarium theaters, and all three are moderate in price.

DAY THREE: MORNING

Breakfast

Head for the neighborhood's western border and **Reva's Place** (1754 West Balmoral; 773–275–1202). This quintessential diner serves up a breakfast that can't be beat, from plenty of hot coffee to authentic hash browns, all for about five bucks per person. And the atmosphere's thicker than the vinyl tablecloths. Reva's major influences include Elvis, Marilyn, jukebox culture, and the Chicago Cubs. Each booth holds magazines to browse, once you've sampled the visual feast of vintage photos and advertising that covers every inch of flat surface. (Reva's is swell for lunch, too.)

An offbeat but genuinely pleasant way to pass the morning is with a long walk through one of the neighborhood's landmarks, **Rosehill Cemetery** (5800 North Ravenswood; 773–561–5940). Some markers show dates reaching back to the eighteenth century, but Rosehill is strictly up-to-date, with monthly programs arranged by the director of its own Civil War Museum. Usually focusing on aspects of Civil War and Victorian culture (neighbors sometimes call police when the cemetery's nineteenth-century cannons boom), the programs range from Civil War reenactments to a summertime Victorian picnic.

Before or after a program, be sure to notice some of the cemetery's silent treasures. At its entrance are neat rows of tombstones commemorating some of the Illinois soldiers who died in the Civil War. Just to the north is a touching monument to Chicago's firefighters, its statue surrounded by a knee-high border that, if you look closely, turns out to be a length of hose. Farther in is a lovely marble statue of Frances M. Pearce and her infant daughter, who died of tuberculosis in 1854. Coming upon this glass-enclosed statue, atop its five-foot-high pedestal, has been described as finding the sleeping Snow White; mother and baby lie together as if napping, their eyes closed, the mother's hand resting over her child's.

Through the cemetery, other statuary and large, ornate mausoleums salute moneyed families, including that of Charles Hull, whose Hull House was Jane Addams's most famous settlement house. A newer Asian area is all colorful ribbons and tombstone inscriptions in characters of other languages. Perversely, wandering through this place of death can make you and your loved one rejoice in being alive and together.

Lunch

When you've walked enough, head back to the cemetery's east entrance and stop for lunch across the street at the **Fireside Restaurant** (5739 North Ravenswood; 773–878–5942). This unpretentious spot offers an enclosed garden area if you're up for more of the great outdoors; if you'd rather warm up, head for the eponymous fireplace. Booths along one wall are cozy, too. The menu is inexpensive to moderate, its items standard but well prepared—burgers, chicken, salads, and some nice entrees, if you're really here for an early dinner. The owner is usually present and eager to please.

ITINERARY 2

Three and two nights

THE GOOD LIFE ON ARMITAGE

*L*iving the good life on Armitage—even if only for a weekend—is a time and place for dreaming about the future together. Here's hoping it's as bright as the gleaming restorations and trendy business you'll enjoy here. You may be surprised to learn that it wasn't always thus. Back in the 1960s, the side streets east and west of North Halsted Street were where the young and impoverished came to find their first apartments in two-flats, brownstones, and frame cottages dating from the turn of the century. In the time-honored Chicago tradition of regarding major streets as impregnable borders, West Armitage Avenue became a sort of "dividing line" separating these hippie-era apartment dwellers from the territory of the notorious Cabrini-Green housing project, a few blocks south.

What a difference thirty years makes. Today Cabrini-Green is on the verge of demolition, and those old buildings north of Armitage, now handsomely restored, commonly fetch seven figures. Many are still residences, but many others have been transformed into chic little shops, restaurants, or bars. And the people in them are, uh, no longer hippies. Nor, however, are they the Gold Coast crowd; even though there's plenty of money in this area, its apartments remain affordable for young career types who keep its style distinctly Lincoln Park, not Water Tower. Spend a weekend exploring the park and a mile or so of West Armitage, and you'll feel pretty darn stylish yourselves.

Romance at a Glance

♥ *Stay at a cozy bed and breakfast in fashionable Lincoln Park.*

♥ *Dine at one of the nation's top restaurants, Charlie Trotter's.*

♥ *Browse at trendy boutiques and shops.*

♥ *Dip into fondue at Geja's, then catch a show at Park West.*

♥ *Enjoy a day in Lincoln Park.*

Practical notes: Expect to plan months in advance for reservations at Charlie Trotter's and weeks ahead for a Park West show. Any time of year is fine for this getaway—but no matter when you choose to do it, bring your Christmas and birthday gift lists. You're going to get a *lot* done.

DAY ONE/EVENING

Book one of the bed and breakfast apartments in a small apartment building on West Wisconsin Avenue, which puts you just a block south of Armitage at its east end. Each of the building's two available apartments offers a working fireplace for chilly days and nights, as well as access to a large outdoor deck in good weather. The first-floor apartment's *two* queen-bedded rooms even let you choose your favorite bedroom. This apartment's guest book holds an entry from a honeymooning couple who wrote (with a smiley-face *and* a little heart): "Everything was lovely—Thanks for spoiling us!" On the second floor, you'll enjoy a bright living room, with a faint, cozy scent of wood from the fireplace, tidy galley kitchen, and a relatively large, queen-bedded bedroom done in cheerful blue and white. Lots of Midwesterners have left warm words of praise in the guest book of this apartment, whose front door holds a welcoming rose pomader. (Both apartments can be booked through Bed & Breakfast Chicago; call 312–951–0085.)

Once you're settled in your weekend home, venture forth for an evening on the town! Both the evenings suggested here will require some planning well in advance, because you're going to see two very different shows on your two evenings—one a food extravaganza at Charlie Trotter's renowned restaurant, the other a show-business performance at the snazzy Park West.

Dinner

In one fan's words, if other restaurants are airplanes, **Charlie Trotter's** (816 West Armitage; 773–248–6228) is the space shuttle. Trotter is a bespectacled, thirtysomething chef who is influenced by everything and inspired by—well, some call it genius, some call it obsession, but nobody goes away hungry. Or bored.

The menu changes constantly, and Trotter's sole concession to simplification is to offer only one set menu per evening. The multicourse degustation, which is available in a regular version ($85 per person) or vegetarian ($65), will guarantee you a sample of everything the chef has on his mind at the moment, prepared with only the very finest, very freshest ingredients. The food is complex, often prepared with incredibly painstaking work, and often resulting in many unexpected flavors. But don't be intimidated—this isn't a food-appreciation class, and the food is never weird or off-putting. Come with an open mind, ready to let your palate be educated, and arrive on time—seating begins at 5:30 P.M. Friday and Saturday, 6:00 P.M. Tuesday, Wednesday, and Thursday. (The restaurant is closed on Sunday and Monday.)

You can opt for a table right in the kitchen, if you want to see how it all comes together. The kitchen table, which books months in advance, is $125 per person weeknights, $150 on Friday or Saturday. And, if the prices take your breath away, consider that dinner here is the entire evening. It's also one of the nation's premier restaurants, so there is some bragging value here, too. Charlie Trotter's is truly the place to take someone you want to impress.

DAY TWO: MORNING/AFTERNOON

After a lazy cup of coffee from your bed and breakfast kitchen, you're ready to wander west. Today is shopping day, to be spent dipping into the many shops lining several blocks of Armitage west of Halsted Street (at 800 west). As you travel west on Armitage, you'll pass a few blocks of residences and Lincoln Park High School, once a divey hangout but now a spruced-up magnet school that draws good students from all over town.

Brunch

To fortify yourselves for a meandering sort of day, settle into a trattoria-style brunch at **Sole Mio** (917 West Armitage Avenue; 773–477–5858). This fashionable yet cozy spot is a neighborhood favorite for risotto, polenta, and pasta; at brunch its horizons broaden to include such delicious diversions as potato pancakes, calamari, and chic little pizzas. On Saturday brunch is served from 11:30 A.M. till 2:30 P.M.; Sunday hours are 10:00 A.M. to 2:30 P.M. Brunch won't cost more than $12 or so for the two of you.

As you emerge, decide whether to start your shopping on the south or the north side of Armitage. Working along the south side from east to west, you'll start at **Cynthia Rowley** (808 West Armitage Avenue; 773–528–6160), the hometown shop where local girl Rowley, a darling of the fashion world, offers her creations. Dresses, multipiece outfits, and accessories are available for a totally personal look that the store's clerks will be happy to help you assemble.

The walk-up storefront at 826 West Armitage Avenue is shared by **Renaissance Buttons** (773–883–9508) and **Mizepah Bead Company** (773–868–0580). These complementary treasure troves offer a wealth of ideas for using their bounty of beads, buttons, and other finery. Why not choose some semiprecious stones and lacy ribbons to create a picture frame that the two of you will look terrific in?

Or find a ready-made frame at **Turtle Creek Antiques** (850 West Armitage; 773–327–2630), where old silver fountain pens, picture frames, and accessories rest alongside vintage linens, velvet, and chintzes. The shop is known for its quilts, so this is the place to look if you're outfitting your bed. For that matter, you can find the bed itself here; furniture and lamps, as well as a tasteful selection of jewelry and beaded bags, are Turtle Creek specialties, too.

Peek in to survey the floral finery at **Fischer** (852 West Armitage Avenue; 773–248–1900) and you might just pick up a posy for your sweetheart. Across the street **Studio 910** (910 West Armitage Avenue; 773–929–2400) is a gift-and-goodies boutique where one-of-a-kind accessories are displayed along with equally distinctive women's clothing. This is the place to find a fancifully decorated little holder for business cards or recipes, or a richly adorned little box, or even a hefty, colorful jar of pickled vegetables. The staff is friendly, chatty, and helpful with gift seekers.

Down at **Urban Gardener** (1006 West Armitage; 773–477–2070), a converted two-floor townhouse now holds absolutely everything the gardener could need, want, or fantasize about. Tools, pots, seeds, bulbs, and all the rest of a gardener's equipment are here, along with gorgeous baskets, wreaths of dried flowers and greenery, stationery, soaps, iron benches, linens, and more. If the two of you are thinking of life in tandem, planting something together is a step in the right direction.

You'll notice that Armitage Avenue seems to end just west of Urban Gardener. Actually, it's just curving a bit to the south, but this does mark the end of the street's shopping strip. So cross the street and head back east, starting at **Faded Rose** (1017 West Armitage Avenue; 773–281–8161), where beautiful slipcovers revive old furniture you just might want to buy. Next door, at **Tabula Tua** (1015 West Armitage Avenue; 773–525–3500), you'll find all sorts of goodies to set your table—some amusing, some exquisite—and cookbooks to help you whip up a gourmet meal. This is a good spot to search out mom-type presents (for your mom or your mate's).

One of the street's very best shops is **Oh Boy** (1013 West Armitage Avenue; 773–248–7954), where you might see an Ed Paschke painting hanging next to a pair of vintage Pendleton wool bathrobes. It's all for sale, from old toys to arty jewelry to the major pieces that should be considered an investment in art. Three owners each contribute an artistic sensibility and unique taste to what they choose to sell, so it's safe to say you can *always* find a gift here—for each other, for your country cousin, even for a really terrific boss. Oh Boy is bigger than many of its neighbors, too, so expect to linger here.

If you're both sufficiently self-indulgent—or is it simply self-preserving?—you can relax under the soothing ministrations of hair, nail, and skin-care experts at **Salon 1800** (1011 West Armitage; 773–929–6010). Schedule his-and-hers massages ($60 for an hour, $40 for half an hour) or even a "day spa" session to primp as long as you like. Relaxing herbal wraps are $35; facials are about $50; and hair procedures, which vary according to the stylist, range from about $20 to about $50.

If one of you isn't in the mood for the full salon treatment, you can take a good book to the neighborhood's own **Coffee & Tea Exchange** (833 West Armitage Avenue; 773–929–6730) or the always cordial **Starbucks** (1001 West Armitage Avenue; 773–528–1340) nearby.

Lunch

Hungry? Stop in at **Bread with Appeal** (1009 West Armitage; 773–244–2700), where sandwiches, pizzas, salads, soups, and focaccia (the house specialty) are made on the premises. So are the luscious desserts displayed at the front counter; for half the calories, share! Prices are reasonable—about $8.00 or less for most selections—and you can watch the passing parade from a window table for two. Another good choice is **Metropolis** (924 West Armitage Avenue; 773–868–9000), where barbecue or rotisserie-roasted chicken vie with pasta and pizza for the lunch bunch. Prices are about the same as at Bread with Appeal; a few eat-in tables are available, or you can carry out your lunch.

Back on the street: How about a shiny aluminum checkbook cover? With an address book to match? These sleek accessories, and lots more in jewelry and art, are at **Ancient Echoes** (1003 West Armitage Avenue; 773–880–1003). Smaller than some stores on the street, Ancient Echoes makes up for its size with a carefully selected range of merchandise. My favorites are the small, wood-framed assemblages that use feathers, dried berries, teeny branches, and other materials to create an outdoorsy scene. Also noteworthy are the "eggheads"—little carved wooden heads by the *other* Paschke, Ed Sr. If you're really daring, choose one that looks like

your beloved—but of course you'll be sure to explain its inner beauty!

Just beyond the Armitage El stop, you'll see everything from overalls to martini glasses in the windows of **Active Endeavors** (935 West Armitage Avenue; 773–281–8100). Several storefronts are bursting with Active Endeavors' sporting gear and chic necessities for the vigorous set. This is the place to rent your in-line skates to whiz around the neighborhood (which can be pretty crowded, so rent helmet and pads, too!). There's also a big bulletin board that holds information on many sports groups around town; it's where to look for tips on pursuing a sport the two of you might want to try together, but not *alone* together.

Another sort of clearinghouse for enthusiasts is the **Old Town School of Folk Music** (909 West Armitage Avenue; 773–525–7793), whose long traditions and loving musicians are steeped not only in the protest strain of folk music, but also in that of many ethnic groups. Celtic music is a particular favorite, and African music has a large coterie of fans as well. Instruments, lessons, sheet music, recorded music, and a huge dose of camaraderie are all available at the school, which is often the first destination of visitors to Chicago from all over the world.

Tea cozies, silk kimonos, and tons of scented soaps are featured at **Findables** (907 West Armitage Avenue; 773–348–0674). The freeze-dried flower arrangements are pretty, and the hats are fun. Amusing hats also are everywhere at **Isis on Armitage** (823 West Armitage Avenue; 773–665–7290), where you'll also find vintage sunglasses and women's clothing in nonmodel sizes—a welcome admission of diversity in an area that sometimes seems to be populated exclusively by fitness buffs.

By now—loaded down with packages and all shopped out—you're ready to taxi back to your bed and breakfast before an evening out. Happily, the rest of the day does not require spending any time on your feet.

DAY TWO: Evening

Dinner

First things first, and that means dinner. One of the most romantic restaurants is conveniently located in the immediate area. Stepping into **Geja's Cafe** (340 West Armitage Avenue; 773–281–9101) is like entering a protected area for the endangered species of diehard romantics. Everything here—secluded alcoves, classical guitar music, dim lighting —is planned to enhance an intimate evening for the two of you. That also goes for the food, which is fondue and salad (so you won't waste much time trying to make decisions). There's no better way to share a meal—and a deliciously sensual experience—than by huddling over a hot pot in which to dip a dinner's worth of tender morsels: bread in fragrant melted cheese to start, meat or chicken in seasoned oil as an entree, and fruit or cake in smooth, luscious chocolate for dessert. Geja's prices are moderate—about $80 for the two of you—and wines are available by the glass; note that the next stop on your agenda, Park West, is likely to have a drink minimum, so you may want to imbibe more moderately here, but at the same time, do allow yourselves plenty of time to linger.

Classic Chicago Couples: Kup and Essee

He's Irv Kupcinet of the Chicago Sun Times, *among the last of the three-dot writers covering the "celebs" in politics, show biz, high society, and other areas of Chicago life. For many years, Kup did play-by-play for the Chicago Bears while hosting a TV talk show on which he routinely sat political types, from presidents and prime ministers to local pols, next to Hollywod stars, artists, and sports figures. Seeing Jesse Jackson converse with Carol Channing was not to be missed.*

Essee Kupcinet has big red hair and a terrific wardrobe, but she's no clotheshorse wife. Known affectionately far and wide as a great broad, Essee is famous for her unstinting support of the arts in town, most notably Chicago theater. She was one of the first pillars of the community to get behind the young actors and writers who developed such companies as Steppenwolf, the Organic Theater, and the old St. Nicholas, early home of David Mamet. She helped with the talk show, too.

Together, the Kups have enriched the city's intellectual and artistic life more than most of us realize. And they've been happily married just about forever. As Kup would write, "it's our one man's opinion" that they're the greatest.

❧

When your fondue, *c'est fini,* head over to **Park West** (322 West Armitage Avenue; 773–929–5959). Naturally, you've done your homework and called well ahead to find a show you and your companion will both enjoy here. The club's streamlined, black-and-silver decor tells you that Park West aspires to be the kind of swanky nightclub Fred and Ginger graced. For the most part, it's successful in attaining that ideal, with good sightlines, a nice balcony and, blessedly, clean washrooms. Depending on the show, a dance floor may be cleared in front, near the stage. Oh, and the bar makes a fine cocktail, too.

Perhaps the best thing about Park West, though, is its booking policy, which is the very definition of eclectic. This snug stage has held practically everyone who's anyone, from Judy Collins to Henry Rollins. I've seen Tom Paxton, Cheap Trick, Steve Earl, Talking Heads, and Laurie Anderson here, to name a few. And there are many sports fans in town who wouldn't attend a pay-per-view sporting event anywhere else.

There *is* a drawback to an evening at Park West: Its no-reservations seating policy could leave you farther from the stage than you want to be. If your priority is getting the best view of the show, arrive early and, as soon as the doors open, claim a couple of stools along the bar area that faces toward the stage. The view also is excellent from the booths, but no one ever seems to know just how you can be *sure* of getting one of those. It's worthwhile to broach the subject with one of the club's many security types, but don't promise your date anything you can't be sure of delivering. Keep in mind that there isn't a truly bad seat in the house—and those rickety little tables for two *are* kind of cute.

After an evening of dinner and a show, you may want to stroll the neighborhood. There are plenty of bars if you're looking for a nightcap—and if your sweet tooth suddenly acts up, stop in at **Ben & Jerry's Ice Cream Parlor** (338 West Armitage Avenue; 773–218–5152) for a scoop or two to share.

DAY THREE: MORNING/AFTERNOON

Here's a low-key finish to a fabulous weekend that will occupy as much or as little time as you care to spend. After coffee in your bed and breakfast kitchen, stroll across Clark Street to wander through **Lincoln Park Zoological Gardens** (Cannon Drive, from North Avenue to Fullerton Avenue; 773–742–2000). More than thirty-five acres of zoo, conservatory, and parkland are open from 9:00 A.M. to 5:00 P.M. daily, free of charge. At the south end of this stretch is the **Chicago Historical Society** (Clark Street at North Avenue; 312–642–4600), which is open from 9:30 A.M. to 4:30 P.M. daily except Sunday, when hours are noon to 5:00 P.M. Admission is a reasonable $3.00 per person (Mondays are free). Be sure to look at exhibits on the American Revolution and the Civil War, as well as the delightful cases of Chicago memorabilia that include full uniforms from beloved members of each of the city's major sports teams. The museum also owns a famous costume collection built largely from local socialites' couture donations. The holdings are more Jackie O than Secondhand Rose, so if you're at all interested in fashion, check out whatever is on display.

Lunch

For lunch stop in at the museum's own **Big Shoulders Cafe** (773–587–7766), where the gateway to the old Chicago Stockyards now lives. The cafe is operated by a local restaurateur and is one of the best museum food-service facilities around; just ask guests at one of the parties held here on many an after-hours evening. Don't miss the terrific millet bread. Daily specials are always worth a try, Sunday brunch is dandy, and prices are very reasonable—a $20 lunch for two is very doable.

Or cross North Avenue to the **Village Theater** (1548 North Clark Avenue; 312–642–2403), a multiscreen movie house that gets the best titles later in their release. It's a great place to catch something you wanted to see for just a couple of bucks, even less before the first show.

ITINERARY 3
Three days and two nights

HYDE PARK HONEYMOON

*W*hen Harry met Sally, it happened here—on the gloriously Gothic campus of the University of Chicago. Their first encounter, you'll recall, set the tone for the relationship: opinionated, brainy, verbal; a tad aggressive, definitely a pairing of differences, if not complete opposites. Totally Hyde Park. And just as Meg Ryan's presence filled the restaurant where she and Billy Crystal discussed sex, so does the University of Chicago fill its lakefront neighborhood. For better or worse, the university's overwhelming presence makes Hyde Park something of a college town.

But let's be fair. There is more to Hyde Park than hyperintellectualization. There's the Museum of Science and Industry, a fabulous entertainment that also tickles the intellect. There's the lovely Jackson Park lagoon. And there's the fact that this community has made racial integration work for nearly half a century. Totally Hyde Park. Come on down and see for yourselves.

Practical notes: You'll want to do some planning for a Hyde Park weekend. For information on entertainment or educational programs that the university opens to the public, call 773–702–9729. This is the Major Activities Board, which programs popular music and the like. The Council of University Programming (773–702–0433) arranges other, more esoteric events. (And you haven't seen esoteric till you've been to Hyde Park.) If you're music lovers, call (773) 702–8068 for a schedule from the **Chamber Music and Early Music Series,** which presents about twenty concerts during its October-to-May season. Tickets are $22.00 ($9.00 with a student ID), and seating is reserved.

Romance at a Glance

♥ *Settle in at a beautiful neighborhood bed and breakfast.*

♥ *Dig into Southern cooking at Dixie Kitchen.*

♥ *Change your pace at the Baby Doll Polka Club.*

♥ *Visit the incredible Museum of Science and Industry, and then stroll Jackson Park lagoon.*

♥ *See a classy bit of theater at Court.*

♥ *Savor an after-theater drink at Jimmy's.*

♥ *Brunch at Medici; explore Rockefeller Chapel and the Smart Gallery.*

DAY ONE: EVENING

One of Hyde Park's greatest charms is its houses, which include some architectural gems and countless proud beauties a century or more old. The area does have hotels, of course, but why not stay in one of those grand old homes? Through **Bed & Breakfast Chicago** (312–951–0085), you can book a room in a hundred-year-old house, restored by its architect owner and his wife. It's a Prairie-style home, filled with antiques and bursting with charm. Go for the second-floor room that has a queen-size bed and its own private bath. Rates are terrific—about $85 per night—with a minimum of two nights' stay.

The house is at the north end of the neighborhood, so begin your stay with a stroll around the area. This is a good place to tackle the delicate subject of safety, ever an issue in Hyde Park. Some very rough areas are close by, but most Hyde Park residents believe their neighborhood is no more dangerous than any other city neighborhood, and I'm inclined to agree. Keep in mind, though, that Hyde Parkers (and I) are longtime urban residents whose antennae never go down. Get yours up, especially after dark. Don't stray from well-lighted streets where others are out and about, and you should be fine.

While you still have some daylight, get out and explore the center of the community—the **University of Chicago campus,** 175 acres of impressive architecture and greenery that's home to scads of scholars, including quite a few Nobel Prize winners. The solidly Oxbridge basis for the campus's design and classical-looking limestone buildings (by Henry Ives Cobb) gives a unified feeling to much of the campus, and its twentieth-century buildings are by such giants as Ludwig Mies van der Rohe (the **School of Social Services Administration Building,** 969 East Sixtieth Street and Eero Saarinen (**Laird Bell Law Quadrangle,** 800 block of East Sixtieth Street, and **Woodward Court residence hall,** 5825 South Woodlawn). Many buildings have lovely courtyards where you can linger.

Dinner

When you get hungry, go north and east of the campus to a lively spot that's a great local favorite. **Dixie Kitchen & Bait Shop** (5225 South Harper Avenue, in Harper Court; 773–363–4943) serves up fabulous soul food and Southern specialties in a setting that looks like a Northerner's idea of Southern living. But there's no quarrel with the food, which includes jambalaya, gumbo, fried chicken, catfish blackened or fried, and all the right side extras: black-eyed peas, coleslaw, collard greens, and johnnycakes. Come hungry and don't leave till you try the pecan pie. Prices are moderate—you may even be able to hold dinner for both of you to under $50, especially if you go easy on that Dixie beer.

Your evening's entertainment may well be on campus (see Practical Notes, earlier in this chapter for how to get information on what's happening). If you want to keep it low-cost, check out what's playing at **Documentary Films,** better known simply as Doc. This student group has been choosing and running film programs for more than thirty years. Sometimes it's totally weird, sometimes it's the greats—but for $3.00, give it a try. Call (773) 702–8574 for information and decide for yourselves.

Maybe you're feeling, well, *frisky*. So hop in the car and drive west, west, west on 55th Street till you reach the **Baby Doll Polka Club** (6102 South Central Avenue; 773–582–9706).

Open seven days a week, the Baby Doll offers live bands on Friday, Saturday, and Sunday evenings for people of the polka persuasion. And there isn't even a cover charge for this wacky, wonderful way to dance up a storm. At fortysomething, the Baby Doll is a South Side institution so hip, so out-there, they don't even have T-shirts. Be the first ones you know to go.

DAY TWO: MORNING/AFTERNOON

Head out early to take in the best of the **Museum of Science and Industry** (Fifty-seventh Street and Lake Shore Drive; 773–684–1414), which includes old kid favorites like the giant walk-through heart and the baby chicks' hatchery, and goes right up to "AIDS: The War Within" and a smashing Omnimax movie theater where any current feature is a don't-miss. Also catch the World War II–era U–505 submarine; the working coal mine (although if you know anything about mining, don't look for authenticity); Yesterday's Main Street, where you can have your picture taken in turn-of-the-century duds; and the Whispering Gallery, where you'll have the chance to whisper sweet nothings to each other from an incredible distance.

Admission to the musem costs $6.00 (Thursday is the free day), and it's open from 9:30 A.M. daily, till 4:00 P.M. weekdays and 5:30 P.M. Saturday and Sunday. You could easily spend the entire day, except for the unfortunate dining situation—a Hobson's choice between vending machines and fast food. One delightful exception has been here forever and qualifies as part of the museum: the old-fashioned, wood-furnished Finnigan's Ice Cream Parlor, which I can never resist. An ice-cream soda isn't *that* much a compromise to your diet, especially if you sip one with two straws, like a couple of kids in a 1940s movie.

Lunch

If you're ready to leave the museum around noontime, have lunch across the street at **Piccolo Mondo** (in the Windermere, 1642 East Fifty-sixth Street; 312–643–1106). This beloved spot features salads and lighter fare, as well as the Chicago original, chicken Vesuvio.

Hitched in Hyde Park

One of the most wonderful weddings I ever attended was a Hyde Park event. The bride was Byelorussian, the groom Japanese; both were artists, and the ceremony took place in the Unitarian church. The reception was held in a slightly shabby but still fine old hotel, where the food was great and the dancing was even better, thanks to the couple's slightly shocking decision to have a jukebox instead of a boring grown-up band. As we all danced the night away, we saluted this fearless pair's faith in themselves, their individualism, and their love and marriage.

There's even spaghetti and meatballs, and prices are moderate—maybe $15 each for dinner, even less for lunch.

Or you might prefer to bring your own lunch. Ask your B&B hosts for a recommendation the evening before, and pick up some sandwiches and stuff on your way to the museum. Then, when you're ready to break, take your lunch outdoors to the **Jackson Park lagoon** (south and east of the museum; officially, 6401 South Stony Island Boulevard). At this rural oasis you'll see people fishing right behind the museum and, on its far-east Wooded Island, find one of the city's finest spots for bird-watching.

You can easily spend hours at the lagoon and the island. Be sure to look for the famous monk parakeets that have lived here for years, even though they're completely unsuited to the climate. They manage by wintering at the steam vents of a nearby building, and moving to the area of the island when weather permits.

On the way back north, you might want to cross Lake Shore Drive near the museum so that you can stroll the beach around **Promontory Point.** It offers a wonderful view of the city's skyline that you won't see anywhere else.

Dinner

As you return to civilization, you'll want to stop back at your B&B before the evening's entertainment. A good choice for dinner is **Orly's** (5498 South Hyde Park Boulevard; 773–643–5500), where many entrees carry a Southwestern accent. Pastas are good, too, especially with a visit to one of the better salad bars around. Prices are moderate, and dinner is served from 5:00 till 10:30 P.M. every night (till midnight on Friday and Saturday).

From Orly's head west to a stimulating evening at **Court Theater** (5536 South Ellis Street; 773–753–4472). An institution in the city as well as the neighborhood, Court provides theater for the demandingly intellectual locals, and it is therefore a good bet for one of the better shows around town at any given time during the theater season. Court sticks to the classics, from Euripides to Tom Stoppard, and often presents works you're not likely to see elsewhere. *Note:* If this makes Court sound stuffy—it's not! A Molière farce here is guaranteed yucks, and even a somber production is a pleasure in its reliable quality. So go. But be sure to call well in advance, because weekend shows often sell out early. Curtain is at 8:00 P.M.

After the show, you can indulge is a quintessential U. of C. pastime by hitting the **Woodlawn Tap and Liquor Store** (1172 East Fifty-fifth Street; 773–643–5516) for a drink and a discussion. But, for heaven's sake, don't refer to the place as anything but Jimmy's. As much a Hyde Park institution as the university itself, Jimmy's is a student hangout where the discourse is as serious as the drinking. And don't expect a nonsmoking section.

DAY THREE: MORNING/AFTERNOON

Sunday morning seems like the perfect time to visit one of the campus's highlights,

Go to the lovely Japanese garden on the island and lose yourself in its serenity. Built for the 1893 Columbian Exposition (which took place in the neighborhood) and abandoned during World War II, the garden has been restored by Chicago's sister city, Osaka, and now features a pavilion, a sparkling waterfall, and a lovely bridge whose arch is meant to suggest the curve of the moon. Another nearby bridge is just as attractive: Three stone arches overlook the harbor and the old Coast Guard auxiliary patrol, just south of a broad lawn-bowling green. You'll never believe you're still in the city!

Rockefeller Memorial Chapel (5850 South Woodlawn Avenue; 773–702–2100). When John D. put up the money for the campus, he specified that its chapel be—always—the tallest building on campus. And so it is. You can see for yourselves from 8:00 A.M. till 4:00 P.M. daily, except when religious services take precedence. These times may vary, so do be sure to call before visiting.

Brunch

For brunch, try yet another Hyde Park tradition. Brunch at **Medici's Pan Pizza** (1327 East Fifty-seventh Street; 773–667–7394) need not involve pizza. In fact, what you want to order here is eggs. Steamed eggs, cooked in the espresso machine when there's a lull in the coffee line. This delicious way to scramble requires no added fat, so what you get is just the eggs—which could include, if you like, mushrooms, cheese, peppers, bacon, or other additions (well, it *is* a pizza place). It's inexpensive, too—you both should be able to leave well-fed for around $15. Sunday brunch is also a delight at the previously mentioned Orly's, which offers a dessert-and-pastry bar, selection of entrees, and a luscious orange-strawberry drink, all for $9.95.

❧❧❧

After brunch pay a visit to the **David and Alfred Smart Gallery of Art** (5550 South Greenwood Avenue; 773–702–0200), a lovely museum that showcases the university's collections—which means you can see ancient Greek vases, modern sculpture by Henry Moore, works by Matisse and Degas, and lots more. The museum also mounts special exhibits, so be sure to find out about these in advance. Best of all, it's free! The Smart Gallery is closed on Monday; Tuesday through Friday, it's open from 10:00 A.M. to 4:00 P.M., and weekends from noon to 6:00 P.M.

FOR MORE ROMANCE

If you happen to be in Hyde Park on a Monday evening, make it your business to be at Fifty-seventh Street and University Avenue, where **Mitchell Tower** holds a set of ten bells rung in changes each week. Not to be confused with the songs typically played on church bells, changes are complex patterns that are a marvel to hear—a spine-tingling audio experience you'll be glad you shared.

ITINERARY 4
Three days and two nights

FIREWORKS FOR TWO

A FOURTH OF JULY WEEKEND

*N*ot many years ago, Chicago's Fourth of July celebration consisted of a classical-music concert in which the Grant Park Symphony performed, among other works, Tchaikovsky's 1812 Overture. The booming cannons that highlight the piece were coordinated with the aural and visual "boom" of fireworks exploding over the lake. It was a spectacular finish to a glorious day spent picnicking and playing in what Chicagoans modestly believe is the world's nicest front yard.

Today the picnicking and playing and music and fireworks have grown to epic proportions. Nobody packs a sandwich anymore; now, there's Taste of Chicago, a massive food fest in Grant Park, which starts a week or so before the Fourth of July and continues through the holiday. The Taste, as it's known, offers bargain-priced samples from the menus of dozens of local restaurants, including some of the very best. Music and contests and countless other amusements surround the feast, which naturally attracts huge crowds and thus may not seem conducive to romance.

But still. The Taste is *such* a well-known Chicago tradition. And wouldn't it be a shame to miss the fireworks and the concert, too? Sure it would. Here's how to join in while creating your own fireworks on this festive holiday.

Practical notes: The city's fireworks display usually is held on July 3. Dates of the Taste vary with where the Fourth falls in the week. Usually, the Taste lasts ten days, including the two weekends before and after the Fourth. Be sure to check well in advance before you start scheduling.

DAY ONE: AFTERNOON/EVENING

Swissotel (323 East Wacker Drive; 312–565–0565) is just the place from which to base your fabulous Fourth. It's located on what downtowners call the New East Side, an area that includes the Navy Pier and North Pier entertainment complexes, lots of hotel and office and apartment buildings, and the massive Illinois Center trio of buildings. In this prosperous area the hotel that is closest to the lake itself and also offers a good view is—you guessed it— Swissotel. This means you'll have a great seat for the Fourth fireworks display, which is launched well out in the lake. The idea is to enjoy the show without having to cope with the crush of humanity.

Therefore, when you book your room (and the farther in advance, the better), ask for one with a lake view. Of course, you won't be the only ones with this idea, so realize that "you can request, but we don't guarantee a lake view," says Swissotel public-relations representative Wallene Blizzard.

Will you want to go, even without a guarantee? *Mais oui!* You'd be caviling to find any Swissotel room with a bad view. Some look out toward the endlessly fascinating cityscape, including a good vantage point from

Romance at a Glance

♥ *Check into the posh Swissotel; ask the concierge for Taste of Chicago tix; dine alfresco nearby.*

♥ *Stroll along Michigan Avenue, stopping for a kiss on the bridge over the river.*

♥ *Sample the Taste when it's least crowded—just as it opens for the day.*

♥ *Play a round of golf right outside your hotel.*

♥ *Return to your room in time for the lakefront fireworks display and a bottle of champagne.*

♥ *Brunch aboard the Odyssey, then explore the site of many slam-bang movie scenes: Lower Wacker Drive.*

which to watch Taste of Chicago. Others look toward the glittering expanse of North Michigan Avenue, where you'll spot the landmark John Hancock building among the towers. And if your room's view fails to satisfy, notice that you would have a great view of the fireworks just by standing in the hall where you'd wait for the elevators.

Swissotel's rooms are spacious and comfortable, recently redecorated in a soothing slate blue. Most offer a mini-bar, and all have fabulously comfy chairs in which to relax while you appreciate that view. Baths have one of my favorite features, a separate shower and tub, plus hair dryers. The health club has a pool and whirlpool, plenty of exercise machines, a separate weight-lifting room, a sauna, and more of that terrific view. Massages, manicures, pedicures, and facials are available as well.

The hotel offers several weekend packages, one of which includes two passes to the health club and two rounds of golf at the adjacent **Illinois Center Golf Course.** At $179 a night, it's an option well worth considering. The basic weekend rate is about $119 per night, which excludes the health club but does provide the services of a helpful (multilingual, even!) front-desk concierge. Ask him or her about getting you tickets to the Taste, which you'll need to exchange for food. (There's no admission or entertainment charge; all you need is the food tickets, but you *don't* want to stand in line on the scene for these.)

Once you've settled into your room, go right back out to enjoy the preholiday afternoon. If the weather cooperates—and anything but a driving thunderstorm counts as good weather during a Chicago summer—give yourselves an hour or two to wander North Michigan Avenue and the beautiful banks of the Chicago River.

The easiest way to get to the river is to descend the stairway just outside the hotel, then walk a block west on Lower Wacker Drive to Columbus Drive. Cross Wacker heading north, and you'll find yourselves at the river. Below is the south bank, which is undeveloped and grassy, perfect for a stroll or for just sitting. Across the Columbus Drive bridge is a lovely river walk, decorated with flowers, trees, and benches for relaxing. If you walk a block east and go

Don't miss this chance to linger on another landmark, the Michigan Avenue bridge. In a recent "best of" issue, Chicago *magazine praised this span as the very best place to feel like you're in Chicago. The magazine specifies sunset, on the west side of the bridge, but there's magic here any time. Examine the historic scenes depicted on the bridge's four pylons; watch the sightseeing boats and pleasure craft along the river. You might even see their blue-collar counterpart, a grimy, hard-working barge, steaming down- or up-river. As you linger on this bridge, if you can resist the urge to hold hands and kiss, it's time to reconsider your relationship.*

upstairs, you'll find yourselves just east of **Pioneer Court,** where fountains and beautiful landscaping invite passersby to linger.

Pioneer Court looks onto Michigan Avenue and, across the street, the landmark **Wrigley Building.** And the court adjoins another Chicago landmark, **Tribune Tower,** home of the redoubtable *Chicago Tribune* newspaper and its corporate sibling, WGN Radio, whose call letters stand for the slogan the *Trib* once proclaimed across the top of its front page—"World's Greatest Newspaper." Modesty remains a foreign concept to this civic pillar, whose other local holdings include a television station (WGN–TV, of course) and the Chicago Cubs. Right across Michigan, just beyond the Wrigley Building, lies the **Chicago Sun-Times Building,** home of the Trib's scrappy rival, so you can see why each paper refers to the other as "across the street" (as in, "We scooped across the street!").

But I digress—from the bustling yet delightful atmosphere of Pioneer Court, where steps away, a line-up of Good Humor trucks is waiting to serve you. They're parked just off the **Michigan Avenue Bridge,** which definitely deserves your attention.

Dinner

When hunger strikes, you're quite close to **Shaw's Crab House** (21 East Hubbard Street; 312–527–2722), a couple of blocks west and north of the bridge. (Note that if you walk west, past the Sun-Times and IBM buildings, you'll need to descend a staircase to street level.) Shaw's has some of the best seafood in town, with oysters and crab cakes as good appetizers and all sorts of wonderful ways to enjoy shrimp. Nonshellfish choices include great pan-fried perch, and you can't go wrong with a side of au gratin potatoes. Even the wine list is arranged according to what goes with which seafood. Dinner will run about $70 for the pair of you here and is available seven days a week till 10 P.M.

If you'd rather head back toward the hotel, consider stopping a block to the west at the Fairmont Hotel, 200 North Columbus Drive. Here, at the elegant **Entre Nous** (312–565–7997), you can watch as daylight dims and the lights of Navy Pier begin to twinkle. (Again, mention your wish for a good view when you make your reservation.) Dinner is served from 5:30 to 10:00 P.M. daily except Sunday, and entree prices range from about $14 to about $33 for the restaurant's French cuisine. But now that you're here, consider being adventurous enough to try one of the more exotic options around: pan-fried medallions of ostrich. These farm-raised critters provide a hearty, flavorful meat that *doesn't* taste like chicken—and it's definitely something to tell the folks back home about!

১৯৩৯

Care for a drink after dinner? The Fairmont's **Metropole Lounge** is comfortably sophisticated and often books cabaret artists whose songs offer just the polished ending you want for the evening. Also just west of Swissotel is **Big** (in the Hyatt Regency Chicago, 151 East Wacker Drive; 312–565–1234). True, it's the world's largest stand-up bar—but you *can* sit down if you want to. And there are literally hundreds of selections to sip or mix into just about any cocktail you dream up.

If you're still wide awake and looking to party, you'll find ample opportunity on another

Chicago institution, **Rush Street.** This Near North strip has long been home to lovers of nightlife, and the current crop of clubs carries on the tradition well. (It's near yet another nightlife institution, **Division Street,** where singles still swing.) Check out **Gibsons Bar and Steak House** (1028 North Rush Street; 312–266–8999), where sports and media celebs often turn up for whopping big martinis, steaks, and the buzz of hyper-trendy atmosphere. It's in the former home of the old Mister Kelly's nightclub and is hugely popular (therefore, not exactly *intimate)* among people who have outgrown singles bars. Also beloved by a similar clientele—and somewhat less noisy, especially when pianist Nick Russo is at work—is **Jilly's** (1007 North Rush Street; 312–664–1001). This sophisticated spot, named for Frank Sinatra's late friend Jilly Rizzo, is a home away from home for fans of the Rat Pack lifestyle. Indeed, the idea here appears to be total preparation for a spur-of-the-moment visit from the Chairman of the Board: a good-looking bar, plenty to drink, a model train in operation (Sinatra is a train fan), and plenty of people ready to party. Again, not exactly a quiet spot for two, but a fun place all the same.

DAY TWO: MORNING/AFTERNOON

Take your pick of two good ways to start the day: a round of golf right next door to Swissotel or an early attack on the **Taste of Chicago** before it's too crowded. You may want to do the Taste first, because when it gets crowded, it's *really* crowded. On the other hand, the postlunch, predinner lull also can be relatively calm. It's your call.

Scope out the Taste before setting foot in Grant Park by asking your concierge for a guide to the food booths and choosing the ones you want to sample. The mix of restaurants always includes more than enough purveyors of pizza, burgers, corn on the cob, and ribs—so be selective, and be sure to visit the top-of-the-line gourmet pavilion, where each day a different fine-dining restaurant takes the spotlight.

At the same time leave some room for spontaneity. Even with a list of good intentions, you'll want to allow yourselves to be distracted. In addition to the food, food, food, the Taste offers musical entertainment, an art fair, cooking demonstrations, and all manner of other fun.

You might as well buy a pair of corny Taste of Chicago T-shirts, too; the longer you're in town, the more you'll notice that *everyone* has one.

Some Tasters like to collect several samples and head for the lake, where you can find a quiet patch of grass to relax with your food and your honey. Here, too, musicians on stage and street will serenade you as the sights, smells, and sounds of the city's biggest festival drift your way.

When you've had enough Taste-ing, head back to your posh, quiet room, or to the relative serenity of the golf course. Ah, yes, the golf course. **Illinois Center Golf** (221 North Columbus Drive; 312–616–1234) is a par-three, Dye-designed, nine-hole beauty that surprises a lot of visitors with its proximity to a bustling downtown area—but here it is, and aren't you glad? Reservations are accepted a week in advance, with green fees at $19.00 for nine holes, $32.00 for eighteen holes. If you're content to stay on the putting green, it's $6.00 per hour; and fees for the ninety-two-station driving range start at $6.00 and go to $14.00. Club rental is $5.00 for a set of four, or $2.00 if you'll need only one. And the course is accessible from Swissotel; just ask a hotel staffer how to get there.

Dinner

After finishing your golf outing, relax with a drink on the adjacent patio or head back to Swissotel to meditate on where you'll have dinner. You may want to stay in-house and dine at the **Palm,** the Chicago outpost of the famous steak-house chain. The steaks here are stunning and the atmosphere studly. It's not cheap (side dishes, especially, can add up), but you're likely to emerge feeling that you got what you paid for at the Palm.

Possibly, however, a major dinner isn't quite what you want after a belly-busting day at Taste of Chicago. In that case stop downstairs at the hotel's **Cafe Suisse.** Its compact, inexpensive menu is available well into the afternoon and provides such lighter fare as sandwiches, salads, pastas, and a vegetable platter. Or take a short cab ride to Navy Pier, where **Riva** (700 East Grand Avenue; 312–644–7482) features steak, seafood, Italian pastas, and more of that great lakefront view. It's on the second floor of Navy Pier and, though the Pier is certain to be crowded, Riva is just as certain to maintain a quiet elegance in which you can enjoy good food and a great vantage point from which to watch a vibrant city at play. Dinner entrees are moderately priced and are served from 5:00 P.M. till midnight daily except Sunday, when dinnertime is 2:00 to 9:00 P.M.

⌒⌒⌒

Nine P.M. is about nightfall and the latest you'll want to get back to your room and catch every bit of the fireworks display. Check with the concierge about which radio or television station will simulcast the fireworks, so you can listen to the music as you watch. And don't forget to have a bottle of champagne on hand to toast the birthday of the U.S.A.!

DAY THREE: MORNING/AFTERNOON

Brunch

Why not make the most of your proximity to the lake by getting right *on* it? The **Odyssey** (708–990–0800) offers a shipshape Sunday brunch that cruises Lake Michigan from 11:45 A.M. till 1:45 P.M. Passengers enjoy a live jazz band while cruising a lavish buffet that includes lots of cold and hot salads, fresh fruits, baked treats, and an entree. The cruise costs $41 per person, and boarding begins at 11:00 A.M. from Navy Pier. (More details about *Odyssey* cruises appear in the subsequent chapter "Swept Away: Romantic Waterfront Cruises.")

⌒⌒⌒

When you return—or, if you're feeling intrepid, even instead of the cruise—explore the scene of many a movie chase along **Lower Wacker Drive.** Running literally right underneath Wacker Drive, Lower Wacker was the brilliant idea of nineteenth-century architect Daniel Burnham, who recognized the need for a downtown "truck route" long before gridlock became an urban curse. Sidewalks are nonexistent along some parts of this winding, eerily green-lit stretch of road, but you can walk along much of it; commuters do it all the time, and you never hear about anyone getting hurt. Beware of traffic, though; it's something of a local sport to drive *very* briskly along Lower Wacker. That doesn't seem to deter a few homeless people who camp here, though it can be nerve-racking when regular drivers, not action-movie stuntmen, are behind the wheel.

As you make your way, notice the many little staircases leading to the surface, and the way Lower Wacker hugs the river. If you get hungry, or want to make the pilgrimage many visitors won't leave town without, stop at **Billy Goat Tavern** (430 North Michigan Avenue; 312–222–1525), home of the "cheezborger, cheezborger" made famous on *Saturday Night Live* and still a popular spot among the newspaper and advertising folk who work nearby. No health food at the Goat, but those burgers are darn good.

Be sure to pause on the *lower* Michigan Avenue bridge, where you can kiss again, right under the spot where you did the same thing the other day. It's a perfect way to say "Happy Fourth" in the city with the great front yard—and a pretty cool basement, too.

FOR MORE ROMANCE

Chicago has *another* fireworks festival every year! It's called **Venetian Night,** and it takes place in late July. If the Fourth of July doesn't work for you, consider taking the itinerary for this chapter (sans the Taste) and applying it to Venetian Night, which also features a virtual flotilla of private boats that take to the lake for the occasion. You, too, can enjoy the evening from Lake Michigan by boarding the Venetian Night cruise on the *Jamaica,* a cruise ship that holds 215 passengers on its open upper deck and enclosed, air-conditioned lower Main Salon. The Venetian Night cruise includes a dinner buffet (ask about the menu when you reserve), open bar, and music played by a disc jockey for those who want to trip the light fantastic. The cruise lasts from 7:00 till 11:00 P.M. and costs $60 per person. Call Wagner Charter Cruises at (708) 653-8690 for information and reservations. And you might even want to do a similar—though daytime—cruise a couple of weeks later for the early-August **Air & Water Show,** a noisy but awesome display of military prowess and civilian stunts. This cruise also offers a buffet, limited open bar, music, and a broadcast of the Air & Water Show's commentary, so you know what's going on. The Air & Water Show cruise is $40 per person; call the same number for details.

ITINERARY 5
Two days and two nights

LET IT SNOW

A COZY WINTER WEEKEND FOR TWO

If you've ever experienced a Chicago winter, you know why Midwesterners seem to be obsessed with the weather. What a delicious fantasy, during these cold and cruel winters, to imagine a whole weekend with your beloved during which you never set foot outdoors.

Here's how to make the fantasy come true in a luxurious way. It isn't cheap, but this is a case of getting what you pay for.

DAY ONE: EVENING

The season doesn't matter once you enter the posh 900 North Michigan building, at the northern end of the city's Magnificent Mile. Inside 900 North, the atmosphere of gracious civility counters whatever miseries nature is inflicting on the unfortunate masses outdoors.

To get to the **Four Seasons Hotel,** you'll use the building's side entrance at 120 East Delaware Avenue. There, a greeter will direct you to the elevators that whisk you to the hotel (it starts on the seventh floor, giving new meaning to the phrase "heaven on seven").

Marble floors, gleaming dark wood, and massive flower arrangements give the Four Seasons its upper-crust look, but what's really special is the blend of friendliness and professionalism

Romance at a Glance

♥ *Indulge yourselves two nights at the Four Seasons Hotel, with room-service breakfast and afternoon tea.*

♥ *Browse Bloomingdale's and other fabulous stores.*

♥ *Dine at Seasons, one of the city's most romantic restaurants.*

♥ *Pamper yourselves with a swim, a personal trainer, a massage.*

♥ *Enjoy an elaborate international Sunday brunch and a movie.*

you'll discover in the staff. And, given the hotel's high level of service and the fact that you aren't planning to leave the premises, you'll see a lot of the staff during your weekend.

Once you've checked in, it would be hard to resist taking some time to appreciate your deluxe accommodations! Even if you don't pop for a suite, a Four Seasons room for two offers a king-size bed with an elegant armoire to house the television set, plus a wonderfully spacious bathroom and, from every window, a stunning view of the city. Suites give you even more space, of course, with French doors separating bedroom from sitting room. Room rates begin at $325 a night—but it's a once-in-a-lifetime extravaganza, right?

If you're celebrating, the hotel can arrange to have flowers and champagne in your room when you arrive. When you're ready to step out, you might enjoy sipping a predinner drink in the lobby—not a single long hall, but a comfortable warren of sitting areas, all furnished with inviting chairs and handy tables to facilitate a lingering chat.

Dinner

Dinner awaits downstairs at **Seasons,** a perennial on the top-ten lists of local critics and a recent entry on *Food & Wine* magazine's list of the most romantic restaurants. The room itself is lovely, its cool pastel color scheme punctuated with more big flowers and underscored with dignified wood paneling. There's a small army of white-coated staff providing service that never misses a beat against a backdrop of tinkling crystal, crisp white linen, delicate bone china, and glamorously hushed conversation.

The menu offers plenty of variety, including the pleasant surprise of more than one vegetarian option (about $24). Fish and meat are about equally represented ($26 to $40) and the card tops out with Japanese Kobe beef (at a breathtaking $95). One unusual touch is an opener of essig, an aperitif wine vinegar that's fashionable among the food cognoscenti.

In surroundings this luxurious, it's easy to make an evening of dinner, perhaps with coffee or an after-dinner drink in the lobby, where a jazz trio will be performing. If you're so inclined, the nearby bar allows smoking, including cigars. (When I visited, a patron couldn't tell me enthusiastically enough just how much he appreciated this accommodation!)

DAY TWO: MORNING/AFTERNOON

Start your day with a leisurely breakfast from room service, and then head for the health club to work off last night's divine dinner! Winter visitors can't take advantage of the hotel's outdoor running track or rooftop sundeck, but the indoor area offers more than enough to keep you busy. Stairmasters, Lifecycles, Nautilus equipment, and much more are available—all ready to plug into the hotel's personal portable stereos, complete with tapes and headsets. Some machines are even equipped with television monitors. Reading racks are here, too, to hold the daily newspapers provided at the entrance, along with juice, coffee, and fruit from a welcoming tray.

The hotel's 50-foot indoor pool looks positively California-ish under a beautiful skylight (it was used in filming the movie *Home Alone 2*), and the level of service is such that you can even borrow workout clothing or get a disposable swimsuit if you've forgotten your own! Other health-club services include a personal trainer who, for $45, will design your very own workout program and help you learn to implement it back home. And massages using various methods—Swedish, acupressure, reflexology, and several others—are available for thirty or sixty minutes ($45 to $65). Saunas and steam rooms, alas, separate men and women, but you can get back together to lounge poolside.

When you're as fit as you can stand to get, shower and get down (via elevator, of course) to some power shopping in the 900 North Michigan building. Tenants include **Bloomingdale's**

(312–440–4460)—hours in itself—as well as **Henri Bendel** (312–642–0140), **Lillie Rubin** (312–337–1444), **Gucci** (312–664–5504), and unusual boutiques to browse. Guests at the Four Seasons receive a "900 Card," which offers discounts at participating merchants in the building. (Although you're probably already in the "if you have to ask, you can't afford it" zone.)

Lunch

Back upstairs, the Four Seasons serves up a relative bargain at lunchtime, with the cafe's pasta buffet setting forth an all-you-can-eat spread for about $11 per person. Soup, salad, antipasto, and two daily specials are included in the buffet, which is available from 11:30 A.M. till 2:00 P.M. daily except Sunday. Or you might prefer to skip lunch and hold out for afternoon tea, a splendid affair served from 3:00 to 5:00 P.M. daily except Sunday in the Seasons Lounge. Choose between a fireside seat or one facing the lakefront near a tinkling waterfall as you sip and chat. Full tea, which includes finger sandwiches and pastries along with a pot of tea, is about $30 for two; add a few dollars more if you want a glass of champagne, too.

DAY TWO: EVENING

Dinner

Those who like to keep their meals on the three-squares program should be pleased that there is a place as casual as Seasons is formal in the 900 building at **Tucci Benucch** (312–266–2500). Thin-crust pizzas, delectable salads, and homemade pastas are served by pleasant, un-tuxed people in this agreeably "rustic" setting. The prices are also a pleasant alternative to 900's rarefied atmosphere, too; dinner could come in at less than $40 for the two of you.

⌘

For a low-key evening, take in a movie at the **900 North Michigan Cinemas** (312–787–1988), where two screens give you a choice and crowds are rarely a problem. Perhaps

Windy City Cinema

You say you'd like to see a Chicago movie that doesn't involve bloodshed? No problem! Here's a strictly subjective list of fun Chicago flicks with what the movie mavens call "a love interest."

While You Were Sleeping: *In this lighter-than-air 1995 romance, Sandra Bullock poses as the fiancee of a comatose mugging victim, becoming entwined with his eccentric family—including an extremely attractive brother who isn't in a coma.*

Continental Divide: *A little-known 1981 romantic gem in which John Belushi plays a hard-boiled newspaper columnist for the* Chicago Sun-Times, *incongruously in love with ornithologist Blair Brown. Watch for Belushi's reaction when his wilderness guide mentions spotting a bear: "Am I pleased or frightened?"*

The Blues Brothers: *Released in 1980, this frenetically funny film features John Belushi, Dan Aykroyd, too many bluesmen to name, and the delicious sight of Jake and Elwood Blues terrorizing the elegant Chez Paul restaurant just by sitting down. Ya gotta love it!*

His Girl Friday: *One of the finest 1940s screwball comedies stars Cary Grant and Rosalind Russell as wisecracking newspaper toughs trying to score the big scoop on a notorious murder case while resolving their on-again, off-again romance.*

About Last Night: *The other Belushi, Jim, stars with a young Demi Moore, Elizabeth Perkins, and Rob Lowe in a funny, touching tale of yuppie love. The 1986 movie has been tamed considerably from its stage origins as David Mamet's "Sexual Perversity in Chicago," although there's still a generous sprinkling of the f-word throughout.*

Ferris Bueller's Day Off: *The very young Matthew Broderick plays a fatally charming high-schooler in this hilarious teen-fantasy romp through the city. Chicago never looked better than it does in director John Hughes' paean to friendship, young love, and a red Ferrari.*

you'd prefer to make it an even cozier evening by retiring to your Four Seasons room to watch a Chicago-made flick. The hotel will provide a VCR if you ask, and the concierge can find you a tape from our list of titles that'll keep you entertained while you try to spot local locations. Snuggle up in the plush terrycloth robes the hotel provides and make this your most memorable movie-watching evening ever.

DAY THREE: MORNING

Brunch

As you prepare to face the outside world again, fortify yourself with one more opulent meal at the Four Seasons. A lavish Sunday brunch is served in the restaurant from 10:30 A.M. to 2:30 P.M. with six "stations" serving Asian, Mediterranean, Midwestern, breakfast, and dessert selections. The toughest decision of the weekend may be choosing whether to try the seaweed salad or roast lamb—or maybe you should just go directly to the chocolate-dipped strawberries. It's all covered in the price of $42 per person, so don't be shy about lingering over cappuccino.

To end your 900 North idyll with a flourish, tell the hotel's concierge that you'd like to take a spin along Michigan Avenue as you depart. Your luggage can wait as you step into a horse-drawn carriage at the hotel's door. Expect this final touch of class to run about $30 for a half-hour ride, which is all you'll want if the day is cold. It's a chilly but charming way to say goodbye to your warm winter weekend.

A ROMANCE WITH HISTORY

AFRICAN-AMERICAN CHICAGO

*L*ove was described by Samuel Johnson as the triumph of hope over experience. Nowhere is this optimistic outlook more appropriate than in Chicago's African-American community, which got its start with the very first non-Native American to settle here. Jean-Baptiste Pointe du Sable, described in a post-Revolutionary War British report as a well-educated "handsome Negro," came around 1779, a successful trader who built his log cabin on the north bank of the Chicago River (demonstrating a good nose for prime real estate) before moving on to the wide-open spaces of Missouri in 1800.

Barely more than half a century later, the white Downstater who became known as the Great Emancipator was nominated here for the presidency. During the Civil War and after, Chicago proved a place of opportunity for freed slaves; and during the first half of the following century, Chicago became by far the most popular destination for southerners making the great migration north, where factory jobs and less blatant discrimination offered the promise of a better life.

Today, the triumph of hope over experience is driving redevelopment in areas such as Bronzeville, where many of the southerners settled. As you explore this and adjacent areas

Romance at a Glance

♥ *Visit Bronzeville, where black Chicago flourished during the great migration from the South.*

♥ *Explore the DuSable Museum of African-American History.*

♥ *Nourish yourselves with soul food at Gladys' Luncheonette and Army & Lou's.*

♥ *Explore opulence for everyone (maybe swim or golf) at South Shore Cultural Center.*

♥ *See a show from one of the nation's most prominent African-American theater companies, ETA Creative Arts Foundation.*

together (keep in mind that you needn't be African-American to do so), you'll be reminded over and over that here, as in *your* hearts and in the heart of every lover, hope springs eternal.

Practical notes: Public transportation is available throughout the South Side, where this itinerary is set. But you'll be able to move along faster—and, it must be said, perhaps more safely—if you're driving.

MORNING

Start your day on the South Side in **Bronzeville,** the community that was a beacon for blacks heading north during the Great Migration of the early twentieth century. Bronzeville was known nationwide as a monument to the economic muscle that African-Americans could amass in unity. Today the neighborhood is no longer prosperous—and nearby public-housing projects should be avoided—but recent efforts to preserve its landmarks and salute its importance hold promise.

Begin at the **Monument to the Great Migration** statue (at Twenty-fifth Street near King Drive and the Interstate 55 overpass), sculptor Alison Saar's larger-than-life bronze of a traveler whose bulging, cord-tied suitcase suggests more dreams than possessions. You can walk south along King Drive and examine, in the sidewalks on both sides of the street, the ninety-one bronze plaques in the **Walk of Fame,** artist Geraldine McCullough's commemorations of notable Bronzeville events and people. On the same route, you'll see twenty-four benches at bus stops and median plazas, each designed by one of twenty-four artists to salute Bronzeville's past and present.

At the symbolic gateway to Bronzeville, Thirty-fifth Street and King Drive, stands a 14-by-7-foot bronze **street map** showing 120 historic sites in the area, including the homes of writer Lorraine Hansberry *(A Raisin in the Sun)* and the great gospel singer Mahalia Jackson, as well as the old Regal Theater and more. At this writing some Bronzeville sites had fallen into disrepair, but public and private efforts are now underway to preserve many.

These include the headquarters of what at the time were the nation's most prosperous black-owned businesses, including the **Supreme Life Insurance** company (3501 South King Drive). The **Eighth Regiment Armory** (at Thirty-fifth and Giles) was the home of an all-black military unit. And at the **Wabash YMCA** (3763 South Wabash Avenue), black historian Carter G. Woodson created what now is celebrated as Black History Month.

One building that has been recycled is the **Chicago Bee Building** (3647 South State Street; 773–747–6872). The *Bee* was a daily newspaper that boosted the Bronzeville promise to African-Americans nationwide. Appropriately its old home now is the Chicago Bee neighborhood branch of the Chicago Public Library.

Lunch

If walking has worked up your appetites, have lunch at a South Side institution that's a little south and west of Bronzeville. At **Gladys' Luncheonette** (4527 South Indiana Avenue; 773–548–4566), the soul food runs from hot links and eggs to salmon croquettes. "It's not fancy," says Gladys' fan Diane Hightower, "but when you sit down there, you really get the feeling that, wow, Louis Armstrong or Duke Ellington sat in this seat, too." The food is inexpensive, and the feeling is free.

AFTERNOON

Going east and south from Gladys', you'll come to Washington Park, which at the turn of the century held a racetrack to which pleasure seekers flocked. Today, it's home to the

DuSable Museum of African–American History (740 East Fifty-sixth Place; 773–947–0600), which got its start as a labor of love by Dr. Margaret Burroughs and her late husband, Charles, back in 1961. Burroughs, a painter and sculptor, wanted to showcase the history and art of her people; and though nowadays she's a civic pillar, it's a measure of how far her mission has come to note that she was the first woman many Chicagoans ever saw in colorful contemporary African dress.

At the museum (which called itself African-American long before the term entered the mainstream) you'll see works by many local artists who attained greater fame. One distinguished example is Archibald Motley, who painted Chicago's Negro life in vibrant compositions that are unmistakably 1930s American while recalling Henri de Toulouse-Lautrec in their clear-eyed, unapologetic focus on the artist's community. Motley was the subject of a major retrospective at the Chicago Historical Society a few years back, and his paintings also hang in the Art Institute as well as other major museums.

The DuSable Museum focuses as much on history as art, with many African artifacts and the stunning Robert Ames Freedom Mural, a 10-foot-tall mahogany carving that depicts highlights in African-American history. Special exhibits are also worth noting; at this writing one on the Douglas-Grand Crossing neighborhood (also known as Bronzeville) closed recently, and an Underground Railroad exhibit was set to open soon. Admission to the museum is $3.00 for adults ($2.00 for seniors and students), except on Thursday, when everyone gets in free. Museum hours are 10:00 A.M. to 5:00 P.M. Monday through Saturday and noon to 5:00 P.M. on Sunday.

A couple of hours in the museum is enough to enjoy its collections and exhibits. Next, take a leisurely drive south through Jackson Park toward the **South Shore Cultural Center** (7059 South South Shore Drive; 773–747–2536). South Shore, once among the city's very best neighborhoods, remains a lovely area of fine old homes. Today's cultural center once was the very tony South Shore Country Club, to which I confess a sentimental attachment by way of my mother's treasured memories of swimming, riding, and playing there as a child.

A few years back my cousin was married at "the club" in one of the most glamorous weddings I've ever attended. The bride wore a vintage green satin short formal; the ceremony was held on the grassy area between the building and its beach, with the lake and city skyline as backdrop. The magic continued as we moved indoors to the ballroom and danced to the music of a local big band, complete with individual bandstands sporting the group's name. After dinner my mother guided us through the building, pointing out the room where movies were screened on Sunday nights, the children's play areas, and the grand staircase, beyond which lay the bedrooms for members who might not make it home!

Even without my mom's travelogue, you'll fall for the magic of South Shore, too. Now operated by the Chicago Park District, the cultural center hosts many events that are open to the public, including dance and music performances that often are free. Call to have a schedule sent to you. And when you visit, notice the stables, at one end of the gravel drive, where the

A Break for Some Action

If you've had the foresight to come in summer and pack your swimsuits, you can take a dip in Lake Michigan at the South Shore beach. Or bring your clubs to the 2,900-acre, par-33 South Shore Golf Course at the Cultural Center. To reserve a tee time, call the twenty-four-hour answering system at (312) 245–0909. Either activity will give you a delicious feeling of playing hooky together as you savor some unexpected pastoral pleasures right in the big, bustling city.

Chicago Police Department's mounted patrol keeps its horses. Indoors, seek out the building's lovely old touches: a mosaic floor, grand windows, dreamy painted details. And savor the fact that what once was *veddy* private is now for everyone.

EVENING

Dinner

Dinner is nearby at another South Side institution: **Army & Lou's** (422 East Seventy-fifth Street; 773–483–3100), where a beautifully refurbished building holds a restaurant that seems to have been here forever. A little more expensive and definitely more upscale than Gladys', Army & Lou's offers its own top-notch soul food, including excellent fried chicken and kosher short ribs. If you're here on Sunday, go for the roast turkey dinner that'll have you giving thanks, even in the heat of summer. And if you're really stuffed, agree on whether you'd rather split the sweet-potato pie or the peach cobbler.

Then take in a performance by the **ETA Creative Arts Foundation** (7558 South South Chicago Avenue; 773–752–3955), a wonderful company that for twenty-five years has been producing shows that explore the African-American experience with heartfelt humor and serious emotion. To wit: the popular recent show, *The Trial of One Short-Sighted Black Woman vs. Mammy Louise and Safreeta Mae,* a funny, pointed courtroom drama in which playwright Marcia L. Leslie tackles the movies' depiction of African-American women. You can see how an ETA show will give you plenty to talk about on the way home! ETA's performances are at 8:00 P.M. Thursday, Friday, and Saturday, and 3:00 and 7:00 P.M. on Sunday. Tickets are $15, and reservations are wise.

ITINERARY 7
Three days and two nights

CHICAGO CHRISTMAS À DEUX

$\mathcal{C}$elebrating the holidays in Chicago is enough to make you believe in Santa. There's magic in the miles of twinkling lights along Michigan Avenue, the towering tree right in the middle of the Loop, the glittering store windows decked out with intricate displays. The shopping is spectacular, even if you never leave North Michigan Avenue. And the festive, anticipatory atmosphere will have you wishing total strangers a happy holiday season. Lucky you, to have a sweetheart with whom to share the revelry!

Practical notes: Here's a weekend when you can leave the car at home! All this itinerary's highlights are within easy reach of each other. You'll definitely need to catch a cab to the Arie Crown for *The Nutcracker,* but everything else is a good walk or a quick bus or cab ride.

DAY ONE: EVENING

Start your holiday weekend at the pinnacle of the Magnificent Mile by checking in at the **Drake Hotel** (140 East Walton Street; 312–787–2200). Although its address and entrance are on a side street, the Drake is something of a crown jewel on Michigan Avenue. It's the northernmost building on one of the city's very best streets, and one of the most venerable. All sorts of royalty have rested here, from Princess Diana to the very prominent society maven who resides in the penthouse. For the rest of us, there's a friendly and helpful staff, a posh afternoon tea, an excellent seafood restaurant that has earned the loyalty of generations of Chicagoans and out-of-towners, and a piano bar where one of the greats holds forth. And when the Drake decorates for the holidays, it does so with enthusiasm plus panache. So give yourselves some time to linger in the lobby and enjoy the environment.

In its rooms as well as its public areas, you'll find the Drake is elegant but not stuffy, comfortable but never assuming. Maid service is provided not once, but twice daily, the better to replenish your supplies of fresh fruit and ice. No two rooms are exactly alike, but all offer a minibar, two telephones, and cozy terrycloth robes in the bathroom. Of course, just about every view is terrific; you can ask for a lake view, or one that looks down on the festive twinkling of Michigan Avenue or Lake Shore Drive. The Drake's rates go as high as $245 for a deluxe room with double bed and lake view, but weekend packages can bring that figure down considerably. Ask about the shoppers' weekend, which is offered during the month of December; you'll do much better on rates this way.

Romance at a Glance

♥ *Check into the poshest hotel—the Drake—and have dinner in the Cape Cod Room and drinks at Coq d'Or with Buddy Charles at the piano.*

♥ *Shop till you drop on Michigan Avenue and Oak Street.*

♥ *Sip high tea at the Drake's Palm Court to soothing harp music.*

♥ *Feast on the Goodman's preshow turkey dinner, and then thrill to* A Christmas Carol.

♥ *Stroll the Loop stores' windows.*

♥ *Make the matinee of* The Nutcracker.

Dinner

Once you've checked in and fully appreciated your accommodations, wander downstairs for a pre-dinner drink at the **Coq d'Or,** where you'll be back later to enjoy pianist Buddy Charles. Then head for a splendid seafood dinner at the **Cape Cod Room** (312–787–2200). The nautical theme here teeters between tasteful and retro, with lots of brass, dark wood, and red-

and-white checked tablecloths. Get in the spirit with Bookbinder's red snapper soup, made famous in Philadelphia and made very well indeed here in the Cape Cod Room. Whatever seafood you favor is sure to be expertly prepared, but do ask your waiter for suggestions. Dinner will run about $40 per person, and you'll want reservations (make them when you book your room for the weekend).

After dinner, if you're feeling festive and the weather isn't forbidding, you might enjoy a **carriage ride** along the side streets of the two neighborhoods in this area, Streeterville and the Gold Coast. Historical sidelight: Streeterville is named for one of the city's genuine characters, a rogue named George "Cap" Streeter, who declared himself ruler of "the District of Lake Michigan" after running his steamboat onto a sandbar east of Michigan Avenue in 1886. Cap and his wife, Ma (I am not making this up), built up the sand bar with junk, remodeled the shipwreck into a shack, and refused to budge for more than twenty years, during which they sold beer on Sundays and performed their own sovereign "state's" marriages. As an irritant and a frustration to their neighbors, who even then included many of the city's very finest citizens (which, then as now, meant its very wealthiest), Cap remains legendary in local lore.

As for that carriage ride, you can make a reservation to be picked up at the hotel by calling the **Noble Horse** (1410 North Orleans Street, 312–266–7878). Rush hour is off-limits, but evening rides are offered from 6:30 till midnight, or 2:00 A.M. weekends. A half-hour ride for two is $30, for a full hour it's $60.

For a swell after-dinner drink, return to the Drake's Coq d'Or room, where pianist Buddy Charles is a local legend. So is the room itself, having opened the day after Prohibition was repealed in 1933. Nowadays one of the city's treasures is performing nightly except for Sundays and Mondays, from 9:00 P.M. till you ought to be in bed, singing and playing the songs people love. The piano man is more artist than entertainer, according to no less an authority than the *Chicago Tribune*'s music critic Howard Reich, who has called Charles's playing "a virtual history of jazz and pop keyboard playing of this century." There's no better way to enjoy him than with the one you love.

DAY TWO: MORNING/AFTERNOON

Dive into a day's worth of holiday shopping by crossing the street to **Arturo Express** (919 North Michigan Avenue; 312–751–2250), where a cappuccino and a bagel or muffin will get you going happily. Then head up the block to start at the top, in terms of browsing, on the fabulous **Oak Street** (1000 North). Oak Street's retailers are the creme de la creme of clothing and accessories, including such star-power names as **Hermès of Paris** (110 East Oak Street; 312–787–8175), **Giorgio Armani** (113 East Oak Street.; 312–751–2244), and **Barneys New York** (25 East Oak Street; 312–587–1700). Representing the cutting edge is 1960s veteran and 1990s star **Betsey Johnson** (72 East Oak Street; 312–664–5901).

Tucked in among Oak Street's heavy hitters are local luminaries that you might actually prefer to scout more closely, since you can get those biggies elsewhere. Don't miss the spectacular **Ultimo** (114 East Oak Street; 312–787–0906), which is a name you can drop among the fashion cognoscenti anywhere. The shop carries high-style, highly sophisticated clothes for men and women, and the staff will help put it together on you. Also extremely stylish, **Hino & Malee Boutique** (50 East Oak Street; 312–664–7475) carries the creations of this Chicago couple, who have made their women's wear a success among the most fashionable ladies in America.

If these high-fashion shops are a bit much for your gift list, tone down the style statement with something a little less haute from **Sugar Magnolia** (34 East Oak Street; 312–944–0885). The overalls are long gone from this onetime Lincoln Park favorite, which has gone uptown gracefully with women's clothing and accessories that are good-looking but less intimidating (and less expensive!) than much of what the neighbors stock.

Beyond clothing Oak Street offers both sexes the kind of personal grooming most of us only dream of—and you might just want to turn over your morning to it. At **Marilyn Miglin**

Hino is the he and Malee (pronounced Molly) is the she in this high-style pair. They met while working for a local fashion designer, eventually joining forces to design and produce their own line of sophisticated women's wear. Both did major overtime for years to build the business from a small, stitch-it-yourself operation to the successful design house it is now. Long after their professional relationship was established, their personal involvement led to that traditional fashion-show closer: a wedding gown. Applause, please. Today they're one of Chicago's hardest-working happily married couples.

(112 East Oak Street; 312–943–1120), you'll find skin-care consultation and products, makeup, and the exotic perfume Pheremone (Miglin's own concoction, and she swears it's every bit as effective as the hormones themselves!). **Ilona of Hungary Skin Care** (45 East Oak Street; 312–337–7161) and **Syd Simons Cosmetics** (2 East Oak Street; 312–943–2333) also offer skin care and cosmetics, and at Simons, you can get lessons in application. Two of the city's top hair salons are on Oak, too: **Marc Benaim** (49 East Oak Street; 312–644–3010) and **Charles Ifergan** (106 East Oak Street; 312–642–4484). A third Oak Street salon, **Chatto** (102 East Oak Street; 312–640–0003) specializes in "multicultural hair," which means your dreadlocks or braids will be handled with care here. And remember—all these salons offer equal-opportunity pampering, so make plans for *two*.

There's lots more on Oak Street, but you don't want to shortchange Michigan Avenue. This is where you'll find **Gucci** (900 North Michigan Avenue; 312–664–5504), **Chanel Boutique** (940 North Michigan Avenue; 312–787–5500), **Tiffany & Co.** (715 North Michigan Avenue; 312–944–7500), **Williams-Sonoma** (700 North Michigan Avenue; 312–787–8991), **Saks Fifth Avenue** (700 North Michigan Avenue; 312–944–6500), **Escada**

USA (840 North Michigan Avenue; 312–915–0500), and many others from the shopping hit parade.

Lunch

When your energy flags, get off the crowded shopping route with a detour to **Mrs. Park's Tavern** (198 East Delaware Place; 312–280–8882). Located in the Doubletree Hotel and Suites, Mrs. Park's atmosphere is pleasant and its menu is American—but everything comes with a bit of a twist. A chicken Caesar salad, for example, comes as a sandwich, and the potato chips are *sweet* potato. Lunch and dinner are served from 11:30 A.M. till 2:00 A.M. daily, and won't cost more than about $30 total.

Revived, give over your afternoon to **Water Tower Place** (845 North Michigan Avenue), with its two anchor stores, **Lord & Taylor** (312–787–7400) and **Marshall Field's** (312–335–7700). Lord & Taylor carries classic clothing and accessories even Aunt Bertha will be happy to receive. And Field's offers a broader selection in the same territory, as well as such surefire gifties as crystal and jewelry. Be sure to stock up on Frango mints, the Field's-made confections you can't get anywhere else. They're a perfect hostess gift, and great to have on hand when you get an unexpected present from someone else.

More gifts? Check out the toy nirvana, **F.A.O. Schwartz** (312–787–8894), which has a Water Tower Place location called F.A.O. Schweetz that's all candy, plus a larger space across the street (840 North Michigan Avenue; 312–587–5000). Gorgeous coffee-table books are all over the place at **Rizzoli Book Store** (312–642–3500), and be sure to browse the selection of international fashion magazines. Everything's pretty at **Laura Ashley** (312–951–8004), and pretty tough at **North Beach Leather** (312–280–9292).

The shopping is unsurpassed, but there's another reason to go to Water Tower: The people-watching is outstanding. The mall—let's face it, this is no more than that—attracts everyone. You'll see power shoppers, mall rats, ladies who lunch, and overstimulated families. I remember to this day a winter evening when I spotted, at a distance, a man I knew slightly, lingering near the sleek glass elevators with a beautiful, curly-haired blonde. Both were wearing head-to-toe black, berets included, and looked as glamorous and lucky in love as you could ever want to look.

Water Tower Place has a way of giving people a patina. Be happy, be in love, and it'll make you shiny, too.

DAY TWO: AFTERNOON/EVENING

When you've finished your shopping (perhaps forever!), rest your plastic and your weary selves back at the Drake. Do it over afternoon tea, a sedate and highly civilized affair held daily in the Palm Court. Scones, finger sandwiches, and pastries will soothe you, as will the strains of harp music played in the court. You can choose a table with elegant upholstered chairs, or sink into a sofa for maximum comfort.

By the time you arise and stop in your room to change, you'll be ready to cab to the southern part of downtown for tonight's main event: a performance of Charles Dickens's *A Christmas Carol* at the Goodman Theater (200 South Columbus Drive; 312–443–3800). For almost twenty years, this show has delighted Chicagoans with its ever-changing production, including whiz-bang special effects that get better every year. It's truly a don't-miss holiday highlight, with shows at 7:30 P.M. (except Friday and Saturday shows at 8:00 P.M.) and tickets ranging from about $23 to about $35. And about dinner: When you get tickets, sign up for the preshow turkey feast served right on the premises. It's a festive dinner that provides a great way to get in the spirit while assuring you'll make it to the theater on time!

Most mortals would be tuckered out by this day and evening, but if you're still going strong after the show, cab over to Wicker Park's extremely hip **Bop Shop** (1807 West Division Street; 312–235–3232), where jazz rules till 2:00 A.M. nightly. Or go upscale at **Green Dolphin Street** (2200 North Ashland Avenue; 312–395–0066), where the jazz is hot and so is the crowd, Wednesday through Saturday, till 2:00 A.M. Both clubs are open later on Saturdays, with cover charges that run around $10 per person.

If you've gotten hungry, choose Green Dolphin Street, and experience one of the more innovative kitchens around town. Moderately priced entrees include a fabulous chicken breast stuffed with portobello mushrooms and sun-dried tomatoes. Smoked scallops and grilled quail are enticing, too, and there's an unusually broad selection of champagnes for that bubbly feeling. If you do eat, remember that the cover charge is waived.

DAY THREE: MORNING

To get an early start on your Sunday, head for the breakfast buffet at **Beau's Bistro** (in the Ambassador West hotel, 1300 North State Parkway; 312–787–3700). From 7:00 A.M. till 1:00 P.M., there's a big buffet of breakfast favorites, including eggs, bacon, hash browns, bakery treats, and more. And the price is right at just $9.95 per person. Beau's is a short cab ride (or walk, if the weather's friendly) west and north from the Drake.

Brunch

For a brunch that's more of an event, consider the American dim sum brunch at **Park Avenue Cafe** (199 East Walton Street; 312–944–4414), where some thirty items give you a chance to sample much of what's coming out of this highly respected kitchen. Meats and fish, baked items, and more are offered in tempting little portions from 10:30 A.M. till 2:00 P.M. At $27.50 per person, it's definitely pricier than your average breakfast—but then, it *isn't* your average breakfast!

This being Sunday morning, even if you're not the churchgoing type, consider stopping in at services in the beautiful **Fourth Presbyterian Church** (126 East Chestnut Street, off Michigan Avenue; 312–787–4570). Its splendid stained-glass windows are worth the trip all by themselves.

Then head south to enjoy the department store windows along State Street. Two big displays are at **Marshall Field's** State Street store (111 North State Street; 312–781–1000) and

Carson Pirie Scott & Co. (1 South State Street; 312–641–7000). If you can stand a bit more time in retail establishments, don't miss Field's giant Christmas tree and Carson's glorious interior. Carson's is a Louis Sullivan building and one of the loveliest works by the city's pre-Prairie master, gracefully decorated and beautifully restored by caring owners.

Next, catch a cab and head farther south for the **Arie Crown Theater** (in McCormick Place, East 23rd Street and the lake; 312–902–1500) to take in the holiday ritual that brings a burst of beauty to the theater's stage every December. This is the city's main production of Tchaikovsky's *The Nutcracker,* a lavish affair featuring professional ballet dancers in principal roles and a happy horde of local kids supporting them. Tickets cost $13 to $37. Take in a 2:00 P.M. matinee and allow yourselves some time, before or after, to gaze out at the icy grandeur of Lake Michigan.

You must be starving by this time, and perhaps a tiny bit sick of sugarplums. Zip over to Dearborn Street Station, in the South Loop, for an early dinner at the romantically dim **Lindas Margaritas** (47 West Polk Street; 312–939–6106). Mexican goes modern in this health-conscious kitchen, which trims fat by grilling meats and using veggies. Entrees range from about $9.00 to about $12.00), and if you happen to come on a Friday evening, you'll even get a mariachi band for extra fun. Sipping margaritas and scratching name after name off your gift-shopping list makes a perfect finale to your weekend of holiday magic in Chicago.

FOR MORE ROMANCE

If you happen to be in town on the right day, do try to take in a performance of Handel's *Messiah.* This magnificent piece has become a holiday tradition here as a do-it-yourself production that's a lot more polished than you might expect. The **Do-It-Yourself** *Messiah.* generally has two performances on a weekend before Christmas, and although admission is free, you need tickets to get in. Write for them at Orchestra Hall (220 South Michigan Avenue, Chicago 60604) or call (312) 776–4300, but do check beforehand to learn when they become available and—very important!—when the performances will be given.

To survey the many *Messiah* performances, as well as other special music programs around town, get a copy of *Chicago* magazine's December issue and consult its listing of holiday programs. They're too specific to discuss here, but it would be a shame to leave town without enjoying something from the rich array of holiday music that's available.

Can you stand one more Chicago Christmas tradition? Make it a visit to the **Museum of Science and Industry's Christmas Around the World** (Fifty-seventh Street and Lake Shore Drive; 312–684–1414), a collection of full-size Christmas trees decorated in the ethnic traditions of many nations. This loving display of pride and memory is sure to squelch any Scroogy tendencies (although I may be biased by the childhood wonder I still recall at seeing the Lithuanian tree, hung with intricate ornaments made entirely from white straws). There are performances of ethnic dance and music, plus all sorts of other special events for the season.

ITINERARY 8
One day and one evening

AMORE!

CHICAGO ROMANCE ITALIAN STYLE

*H*ere's a question for you and your beloved to ponder: If we were planning a trip to the land of romance, where would we be going? If you're from Chicago, the answer is likely to be Italy. Leave snooty France, humid Florida, and all those overcommercialized tropical islands to other, less discerning lovers. If you want great food, great culture, great people, and great regard for *amore,* you've got to go for Italy.

Or the next best thing, which is immersion in Italia, Chicago-style, and does *not* include anything pertaining to Al Capone, thank you. Here's a lighthearted look at la dolce vita, according to one of the city's proudest ethnic groups.

Practical note: This itinerary calls for a car to permit traveling from the western suburb of Stone Park to downtown locations. The drive is about a half-hour from downtown on Interstate 290; exit northbound at Mannheim Road and look for signs.

MORNING/AFTERNOON

Get your cappuccinos *per andare* (to go) and head out to the **Italian Cultural Center** (1621 North Thirty-ninth Avenue, Stone Park; 708–345–3842), where loving Italian-Americans have assembled "Italians in Chicago," a photo exhibit displaying hundreds of nineteenth- and twentieth-century pictures of their compatriots at work, church, and home. An art gallery features paintings, sculptures, and lithographs by Italian artists, as well as the little puppet mouse, Topo Gigio (think 1960s, *Ed Sullivan Show*). Other exhibits include a stunning, built-to-scale wooden model of the Vatican's Basilica of St. Peter and its columned courtyard, as well as miniatures of Pisa's Cathedral, Baptistry, and famous Leaning Tower. A library of some eight hundred volumes, about one-fourth of them in Italian, is open to the public but doesn't allow books to circulate, librarian Florence Roselli explains, because too many have been lost.

The center's hours are 10:00 A.M. to 4:00 P.M. weekdays; usually the center's closed on weekends, except for the annual Italian Day picnic, which is held on the first Sunday of August. An outdoor mass is celebrated in Italian before revelers settle down to catered food, tours of the center, and serious competition in bocce (an Italian version of bowling). If you want to make the picnic, call the center during its open hours for information.

Romance at a Glance

♥ *Visit the Italian-American Cultural Center.*

♥ *Sample Chicago's legendary deep-dish pizza.*

♥ *Learn to play bocce at McGuane Park.*

♥ *Be a "guest" at* Tony 'n' Tina's Wedding.

♥ *Nibble and sip a nightcap at Spiaggia.*

Lunch

Pretend you're in a little red Ferrari as you hit the Eisenhower Expressway (only out-of-towners and map readers call it Interstate 290) and zoom downtown. You're headed for one of Chicago's premier destinations: **Pizzeria Uno** (29 East Ohio Street; 312–321–1000). At Uno's and its down-the-block sister spot, **Pizzeria Due** (619 North Wabash Avenue; 312–943–2400), what a grateful world knows as Chicago-style pizza was introduced by the late man-about-town Ike Sewell. This splendid slice of heaven starts with a crust thick enough to constitute a meal itself, topped abundantly with gooey mozzarella, a sauce that's more tomato than sauce, and, if you like, satisfying lumps of spicy sausage. Add a side salad (for health reasons) and a pitcher of soda or beer, and you'll know you're in Chicago.

Rolling out of these pizza palaces, you're likely to feel like a bocce ball yourselves. And you might just like to try your hand at this little-known but pleasantly undemanding sport. Many Chicago Park District parks have bocce courts, and the accommodating staffers will even teach you the basics—with the park's balls—at **McGuane Park** (2901 South Poplar; 312–747–6497). Be sure to call in advance and ask if someone is available when you plan to come.

If you want to explore a little-known corner of the city, take some time to look around the park's neighborhood. This quiet old Italian area lies about a mile south of the Near West Side's better-known Little Italy, an immigrant haven where Jane Addams began modern social work with Hull House. As that neighborhood now is dominated by the University of Illinois-Chicago campus, so was this area once dominated by International Harvester's huge McCormick factory, whose jobs allowed many local Italians to buy the tidy homes that still stand today. Some are owned by newer arrivals to the United States, while others remain in the families of those long-gone Italian factory workers.

EVENING

Witness the most memorable nuptials ever. ***Tony 'n' Tina's Wedding*** (Piper's Alley Theater, 230 West North Avenue; 312–664–8844) is a participatory piece of comical theater that makes the audience the guests at a loony Italian-American wedding reception, complete with crackpot cousins, a champagne toast to the happy couple, a full buffet, dancing, and wedding cake for everybody. The cast makes it their business to draw audience members into the action, although you don't *have* to join the bunny hop to yuck it up at this goofy "occasion."

And if it sounds totally *not* your cup of tea, consider going anyway. Every reviewer in town has been surprised at how much they liked this wacky evening—especially when they didn't expect to. To make your grab for the bouquet early, plan to catch the 5:00 P.M. show on Saturday or Sunday (Tuesday through Friday, it's at 7:30 P.M.; tickets range from $47 to $60 apiece).

Joseph Sylvester Figliulo's family came from Naples, Italy, to Chicago's South Side neighboorhood of Englewood. There he played as a child with Olivia Teresa Coleman, whose family had come from all over Ireland to the same neighborhood. Joe and Teresa grew up, fell in love, married, produced two sons, worked, traveled, and doted on their seventeen grandchildren. They lived into their nineties and celebrated sixty-eight years of marriage.

Grandma and Grandpa Figliulo would have been a great couple anywhere. How lucky for me they that lived in Chicago.

Dinner

When you're ready to end your day of la dolce vita on a more sedate note, head back downtown toward the glittery stretch of North Michigan Avenue that holds **Spiaggia** (980 North Michigan Avenue; 312–280–2750) and **Cafe Spiaggia** (same address; 312–280–2764). Either of these extremely chic sibling restaurants can serve you the signature thin-crust pizza, with toppings as rich as the clientele. There are many variations, but the combo I like best is duck sausage and goat cheese. It's definitely different from pepperoni and anchovies, but trust me: You'll love it, too. Follow it by toasting each other with one of those bracing Italian liqueurs, such as Strega or grappa, and you'll feel like Mastroianni and Ekberg wading recklessly in the fountain of Trevi—except your fountain is more likely to be Buckingham. And, of course, *you* still believe in *amore.*

FOR MORE ROMANCE

Another Italian treat might be waiting for you at the **Fine Arts** (418 South Michigan Avenue; 312–939–3700), a cinema where art films have a happy home. Check the newspaper listings to see whether there's an Italian movie among them. If so, you can enjoy listening to the language (but reading the English subtitles) as you steep yourselves in the culture.

NATURAL WONDERS

ITINERARY 9

One day and one evening

ADVENTURES IN LOVE

AN OUTDOOR AFFAIR

*B*eing in love makes you feel as if you can do anything—so why not try it? Trust the one you love to be a boon companion, in adventure as well as in love. Do something neither of you has ever tried before and give yourselves a memory that will last forever.

Notice that this itinerary differs from others in that, although two days are outlined, they're alternative rather than consecutive. You could do one day after the other—but be sure to plan some recovery time afterward!

Practical notes: Whether you're kayaking or canoeing, dress for the outdoors and be prepared to get wet! And remember that these activities are weather dependent. Rain, high winds, or other inhospitable weather can delay your ballooning plans (although of course you'll be rescheduled). Canoeing or kayaking can be done in bad weather—but do be realistic in deciding what constitutes bad.

MORNING/AFTERNOON

Taking to the water needn't mean a dip in Lake Michigan. The other Chicago waterfront is a river, and there are several. You already know the Chicago River and its branches, of course; out in the 'burbs, there are the Fox River, the Kankakee, and perhaps the most user-friendly, especially for novice canoers, the **Des Plaines River,** which reaches into the north and northwest suburbs.

Along these suburban stretches, "anything in the Vernon Hills area is safe, because the river is only about four feet at its deepest point," explains Matt O'Brien of the north suburban outpost of **Offshore Marine** (Milwaukee Avenue and Route 60, Vernon Hills; 847–362–4880). Located about an hour from downtown, Offshore is where you go to get outfitted for a canoeing expedition on the Des Plaines. The store provides everything you'll need, even if you don't know what to ask for. And if you're hesitant about your minimal skills, O'Brien is reassuring.

Romance at a Glance

♥ *Learn to kayak, then go tandem on the placid Des Plaines River.*

♥ *Canoe the Chicago River—or kayak unpredictable Lake Michigan.*

♥ *Balloon into the sunset over rural countryside.*

♥ *Learn to windsurf together.*

"Most canoe renters do fine, because there's not much to know," he says. "A canoe is a pretty stable craft, and if you're in calm waters, things should be OK." Just remember not to stand up and dance while afloat, and you should find yourselves enjoying a congenial paddle.

Lunch

As for sustenance (food, not each other), pick up a *bellissima* picnic from **Convito Italiano** (Plaza del Lago, 1515 Sheridan Road, Wilmette; 847–251–3654). This Italian food-and-wine shop offers six take-out lunch menus, ranging in price from about $8.00 to $30.00 each, and not everything is pasta; plenty of salads and sandwiches are available, too. Be sure to call a couple of days in advance to order your picnic pick.

EVENING

Want to celebrate your day together at the top of the world? Do it in a balloon!

Champagne Flights (208 Harding Street, Libertyville; 847–604–1451) offers sunrise and sunset rides on its colorful hot air balloons over its northern Illinois territory.

When you schedule your flight, you'll be told where to meet your pilot—maybe Champagne owner Ron Briley or maybe one of his employees, who average about seventeen years' experience aloft, Briley says. "Usually we meet at Hawthorne Mall," he notes, which lets you return your Offshore Marine gear conveniently. "From the time we start out till the time we bring you back where we met, it's about two, two and a half hours."

As you prepare to ascend, you're welcome to help your pilot make preparations as well, Briley says. Then, as you climb into the traditional wicker basket, drift skyward and watch the earth recede, see if you don't feel like the Great and Powerful Oz floating above the Emerald City!

Returning to terra firma, you're again welcome to help your pilot deflate and pack up the balloon. Then you'll pop the cork on a celebratory bottle of champagne before returning to your point of origin. It's all pretty dreamlike, although there are a couple of practical points involved. One, of course, is price: about $150 per person for a weekend flight (weekdays are $130). Another is the rendezvous factor: Briley will notify you about your meeting place an hour or two before you fly, so you'll need a reliable answering machine you can call in to or a place where someone will take a message for you. (Maybe Offshore Marine will help!)

As you end your adventure, you'll probably be starving—so scout around for the mall's rest rooms, slip into the fresh clothes you presciently packed in the car, and you're off to a cozy dinner for two.

Dinner

At the charming **Cafe Pyrenees** (River Tree Court, Milwaukee Avenue at Rt. 60, Vernon Hills; 847–918–8850), the French food is lovingly prepared and beautifully presented in a setting that's trés romantique. You'll find a terrific bargain in the $20 fixed-price dinner, which gives you four courses and takes nicely to an American or French wine from the list. If you go a la carte, consider the napoleon of grilled vegetables and goat cheese. Carnivores adore the grilled beef tournedos from the bistro-style menu. And chalk up the day's activity as justification for dessert if you're tempted by the luscious chocolate-caramel mousse cake.

ALTERNATIVE MORNING/AFTERNOON

What if you're up for a more challenging adventure? Make it kayaking in Lake Michigan! You can learn at the Thursday evening classes offered by Offshore's Chicago location (2333 West North Avenue; 312–486-9875). "These classes are about three hours, and they're for the person who has never been in a kayak, or has minimal experience," O'Brien says. "We teach forward paddle strokes, turning techniques, and how to handle wet exits in an emergency" (in other words, what to do if you dump!)

All lessons are offered in solo kayaks, "because it's always better to start in a solo," O'Brien explains. "You can control it better if you're alone. After a lesson, we'll rent you a tandem kayak, but you need to know what to expect. The tandems are short, wide and not speedy." They're also less stable than solo craft, so be ready to dump and recover.

To sign up for Offshore's lessons, call a week or two ahead. Lessons are $39 per person, starting at 5:30 P.M. Thursday at **Lincoln Park Boat Club** (in Diversey Harbor, 2800 north). When you're ready for that tandem kayak, plan to paddle in the North Side shore area. "Most people go roughly from Diversey to North Avenue, or between Fullerton and Belmont," O'Brien says. Everything you'll need for your day will cost about $125—except for lunch, which you could pick up on the way from Offshore to the lake at **Whole Foods Market** (1000 West North Avenue; 773–587–0648). There's a fabulous array of salads, sandwiches, and desserts at this big alternative supermarket, and you can assemble a dandy meal for two for about $15.

If you'd prefer to canoe the Chicago River or another nearby river, call **Chicagoland Canoe Base** (4019 North Narragansett Avenue; 773–777-1489), where the legendary Ralph Frese makes 'em himself. An expert on the seventeenth-century *voyageurs* who explored the Great Lakes and many area rivers, Frese might have time to chat with you about his work and

When is a poncho the most romantic gift imaginable? When it's from my next-door neighbor, Bill, to his wife, Lori. He adores the great outdoors; she likes all that, but she likes comfort, too. So the toasty-warm, water-resistant, top-of-the-line poncho Bill gave Lori last birthday was more than a raincoat, it was a thoughtful gesture from a guy who understands what a woman needs to cope.

passion for local waterways. Or he might just get you outfitted and heading for a good spot to put in along the river of your choice. Everything you'll need—canoe, paddles, life jackets, and rigging to carry the canoe on your car—costs $35 per person for the day, plus a $25 cash deposit.

Lunch

Again you'll want to pack a lunch; Whole Foods is an option, as is **Foodstuffs** (north and east of Chicagoland Canoe Base, at 2106 Central Street, Evanston; 847–328–7704), where you can get a succulently roasted half chicken, side goodies, and dessert for $11.95.

ALTERNATIVE EVENING

Dinner

When you've returned your gear to Chicagoland Canoe Base, get cleaned up and do a little carbo-loading at **Lutnia** (5532 West Belmont Avenue; 773–282–5335). This is a slice of Chicago's Polonia, an old-fashioned restaurant where the service is proud and the pierogi even prouder. If you know Polish food, try the bigos (hunter's stew) or other familiar foods; if you don't, sip some borscht and ask for guidance. Prices are moderate; dinner for two shouldn't run more than $50, depending on your taste for vodka.

FOR MORE ROMANCE

Here's a great way to impress an athletic sweetheart: Arrange a private lesson in windsurfing for the two of you. Lessons are scheduled from Memorial Day to Labor Day at **Windward Sports** (3317 North Clark Street; 773–472–6868). They'll outfit you with all the gear, transport it to a nearby Lake Michigan beach, teach you how to put it together and take it apart, then get you up and moving—all for $45 per hour, per person. You can master the whole thing in a couple of hours if you have sailing experience.

To do it at less expense, sign up for the group lessons offered weekends at Wolf Lake in Hammond, Indiana, about an hour southeast of downtown via Interstate 90. They run about three and a half hours, and with a maximum of ten to a class with two teachers, you'll learn fast. Two lessons—which include guaranteed certification, a book, and five subsequent rentals—run $120 per person and needn't be booked more than a few days in advance.

ITINERARY 10
Two nights and two days

LOVE IN BLOOM
A GARDEN LOVERS' WEEKEND

*C*hicago's official motto is *urbs in horto,* Latin for "city in a garden," and if you're here during the summer, you'll see just how appropriate that is. The city's "front yard" runs from the South Side's Jackson Park to Grant Park downtown to Lincoln Park on the North Side. At the city's outer edges and into the suburbs, the Cook County Forest Preserve maintains miles and miles of natural and recreational space. Beyond the city limits are gorgeous, growing monuments to nature, notably the Chicago Botanic Garden in north suburban Glencoe and the splendid Morton Arboretum in west suburban Lisle.

Chicago and its environs truly are in full bloom during late spring and well into fall. Sure, the weather can be wicked—too hot, too cold, too rainy, too dry—but when you're with the one you love, it all fades. And when the weather is good—as it often *is!*—this glorious garden city is unbeatable. Here's a weekend and more of outdoor bliss.

Practical notes: This is a sunscreen-and-sensible shoes itinerary! Much of this itinerary requires that you visit during the summer, but not all of it; attractions that remain available during the winter are noted. You could spend a whole weekend outdoors reveling in Grant Park and Lincoln Park, which would require only CTA public transportation. Going farther afield, the Metra-Union Pacific North Line (formerly the Chicago and North Western railway's North Line) serves Ravinia Park on the North Shore. The Chicago Botanic Garden and Morton Arboretum, however, can only be reached by car.

DAY ONE: EVENING

Enjoy a lovely garden right on the premises at the charming **Gold Coast Guest House,** a freshly rehabbed home just west of Michigan Avenue whose rooms are booked through **Bed & Breakfast/Chicago** (312–951–0080). The comforts of a queen-size bed and your private bath are considerable, and the house is full of delightful details like the spiral staircases connecting its levels. The price is right, too, with rooms ranging from $85 to $125 per night.

Romance at a Glance

♥ *Savor music and a picnic under the stars at a Grant Park concert—and don't miss Buckingham Fountain.*

♥ *Visit the Chicago Botanic Garden, and then toast your romance at Ravinia.*

♥ *Spend a day among the trees at the Morton Arboretum.*

♥ *Find your own "secret garden" in the lovely little Shakespeare Garden.*

You can explore the garden at your home base in the morning, when breakfast is served there (weather permitting, so pray for sun!). Tonight, you're off to enjoy a picnic in the park—Grant Park, that is, where one of the city's great summer pleasures awaits. The **Grant Park Music Festival** (Petrillo Music Shell, Columbus Drive and Jackson Boulevard; 312–742–7638) starts in spring and continues, five nights a week, through a season of top-quality music. Most evenings the Grant Park Symphony performs classical programs, but you'll also find plenty of popular music. Show tunes are a frequent feature, as are jazz and even the occasional rock program. If there's a "Night at the Movies," don't miss it; for example, one program featured a score by Dmitri Shostakovich accompanying a screening of Sergei Eisenstein's *The Battleship Potemkin.* Dance, too, has a place in this eclectic lineup. And the amazing, wonderful part is that it's *free.*

So pack your picnic basket and come on over. Music starts at 7:00 P.M. Wednesday, Thursday, and Sunday evenings, and at 8:00 P.M. Friday and Saturday. If you can arrive early, by all means do so, and start your evening at the northern end of the park. That way you can appreciate another wonderful aspect of Grant Park, which is its **Wildflower Works** garden (Columbus Drive between Randolph and Monroe Streets). Some would call them weeds, but you know better. These indigenous beauties include pink evening primroses, purple coneflower, and the odoriferous wild onions from which Chicago takes its name. The park's **Rose Garden** is on your way south, so take the time to examine this gorgeous display.

Dinner

About that picnic basket: Call ahead and they'll do it for you at **St. Germain** (1210 North State Parkway; 312–266–9900), packing delicious sandwiches and salads, and pastries for dessert. The bakery is a slice of Paris, turning out baguette, croissant, pain brioche, and more—not to mention those desserts! You can also go for a selection of pâtés, a cheese plate, and even a genuine croque monsieur (although it'll be cold by the time you eat). Prices are relatively inexpensive—$7.00 or so for a sandwich, $8.00 for the pâtés—and you can even have the whole thing delivered via **Room Service** (312–644–6100). Pick up a bottle of wine on the way down (ask where to go before leaving Gold Coast Guest House) and you're set for a totally romantic evening.

⁂

Well, there *is* one more thing: Before heading back north, stroll over to **Buckingham Fountain** and enjoy the marvelous sight of its multicolored lights playing across spouts and streams of water. It's one of the city's favorite landmarks, and not to be missed at night. The fountain operates from Memorial Day through Labor Day and is a magical way to wrap up your visit to the city's spectacular lakefront.

DAY TWO: MORNING/AFTERNOON

Enjoy your coffee in your B&B garden, and then head up and out to the north. It's a short hop to the **Lincoln Park Conservatory** (Stockton Drive near Fullerton Avenue; 773–742–7736), where formal outdoor gardens complement the indoor cultivation. All is not hopeless if you happen to visit in the winter; you can refresh your spirits in the conservatory, which presents a special poinsettia display in December and a chrysanthemum show late in the winter. Like nearly all of its Chicago Park District siblings, the conservatory is free.

Another kind of complement to the formal gardens is just across the street and often overlooked when people visit Lincoln Park. Look for the **Grandmother Gardens** at the northwest corner of Webster Avenue and Stockton Drive, and enjoy its naturalistic stretch of ornamental grasses and flower beds. Most are perennials, and they're arranged as a freewheeling counterpoint to the orderly plantings across the street. Irregularly shaped beds give an unstructured feeling, and a long lawn "flows" down the garden's center, suggesting the curves of a river bordering the "banks" of flowers.

When you're ready to move on, drive a few miles west on Fullerton to the Kennedy Expressway, where you'll head about 30 miles north on Interstate 94 to its Lake Cook Road exit. Go a half mile or so east after exiting, and you're at the **Chicago Botanic Garden** (1000 Lake Cook Road, Glencoe; 847–835–5440).

The Chicago Botanic Garden, which is open year-round from 8:00 A.M. to sunset, charges no admission fee, but parking costs $4.00. The easiest way to get an overview of its three hundred acres is to take a tram tour ($3.50) and note which areas you want to explore more fully. Some don't-miss parts include the splendid rose garden, the six-room English walled garden, the three areas of Sansho-En (a Japanese garden), and the six prairie types that reflect the state's natural beauty and heritage.

A Hidden Garden

If you don't mind a meandering drive to the Chicago Botanic Garden, go north on Lake Shore Drive to Sheridan Road and then continue north to Touhy Avenue. There, head west (away from the lake) and be patient for several miles, just until you cross the Chicago River. Turn to the north onto McCormick Boulevard and, along the grassy area atop the riverbank, you'll see a garden that is little known beyond this neck of the woods: the Sculpture Garden. Park the car and stroll north through this pleasant expanse, with its large-scale modern works, and take a bit of time to enjoy this variation on cultivation, which remains available year-round, unaffected by the vicissitudes of weather that harm living things.

Lunch

Plan to have lunch in the Botanic Garden's inexpensive cafeteria, which is open till 5:30 P.M. to serve soups, sandwiches, and salads. (If you're moving at breakneck speed, you might get here in time for breakfast, which is served till 11:00 A.M.) If you are interested in particular aspects of gardening, call the garden before you come to ask what programs are scheduled for the time you'll be there. Flower shows, sales, talks, classes, and demonstrations are offered year-round.

❧

Which brings us to the fact that the garden is well worth a visit, even in the dead of winter. The garden's extensive greenhouses are filled with rare cacti, amusing topiary designs and figures, and lush, warming tropical plants. The Japanese garden, surprisingly, is also a joy during winter. Needless to say, you'll contend with drastically fewer fellow visitors during the winter, too.

DAY TWO: EVENING

As you leave the Botanic Garden, head east on Lake Cook Road till it bends into Green Bay Road. Look for signs directing you to parking for Ravinia, and watch out for the traffic jam you could find (especially on weekends).

While not itself a garden, **Ravinia Park** (Green Bay Road, Highland Park; 847–728–4642) nestles in the tangled expanse of green that is the North Shore, providing a civilized, open-air haven for the entire Chicago area. Like the Grant Park music programs, the Ravinia Festival offers predominantly classical music, with enough jazz and other popular styles to attract the nonclassical crowd. Unlike Grant Park, Ravinia charges admission and, in addition to its expansive, well-groomed lawns, has a pavilion which you'll be glad you're sitting under if it rains.

Ravinia is the summertime home of the Chicago Symphony Orchestra, so you know you'll be hearing the best there is. The Ravinia Festival Orchestra also is featured, and both orchestras frequently welcome such guest artists as violinist Itzhak Perlman, pianists Mischa Dichter and Andre Watts, cellist Yo-Yo Ma, and vocal luminaries from soprano Jessye Norman to basso Franz-Josef Selig. Programs come from the repertory, but you'll be enchanted at hearing them unfold under the stars.

Nonclassical programs include a long weekend of jazz, a week of dance toward the end of summer, and a season-long sprinkling of popular artists—for example, country stars Willie Nelson and Kathy Mattea, pop rockers Jackson Browne and Anne Murray, Broadway chanteuse Bernadette Peters, Motown groups the Temptations and the Four Tops, and festival favorite Tony Bennett graced the Ravinia stage in 1996.

Dinner

OK, there's the musical picture. Let's talk about food, which you'll want to have planned before you get here. My favorite dining option is **Instant Ravinia** (847–432–7550), which gives you a boxed supper, ticket for the evening's entertainment, and even a chair for comfort.

It's all just $22, and your choices for dinner are universally yummy: vegetarian baguette with goat cheese, Asian shrimp pasta salad, chicken baguette, and Tuscan steak sandwich (grilled beef tenderloin, smoked Provolone, and sun-dried tomato pesto on focaccia). All come with fresh fruit, a soft drink, and a giant cookie. (Alcohol is allowed at Ravinia, so feel free to bring your own; it just isn't included in this dinner.) You must allow at least twenty-four hours' notice, so be sure to call ahead on this.

One more thing about Ravinia: I think it's one of the most romantic places in the entire Chicago area. I'd never want to have to choose between Ravinia and Grant Park, but there's an atmosphere of gentility here at Ravinia that makes you want to straighten your shoulders as you lean over to kiss.

DAY THREE: MORNING/AFTERNOON

You've done the lakefront, the prairie, the wildflowers, and the cultivated gardens. Now, you're off to the woodlands at the west-suburban **Morton Arboretum** (Illinois Route 53 at Interstate 88, Lisle; 630–719–2400). The Arboretum's fifteen hundred acres hold more than three thousand kinds of woody plants from around the world, with special strengths in such geographical groups as Appalachia, the Balkans, central and western Asia, China, Japan, Korea, and, of course, northern Illinois.

While there is some overlap with the area's other major gardens—a prairie/savanna reconstruction, a fragrance garden, landscaping galore—the arboretum is quite clear in its identity as a place of trees, shrubs, and vines. Come around Arbor Day (April 26), and you'll see that identity in full, uh, flower, with special programs and tree plantings.

First-timers usually start at the Visitors' Center, then strike out on the 13 miles of trails that are marked for easy self-education. You're even allowed to drive through on paved roads if you prefer (though bicycles and in-line skates are banned). And bird-watchers should be sure to bring their binoculars.

Morton Arboretum is open daily, year-round, from 7:00 A.M. till 7:00 P.M. or sunset, whichever comes earlier. Bring any questions about your woody plants back home, and you'll get polite, informed discussion. You can even use the scholarly Sterling Morton Library from 9:00 A.M. to 5:00 P.M. Tuesday through Friday, and from 10:00 A.M. to 4:00 P.M. Saturday. Parking is $6.00. You'll probably want to stay for lunch at the restaurant, which is inexpensively priced and open from 11:00 A.M. to 3:00 P.M.

FOR MORE ROMANCE

If you return to the city from the Botanic Gardens in daylight, detour east to the **Shakespeare Garden** (east end of Garrett Place at Sheridan Road, on the Northwestern University campus, Evanston). This exquisite nook, only 70 by 100 feet, is planted by thirty-five local Garden Club volunteers with flowers, herbs, shrubs and trees mentioned in the Bard's works. These include lavender, daisies, columbine, poppies, yarrow, hollyhocks, pansies, rosemary ("That's for remembrance—pray you, love, remember" said Ophelia), and more. The garden, designed by the landscape architect Jens Jensen, is ringed with a double row of hawthorn hedges original to the site. And the flower beds are set off with a bronze relief of Shakespeare, a stone bench for sitting, a sundial—and the play of sunlight and shadow that was Jensen's trademark.

Nothing comforts the winter-weary Chicagoan like the **Chicago Flower & Garden Show,** held every year in March at downtown Navy Pier (East Grand Avenue at Lake Michigan; call either the Chicago Botanic Garden or the Morton Arboretum for specifics). You needn't be a gardener to enjoy this optimistic look at the green season, which includes exhibits from the area's garden centers and educational institutions, special programs for orchid enthusiasts, and sessions on many topics for everyone. Admission is $8.00—worth every penny during a Midwestern winter—and there's a *lot* of walking involved.

ITINERARY 11
Three days and two nights

SWEPT AWAY

ROMANTIC LAKEFRONT CRUISES

*A*hoy, young lovers! Get one look at the panoramic beauty of Lake Michigan and you'll understand immediately why some Chicagoans leave home every summer. They don't go far, though — just to their boats, which they dock along the lakefront and live in till cold weather prevails. It's a totally romantic way to live — and you can get a taste of it by spending a weekend *practically* living in the lake.

Practical notes: Obviously this weekend is intended for a summer visit to Chicago. It's quite a bit of cruising, but don't feel you must spend an entire weekend on the water. Any one of the options here will give you a terrific date without a weekend's commitment.

DAY ONE: AFTERNOON

Even the street address will get you in the mood at the **Sheraton Chicago Hotel & Towers** (301 East North Water Street; 312–464–1000 or 800–325–3535). Located at the far east stretch of the Chicago River on its north bank, the hotel takes full advantage of its setting with gorgeous views and a charming, landscaped river walk at ground level. And, while it's fully fitted with exercise equipment, the swimming pool and sundeck are what you'll really enjoy in the hotel's health club.

Warm tones and lots of wood dominate the hotel's decor, the better to emphasize its magnificent views of lake and river. Nearly every room has a great view (ask for one when you reserve, just to make sure), and a really nice touch is in-room Starbucks coffee. The Towers rooms and suites offer extra luxury, and you can even book the presidential suite where Bill and Hillary stayed during the 1996 Democratic National Convention. (Of the hotel's three presidential suites, the Clintons' favorite is the one with contemporary decor, says marketing coordinator Alexandra Gorin.)

Room rates vary widely depending on when you're here and whether you want a suite. But you're likely to find a weekend package that will give you a rate as low as $119 per night (for a two-night minimum) or a $144 nightly rate that includes some nice perks.

Since you're heading for an aquaphilic weekend, you'll appreciate one more advantage the Sheraton provides: It's the only hotel in town with docking facilities. That means you can ask to be picked up right at the hotel when you take one of the cruises described in this chapter. (The *Odyssey* does this routinely, although usually for groups; others may need a bit of explaining.) Or ask the concierge to make your arrangements, and you'll *really* feel like royalty!

Romance at a Glance

♥ *Practically sleep on the water at the riverside* Sheraton Hotel.

♥ *Dine and dance aboard the sleek* Spirit of Chicago.

♥ *Learn about local ecology on the Friends of the Chicago River cruise.*

♥ *Board a fabulous old schooner, then enjoy a Summer Sunset Cruise on the lakefront.*

♥ *Fish on your own private cabin cruiser; swing to the tunes on a Sunday jazz brunch.*

♥ *Stalk soggy spooks on the Chicago Supernatural Cruise.*

Dinner

Be sure to check out this possibility for your first evening's excursion: a dinner-dancing cruise aboard the sleek ***Spirit of Chicago*** (at Navy Pier; 312–836–7899). This black-and-white beauty is instantly recognizable when you see it from the lake, with its "striped" look and streamlined feeling. When you board for the evening's cruise (Navy Pier is a short cab ride from the Sheraton, if you can't get the *Spirit* to pick you up there), you can choose between taking in the fresh air on deck or heading to the air-conditioned comfort waiting below. To do both, check out the cash bar below and then take your purchases out to a table on deck.

When dinner is served, you'll find yourselves seated with several other passengers (as on a cruise ship) and perusing a menu that offers three entrees: prime rib, chicken with a selection of sauces, or the day's fish or seafood specialty. Dinner also includes salad, vegetables, a variety of desserts, and more.

After serving dinner, dessert, and coffee, the ship's waiters and waitresses sing and dance in a cabaret-style show. Then you and your fellow passengers can dance to a live band—and all the while, the *Spirit* slices through the lake, going as far south as McCormick Place and as far north as Montrose Harbor. Altogether, it's a fun little getaway, a three-hour version of the kind of festive, "real" cruise you just might take together one day.

Boarding for the *Spirit*'s dinnner cruise is at 6:15 P.M. every day, with departure at 6:45 P.M. and return at 9:45 P.M. The dress code is casual but "nice"—no jeans or gym shoes, but ties and jackets aren't required. And do consider one of the *Spirit*'s special packages for passengers celebrating some occasion. Balloons, a special photo, souvenirs, a cake, and more can all be yours if you want to surprise your sweetheart. Ask when you book. The cruise itself costs $60.30 per person for Monday through Thursday evenings; $67.55 on Friday and Sunday, and $77.20 for Saturday night. These prices cover everything except tips to the waitstaff.

If you've *really* enjoyed the trip, come back for more a few hours later! The *Spirit* runs moonlight cruises on Friday and Saturday nights during the summer, leaving Navy Pier just after midnight and returning about 2:30 A.M. These cruises cost $24.95 per person; again, ask about special celebrations. Bring a sweater or jacket if you want to stroll on deck; the night air can get a tad nippy—or maybe you'll just have to hold each other a little closer . . .

DAY TWO: MORNING

Cruises can be more than just a good time, as you'll learn on the **Friends of the Chicago River Cruise** (Wagner Charter Cruises, 708–653–8690). This Saturday-morning special trip takes you through the river's main, North and South branches, with commentary from a trained Friend as you cruise. Going all the way back to pre-European settlement by Native Americans, this short history course also addresses the river's ecology, which took a beating during industrialization but now has recovered somewhat (in no small part because of the Friends' efforts). The tour also describes the many recreational uses of the river, including the fishing that seemed like a pipe dream back when Mayor Daley (the powerful first one, who reigned from the 1955 until his death in 1976) announced a plan to stock the river with sport fish. People were skeptical, but you'll see the late mayor's legacy in the quiet anglers dotting the riverbanks.

The two-hour Friends cruise is offered once or twice each month during the summer, with starting times at either 9:30 or 10:00 A.M. (There's a ninety-minute version of the cruise, too, if you're pressed for time.) You'll travel on the *Jamaica*, a 105-foot boat with an enclosed lower deck and open upper deck and bow. The *Jamaica* holds well over one hundred passengers, but the Friends cruise usually is a smaller crowd, so you won't feel cramped.

The *Jamaica* boards at Lower Wacker Drive and Wells Street, which you can reach by walking along the river from the Sheraton. (You'll need to wind up on the south side of the river, so even if you walk on the north side most of the way, cross a bridge somewhere.) The $18 per person fee includes coffee and muffins, so you don't even have to get breakfast beforehand. Reservations are essential, though; call a month or so in advance.

DAY TWO: AFTERNOON

Lunch

Break for lunch before boarding another craft! Since you'll debark from the *Jamaica* at

Lower Wacker and Wells Street—and since you're likely to be hungry after all that fresh air—let's consider a lunch spot around the area. An obvious choice is the **Crab House** (745 North Wells Street; 312–664–2722), where the best lunch bargain is a seafood salad bar that offers all you can eat for $9.95 per person. The dinner menu is also available at lunch, so you can find just about anything you might be in the mood for (except prime rib, which is served only at dinner—but you didn't want that for lunch anyhow). Crab cakes are delicious, and the filet of salmon can be prepared any way you like it, from simple broiling to a scorchy blackening.

Or you can head back toward Navy Pier (the better to catch your next cruise on time), where you'll be happy with lunch from **Charlie's Ale House** (on Navy Pier; 312–595–1440). This sibling of an old-time pub on the North Side offers a super hamburger: half a pound of meat, plus a topping and potatoes and coleslaw, all for $6.50. There's a solid chili, made with chunks of sirloin instead of ground beef, for $4.50. The ubiquitous Buffalo wings are here, too, and there's even a meat loaf dinner for $8.95.

Thus fortified, you might need a snooze out in the sun before picking up the pace again. Or you might even snooze during your next excursion, which offers a leisurely contrast to the morning's lessons. When you board the 145-foot schooner *Windy* (at Navy Pier; 312–595–5555), you're on a bit of nineteenth-century romance for folks who love the water. Holding some 150 passengers for three lake cruises daily, this tall ship will get the wind stirring your hair and your hearts—*and* it has modern conveniences (like plumbing!). Two-hour cruises are at 2:00, 4:30, and 7:00 P.M. daily, boarding at Navy Pier. Boarding passes cost $20 per person ($15 for seniors or children) and are available at the dock, although you can't go wrong by reserving in advance.

To get the most water time from the remainder of the day and evening, figure on taking the 2:00 P.M. *Windy* cruise. You'll be on land by 4:00 or 4:30 P.M.—plenty of time to head back to the Sheraton, grab a nap or an early dinner, and walk over to the Michigan Avenue bridge.

DAY TWO: EVENING

Descend the old metal staircase near the bridge, on the south side of the river, and you're ready to see the city's skyline fade into the sunset. The **Summer Sunset Cruise** (Mercury Cruiseline, on the south side of the river, Michigan Avenue and Wacker Drive; 312–332–1353) travels the lakefront for two twilight hours, starting at 7:30 P.M., when it's still light out. Much of the territory is what the *Spirit of Chicago* covers in its dinner cruise, but tonight, you're able to focus all your attention on the sights.

And they're grand! The skyline, backlit by the setting sun, is one of those star-struck, "how ya gonna keep 'em down on the farm" sights. Grant Park is visible, too, its swath of green and gardens spreading before the lake like a country estate's grounds. The highlight of the cruise is its lingering look at the light display at Buckingham Fountain, which assumes a magic all its own when viewed from the river. See if you don't agree after visiting on land and then taking this cruise. Of course, you'll also enjoy the twinkling lights of downtown's buildings and the glittery Gold Coast. At $11 per person, the sunset cruise is one of the loveliest bargains in town. (Important note: Be at the dock an hour before departure to pick up your tickets.)

Dinner

If you're not completely starry-eyed when you dock, you will be after a late supper at **Redfish** (40 North State Street; 312–467–1600), where live music and a Louisiana menu keep the joint jumping till 2:00 A.M. Landlubbers can choose hickory-smoked barbecue, Southern fried chicken, or Cajun-spiced meats and poultry, while fans of the fin will always find seafood and a blackened-fish daily special. Of course, everyone saves room for the pecan pie. Entrees average about $15, and the kitchen is open until 11:00 P.M. weekend evenings. The bar stays open later, if you want to linger and enjoy the live music weekends bring, usually from a rhythm-and-blues band. Redfish is just a couple of blocks west of Michigan Avenue and a little

north of the river, across the street from Marina City—a short walk from where the sunset cruise docks, and not too far from the Sheraton, either.

DAY THREE: MORNING/AFTERNOON

Here's a tough call: Should you spend Sunday fishing, or take one more fabulous cruise to round out a watery weekend?

If you want nothing so much as a quiet (albeit pricey) day of angling, call **Chicago Sport-fishing Charter** (312–922–1100) and arrange your very own expedition on your very own cabin cruiser. Salmon and trout are the usual catch on these junkets. All the equipment you'll need is provided, and if you haven't gotten your annual Illinois fishing license and stamp, the charter company will sell you that, too. All you bring is yourselves and your lunch.

Boats accommodate up to six people, but the price is the same whether it's just the two of you or a group. Five hours on the water runs $395, and a six-hour trip is $475. Early birds go out at 7:00 A.M. and return at noon, and late risers' fishing goes from 1:00 to 6:00 p.m; six-hour trips are flexible.

Lunch

And about that lunch: Maybe you can get your captain to put in at **South Pier Restaurant** (6401 South Coast Guard Drive; 312–241–7437). The restaurant, located in a former Coast Guard station, provides free docking for hungry boaters and features a menu of pastas, seafood, salads, sandwiches. There's a bar, too, and even a jukebox, if you'd like to linger (although you're apt to hear a metaphoric meter ticking on that cabin cruiser). South Pier is open daily from 11:00 A.M. to 11:00 P.M., and lunch for two costs around $40.

⁣⌒⌒⁣

If fishing isn't your sport of choice, close out your weekend by sleeping in, then enjoying a final fling on the lake with the ***Odyssey* jazz brunch** (from 401 East Illinois Street; 630–990–0800). Cruise connoisseurs around town agree this is one of the very nicest. The ship is beautiful, a streamlined beauty in black and white, and the food and music are just as distinctive. "The food is wonderful, and I should know—I work in catering," says one anonymous informant.

The brunch buffet features lots of fresh fruit, pastries, hot and cold salads, and desserts. Entrees (one per person) span all three meals, ranging from poached eggs with smoked salmon or scrambled-egg quesadillas to chicken or pork chops. A cash bar is open during the cruise (although you can't buy liquor until noon on Sunday).

Music comes from three different jazz combos, one on each deck. On the outdoor observation deck, you'll hear music from one of these piped out. Boarding starts at 11:00 A.M., and the cruise runs from 11:45 A.M. till 1:45 P.M. The whole thing, taxes and tips included, costs

$53.30 per person, and reservations are a good idea. The jazz brunch cruises the lake from March through October, and since nearly all the ship is enclosed, cruises run even in the rain.

FOR MORE ROMANCE

Devote a fall day to learning more about the area's waterways on a **National Heritage Corridor Cruise** (through Mercury Cruiseline; 312–332–1366). This cruise, which leaves Michigan Avenue and Wacker Drive at 9:00 A.M. and returns at 4:00 P.M., constitutes a sort of minicourse in the natural history and development of Chicago's lake, rivers, and canals. It's conducted by Dr. David Solzman, who is professor of urban geography at the University of Illinois Chicago. He's also a genial host and raconteur. (I knew him slightly as an undergraduate and remember how popular his classes were!).

You'll gather for a continental breakfast as you board, but you must bring your own lunch and beverage. To take the aggravation out of that, order a spiffy lunch in advance from the **Corner Bakery** (516 North Clark Street; 312–644–8100, or for the catering department, 312–527–1956). This chic spot will put together a basket holding sandwiches, salads, and desserts for both of you. This package runs $40, but it includes a complete picnic setup, from tablecloth to cutlery. You'll want to scale down to a cruise-size basket, so let the kitchen know you don't need some of the accoutrements and they'll oblige. Tickets for the National Heritage Corridor Cruise are $45 per person for each Saturday in September. Reservations are essential, and the further in advance, the better.

ITINERARY 12
Two days and one night

THE ZOO FOR TWO

*W*hat is it about being in love that makes people want to go to the zoo? Maybe it's the animals' antics, which give you plenty to talk about when you're getting to know someone. Or maybe it's the free-spirited wandering that's so pleasant to do in a zoo. Or the cotton candy and popcorn to snack on, or the silly souvenirs you take home. Whatever the attraction, a zoo is a terrific place to while away a day with your sweetheart. And in Chicago, you can do it two days in a row, at two outstanding zoos.

Practical notes: This itinerary really calls for fair weather, although you don't need summery heat as long as you're not getting rained on. Both zoos are open year-round and are far less crowded in the cooler (spring, fall, and winter) months; weekdays, too, are less crowded than weekends.

DAY ONE: MORNING/AFTERNOON

Visiting **Lincoln Park Zoo** (2200 North Cannon Drive; 773–742–2200) always reminds me of how I felt on discovering the Berlin Zoo—right in the middle of town, right across the *strasse* from the train station. How astonishing to find, at the heart of this bustling, aggressive city, a leafy, self-contained alternative world of animal life. Lincoln Park Zoo isn't quite in the middle of downtown, but it's about as close to that as you can get. It's a very doable, pleasant walk from the posh shopping strip of North Michigan Avenue. In fact, you could even walk to it without ever leaving the park and beach areas right along the lake shore.

Romance at a Glance

♥ *Wander the Lincoln Park Zoo—and rent a paddleboat for floating fun.*

♥ *Dine at the spectacular Ambria, just across the street from the zoo.*

♥ *Spend a leisurely day at the world-class Brookfield Zoo, with a new swampland and other unique exhibits.*

Even closer, however, is staying in a bed and breakfast on West Menomonee, just a little west of the zoo's south entrance. A couple of bed and breakfast apartments are available on this quiet little side street, and both are booked through **Bed and Breakfast Chicago** (312–951–0085). One is worth asking for if you're interested in art. This apartment's owners have filled their home with folk and primitive art that will make you feel as if you're inhabiting your own private museum. If you do stay here, be sure to allow yourselves plenty of time to peruse and appreciate this amazing collection. You'll enjoy the whimsical sensibility that's evident throughout, right down to the mirror-lined bathroom: All those mirrors are vintage handheld types, and they're mounted on the walls so you see their backs, not their reflecting sides.

This apartment's appeal is augmented by a wood-burning fireplace and upstairs bedroom with double bed. On the same street a second building offers two apartments. One is at the garden level (where a stone floor keeps things cool, even in summer). In the other a working fireplace graces one bedroom, and a second bedroom faces a quaint little courtyard. Often the whole apartment is available (the owner-architect travels), and if that's the case, you might prefer the owner's bedroom, which is flooded with light on a sunny day.

Whichever apartment you choose, you can head right back out to the park after settling into your weekend home. You're closest to the south end of the zoo, where generations of children have enjoyed the **Farm in the Zoo.** Cows, horses, pigs, and chickens are all here—but the most fun is in watching the hatching baby chicks. If you've never seen a tiny beak peck its way through a shell, take time to do it now. And visit the big barn, where several educational exhibits coexist with one of those two-dimensional cut-out models that let you photograph your head on a farmer's body. Bring a camera and get a fellow zoo lover to shoot the two of you; you'll giggle over the picture forever.

The nicest way to do Lincoln Park Zoo's 35 or so acres is in a wandering mode. If you're knowledgeable about the animals, you'll appreciate one of the world's largest collections of gorillas here. The Primate House also holds an impressive colony of mandrills, colobus monkeys, and lemurs. The big cats are plentiful as well, and it's fun to watch the flamingos in their dome home.

One of the best entertainments at the zoo is renting a paddleboat on the pond where ducks vie for space with passing paddlers. It's easy to keep these big yellow boats moving, and you're considerably less likely to "dump" than in a canoe or kayak. Paddleboats rent for about $13.00 for a full hour, or $8.00 for half an hour. And even if you don't want to hop in and paddle, linger to watch the adventures of those who do.

Lunch

If you're hungry by now, you're in the right place. The zoo's **Cafe Brauer** is right at the paddleboat pond. This nineteenth-century building fell into disrepair over the years but was restored to its original beauty during the 1980s. Today it is a focal point of special events at the zoo. If crews are setting up or clearing an event, you may be able to peek upstairs for a look at the building's elegant spaces and lovely mosaics.

Back downstairs, the lunch menu offers pizzas, salads, sandwiches, and a zoo specialty of animal-shaped french fries. Lunch won't run more than about $12 for both of you, although Cafe Brauer is likely to be crowded if the weather's good. You might prefer to leave the zoo and walk west to the Clark Street strip of shops and restaurants, returning to the zoo after a sit-down lunch.

Another good spot to take a break is the central area around the sea lions' pool (do go down the ramp to watch them zipping by underwater). Popcorn, cotton candy, and similar snacks are available from colorful vendors' carts here, and it's a good place to sit in the sun and enjoy them. When it's *too* sunny, head for the reptiles' building, which is cool and dim.

As you head toward the zoo's northern end, stop at the gift shop for a souvenir (rubber snakes, anyone?). And don't miss the wild, wooded rookery, which counts several severely endangered species among its who-knows-how-many birds. Two rookery inhabitants—the Guam rail and the Micronesian kingfisher—are extinct in the wild. If you're lucky, your visit may coincide with a spring or fall migratory period, which gives you the opportunity to see even more aviary rarities.

Just south of Fullerton Parkway, you'll come to the **Lincoln Park Conservatory** (773–284–4770), where you may find a special event highlighting some of its gorgeous flora. You don't need a special event to fall for this intoxicating atmosphere of color and scent, though; just linger and enjoy. Admission is free; hours are 9:00 A.M. to 5:00 P.M. daily.

DAY ONE: Evening

Dinner

When you're ready to head back to your bed and breakfast, be sure you've brought something great-looking to change into. You're going to dinner at one of the most romantic restaurants in town. I know of at least two couples who got engaged at **Ambria** (2300 North Lincoln Park West; 773–472–5959), and there's no doubt they aren't the only ones. You could find yourselves in the mood for just about anything as you luxuriate in this lovely room's cozy booths, wonderful service, and sublime food. Ambria is elegant yet friendly, posh yet comfortable, top-drawer yet accessible. It's expensive, too—expect to spend upwards of $100 total—but worth every penny to spend several hours with the one you love while savoring marvelous specialties from chef Gabino Sotelino. Let your waiter be your guide, to the restaurant's many fine wines as well as its cuisine; or make it easy by choosing the degustation, which serves up five courses for about $50 per person or a more elaborate version at about $65 per person.

Maybe you're not up for such a splurge—or maybe your day at the zoo has left you feeling too connected to eat meat. Consider a dinner that's more informal and makes a dandy vegetarian spread. **Uncle Tannous** (2626 North Halsted; 773–929–1333) offers Middle Eastern specialties such as hummus, baba ghannouj, and little pastries stuffed with cheese or spinach. You'll do fine by making a dinner of appetizers, sharing if you like. Prices are reasonable—not more than about $25 per person, especially if you go vegetarian. It is a hike from your bed and breakfast, however, so you'll probably want to take a cab or drive there and back.

For a swanky way to while away the remainder of the evening, stop in at the **Cognac Bar** (2140 North Lincoln Park West; 773–665–9071), which is adjacent to the restaurant **Toulouse on the Park.** The bar is a cozy room that presents top-notch cabaret artists as such as Julie London, Spider Saloff, and Ann Hampton Callaway, usually in three shows a night, with varying cover charges (rarely topping $10 apiece). The sophisticated setting—don't come in jeans—and ultraromantic music are guaranteed to smooth a shiny gloss over your evening.

DAY TWO: MORNING/AFTERNOON

After breakfasting in your own B&B kitchen, hop into the car and head south on Lake Shore Drive to Interstate 290 (known locally as the Eisenhower Expressway), and travel about an hour to the western suburb of Brookfield for something completely different: another day at another zoo. **Brookfield Zoo** (First Avenue and Thirty-first Street, Brookfield; 708–242–2630) is one of the area's major cultural institutions, with just about everything on a scale far larger than what you saw at the comparatively snug Lincoln Park Zoo. Unlike Lincoln Park, Brookfield charges $5.50 per person ($3.50 on Tuesday and Thursday) for admission, plus $4.00 for parking; some exhibits carry an extra charge, too. (Zoo membership is $35 annually, so if you expect to come back, joining might be worthwhile.) Once you're in, however, the two of you will agree that it is money well spent. The zoo is nearly cageless, its many areas are beautifully kept, and its exhibits are fascinating.

Among Brookfield's newest attractions is "The Swamp: Wonders of Our Wetlands," which re-creates an Illinois wetland and a Southern cypress swamp, complete with alligators. "Tropic World: A Primate's Journey" and "Habitat Africa!" explore animals' habitats in a larger context, reflecting the zoo's overall emphasis on environmental preservation and protection of fauna. The "Seven Seas Panorama" was the first local showcase for the dolphin presentations that are commonplace today; many Chicagoans treasure childhood memories of the mammals' splashing antics. Newest of all is "The Living Coast," scheduled to open in early 1997, which is designed to depict the interrelationships linking plants, animals, people, and the environment along South America's western shores.

In other words, you'll probably learn a lot during your visit to Brookfield! But the nicest thing about Brookfield is its air of a day outing. You'll feel like kids again as you approach the big gates, anticipating the fun of observing our near and distant relatives in the animal kingdom. It's definitely a day's worth of attractions, and more. "Habitat Africa!" alone covers five acres, and "Tropic World" is one of the largest indoor exhibits in the world. The zoo's wide boulevards intersect at a lovely fountain ringed with bright flowers. One good way to scope out the zoo is by boarding its Motor Safari train; stay on for the entire ride if you like, or exit at one of its four stops to take in an exhibit. (The ride costs $3.00 per person and it can save some wear on your feet.)

Lunch

Brookfield offers some welcome variations on the typical burgers-and-pizza lunch possibilities. Breakfast is available until 11:00 A.M., if you're hungry early. There's Mexican food at Café Olé, beer and wine coolers to wash down brats in a summertime beer garden, and gyros or

Edy's ice cream for the indulgent. Lunches won't total more than $7.00 or so per person (although beer will add up). Intriguingly, when "The Living Coast" opens, its restaurant is slated to feature a Peruvian menu, so the adventurous will want to plan for it.

And be sure, while you're here, to find your way to **Indian Lake,** where you can sit on a shady bench and commune with each other in silence. A few ducks might come by, but you're likely to be the only humans at this quiet haven. Unleash a little animal passion on each other's lips!

FOR MORE ROMANCE

Animal-loving Chicagoans eagerly anticipate annual events at each zoo. One that's especaially popular takes place on a Sunday afternoon early in December, when animal lovers come to Lincoln Park Zoo for "Caroling to the Animals." Singers of all ages and persuasions make a number of stops throughout the zoo, then repair to Cafe Brauer for cocoa and camaraderie. It's a wonderful way to enjoy the season and the zoo with someone you love. Watch the local newspapers for a date, or call the zoo at (312) 742–2000.

Another jolly celebration comes around every year on March 1, which the uninitiated may not recognize as National Pig Day. Brookfield Zoo celebrates what it dubs "the holler-day" with a pig-calling contest, pig polka music, and a program starring some of its most talented porcine population. Also popular (and very big with children) is the daylong Teddy Bears' Picnic, which takes place in early September each year. Call the zoo at (773) 242–2630 for more information on either event.

ARTS AND HEARTS

LOVE BUILT ON BEAUTY

ARCHITECTURE IN CHICAGO

*P*oetic thoughts on architecture and romance:

"Love built on beauty, soon as beauty, dies."
—John Donne, *Elegies*

"When we build, let us think that we build for ever."
—John Ruskin, *The Lamp of Memory*

You're building "for ever," and your solid-as-granite love will be richer for an immersion in Chicago's architectural riches. They're too great (and too scattered) to pack into one weekend—but that's no reason not to try! You'll find plenty of knowledgeable help in tours offered by the Chicago Architecture Foundation, whose volunteers are trained to explain how and why the work they show is important.

Take a full day to explore west suburban Oak Park, where architectural consciousness is incredibly high because the Prairie giant, Frank Lloyd Wright, lived and worked there. You can visit his home and studio, walk through a neighborhood where many other Wright works are located, and even stay in a bed and breakfast home designed by the master. Then come downtown to experience those who came before and after Wright. There's the great Louis Sullivan, Wright's mentor, perhaps the last architect to enjoy ornament unself-consciously. There's Sullivan's contemporary, Daniel Burnham, who is remembered not only for his buildings, but his statement about his bold, virtually citywide plan for Chicago: "Make no little plans; they have no magic to stir men's blood." And there are the later greats, most notably Mies van der Rohe, whose credo "less is more" dictated the shape and feel of the later twentieth-century world. All of them lived and worked here in Chicago. Come and see what they did.

Romance at a Glance

♥ *Spend a day in Oak Park among Frank Lloyd Wright's residential master-pieces and Unity Temple.*

♥ *Stay in Cheney House Bed and Breakfast.*

♥ *View downtown highlights from the comfort of the Chicago Architecture Foundation River Cruise on Chicago's First Lady.*

♥ *Stroll among the architec-tural masterpieces downtown; pause at the river, where nature counters architectural perfectionism.*

DAY ONE: MORNING/AFTERNOON

Start a self-designed architecture appreciation course in the first suburb to Chicago's west, **Oak Park,** which native son Ernest Hemingway scorned as a town of "broad lawns and narrow minds." Of course, Papa was a rolling stone who couldn't leave home fast enough, and he might just be surprised by the liberal bent of many Oak Parkers today.

But we're not talking politics here, we're talking architecture. And Wright is a good starting point not just because of Oak Park's concentration of his early work, but because Wright himself is a pivotal figure in the city's architecture. His mentor was Louis Sullivan, the hard-luck genius of the late nineteenth century, whose belief in functional yet beautiful buildings was carried out with an impeccable taste in decoration and absolute acceptance of the commercial nature of his work (which dictated a tall, proud appearance for the office buildings of the day). Like most artists, Sullivan relied on an underlying, romantic faith that his work would make the world a better place; he considered architecture essential to democracy, an art form that would reinforce the dignity of humanity and endow the commercial world with some of the same.

Wright and his like-minded contemporaries came to believe in buildings as horizontal as Sullivan's were vertical. Wright's principle of beauty in a building relied on taking the visual cues of its setting, and his setting was the prairie, a vast stretch of horizontal planes decorated by vegetation in muted shades (which Wright and other Prairie School architects represented with the stained glass that is one of their hallmarks). The geometric precision that assumes ever-greater importance in Wright's work comes into fullness in the work of a third, post-Wright giant of Chicago architecture, the Bauhaus master Mies Van der Rohe. Here decoration comes to a halt; sleek, soaring lines are all, and the untrained eye is challenged to find the details in which Mies is said to have seen God.

OK, there's Chicago architecture in two paragraphs. You can plunge right into the subject by booking a room at **Cheney House Bed and Breakfast** (520 North East Avenue, Oak Park; 708–524– 2067), a ninety-three-year-old home designed by Wright that is furnished with the master's furniture and fabrics. (Perfectionist that he was, Wright left nothing to the vicissitudes of others' taste!) "The happiest people who stay with me are those who are Wright fans," says owner Dale Smirl. "Everything is vintage Frank Lloyd Wright, nothing new or reproduced."

Cheney House has three B&B possibilities, two suites and one double bedroom. Both suites offer two bedrooms, a living room with a fireplace, dining room, kitchenette, and whirlpool-equipped bath. You can see why Smirl says he sometimes has honeymooners who spend a week without his ever seeing them! Then there's the double bedroom, which also has a king-size bed and private bath (sans whirlpool), and offers the greatest degree of privacy, including breakfast service in the dining room (suite guests make their own). Weigh your options and talk it over with Smirl before deciding which suits you best. Suites are $155 a night, and the double room is $100.

Smirl, who by day is a downtown attorney, likes to give guests tours of his home, which he has owned for almost twenty years (running the bed and breakfast business for the past four). Like many local Wright owners, he has his share of difficulties in keeping up the structure, but he considers every bit of work, worry, and expense a good investment in history and beauty.

When you've seen Cheney House, head out to immerse yourselves in Wright's works. Discuss beforehand whether you prefer to go on your own or join a tour. If you don't know much about the subject, you're likely to learn more on a tour; but if you want an experience that's just for the two of you, you'll find plenty of printed material to help you along the way.

The excellent Chicago Architecture Foundation offers two Oak Park Wright tours: a walking tour and **Frank Lloyd Wright by Bus,** a three-and-a-half-hour junket that takes you into the neighboring suburb of River Forest to view Wright homes there. The bus tour is offered at 9:00 A.M. on the first Saturday of every month, and note that it departs from the downtown Chicago Architecture Foundation Tour Center (224 South Michigan Avenue; 312–922–3432, ext. 140). It costs $25 per person.

Once you're in Oak Park, though, the logical place to start is the master's own home, **Frank Lloyd Wright Home and Studio** (951 Chicago Avenue, Oak Park; 708–848–1976). Tours are offered weekdays at 11:00 A.M. and 1:00 and 3:00 P.M.; Saturday and Sunday tours are ongoing, from 11:00 A.M. to 4:00 P.M. Admission is $6.00 per person. As you tour the house the master designed for his own family, you'll see the development of his ideas about the organic arrangement of space—and you'll feel the rightness of how he did it. Enjoy, too, the gorgeous yet restrained beauty he created by using stained glass to suggest prairie flowers. Imagine yourselves taking root—together—in this warm, enchanting space.

The house's **Ginkgo Tree Bookshop** is the starting point for various, more wide-ranging tours of the **Frank Lloyd Wright Prairie School of Architecture National Historic**

Flawed Genius

When you visit Frank Lloyd Wright's home, you'll surely be touched by the majestic quality of the house and especially by the beauty of the playroom he built for his six children there. What you may not know is the scandal surrounding Wright's departure from the house. Domestic life apparently did not suit the architect, who left his wife and all six children when he ran off to Europe with the wife of a client. The Wrights continued to live in the house minus Dad, and the house you see today has been restored to its state in 1909—the last year he lived there.

District, which includes thirteen Wright-designed homes. You can do your own self-guided map tour from 10:00 A.M. to 5:00 P.M. daily; choose an audiocassette-guided tour from 10:00 A.M. to 3:30 P.M. daily; or sign up for a guided Chicago Architecture Foundation walking tour, which is offered at noon and 2:00 P.M. Saturday and Sunday year-round, as well as an extra 10:30 A.M. tour offered March through October. This tour costs $9.00 per person.

On your own or with a group, what you'll see here in Oak Park is a remarkable, living museum of architecture. The area's thirty-plus Wright buildings constitute a treasure trove of the master's work, and more: a real-world context in which to view the works. These are the streets for which the houses were designed, the sites on which they were built, the neighbors with which they lived—and except for Wright's own house, every one of these remains a privately owned home. Seeing so many, one after another, is a sort of intellectual voyage during which you can watch the development of ideas and the flowering of brilliance. Architecture can be appreciated adequately only in situ; here is Wright's.

The two most important Wright buildings in Oak Park are Wright's home and studio, and one of his greatest works, **Unity Temple** (875 Lake Street, Oak Park; 708–383–8873). Wright himself called the structure his "little jewel," and its smooth, straight, graceful lines belie the

[113]

complex assemblage of spaces that together create a massive yet intimate whole. This is still a functioning church, so tours are sometimes modified to meet the congregation's needs. The basic schedule, however, includes guided tours at 1:00, 2:00, and 3:00 P.M. Saturday and Sunday, plus self-guided audiocassette tours from 1:00 to 4:00 P.M. weekdays. Cassette tours are $3.00, guided tours $5.00 per person.

Between the Wright home and Unity Temple are many Wright designs; sorting them out is best done on a tour, which helps assure you won't miss anything. If you're going solo, be sure to note the **Arthur Heurtley House** (318 Forest Avenue), which is near the Wright home and, having been built in 1902, is one of the very earliest and finest examples of Prairie design. At the corner of Forest and Superior Street is the **Nathan Moore House** (333 Forest Avenue), Wright's 1895 blend of Prairie and Tudor. Forest Avenue also holds the 1906 **Hills–DeCaro House** (313 Forest Avenue), the **Peter A. Beachy House** (238 Forest Avenue), and the 1901 **Frank W. Thomas House** (210 Forest Avenue). As you travel Forest Avenue, keep an eye out for Elizabeth Court, where at the bend you'll find the lovely **Mrs. Thomas Gale House,** a 1909 design that shows the way to what many consider Wright's greatest house, Fallingwater (which unfortunately is not in Oak Park, but in Bear Run, Pennsylvania).

Lunch

When the two of you are ready to sit down and break from this architectural overload, do it with lunch at **Petersen's Restaurant & Ice Cream Parlor** (1100 Chicago Avenue, Oak Park; 708–386–6130). Sandwiches, soups, and other lunch fare here are good, but greatness is in the ice cream. Petersen's creamy, butterfat-laden treat has kept Oak Parkers and others coming here for seventy-five years.

Back on the architecture beat, do make time for a stop at the **Pleasant Home Mansion** (217 Home Avenue, Oak Park; 708–383–2654). It's a good reminder that Wright wasn't the only practitioner of Prairie; this thirty-room mansion, done in 1897 by Prairie School member George W. Maher, now belongs to the Historical Society of Oak Park and River Forest, which opens it to the public. Admission is $3.00 per person, and tours are offered at 1:00, 2:00, and 3:00 P.M. Thursday through Sunday.

If you're Hemingway fans—and what lovers aren't, once they've read *For Whom the Bell Tolls*?—do visit his birthplace in the family's Victorian home (339 North Oak Park Avenue, Oak Park) and the **Ernest Hemingway Museum** (200 North Oak Park Avenue, Oak Park; phone 708–848–2222 for both sites). The home focuses on his family, while the museum holds his childhood diary, early writings, letters, photos, and more. Admission is $3.00 per person for the home, or $5.00 per person for both sites, and home tours are offered from 1:00 to 5:00 P.M. Friday and Sunday, and from 10:00 A.M. to 5:00 P.M. on Saturday.

DAY ONE: EVENING

Dinner

After your wanderings, go to dinner at one of the town's favorite spots, **Philander's Oak Park** (in the Carleton Hotel, 1120 Pleasant Street, Oak Park; 708–848–4250). This elegant restaurant was among the first to take advantage of the repeal of Oak Park's dry laws, not so very long ago, and has since prospered sufficiently to add **Poor Phil's Shell Bar** (round the corner, 139 Marion Street, Oak Park; 708–848–0871). Either can give you top-notch seafood, and Philander's often adds a live jazz band to entertain its patrons. Dinner will run about $60 for the two of you.

❧◕❧

Nightlife tends to be quiet in Oak Park, but summer brings the treasured institution of **Shakespeare in the Park** (Austin Gardens Park, Lake Street and Forest Avenue, Oak Park; 708–524–2050) The mosquitoes can be vicious, but the shows are a pleasure, especially with ticket prices comfortably under $20 apiece.

DAY TWO: MORNING/AFTERNOON

Depart Oak Park for downtown Chicago and a whole different perspective on the Windy City's architectural life! When you arrive downtown, check in at the **Inter-Continental Hotel** (505 North Michigan Avenue; 312–944–4100), where the Art Deco atmosphere will lure you right out of the Wright world and back into a richly decorated look of luxury, 1930s-style. Beautifully restored in recent years, the Inter-Continental is right in the middle of the famous Michigan Avenue shopping zone, the Magnificent Mile, and thus a good location from which to survey this high end of downtown.

The hotel also offers a fully equipped fitness center, but its real attraction—in looks as well as the pursuit of fitness—is a stunning, junior Olympic-size swimming pool whose cool green tempts the tired traveler. Be sure to get a look, at the very least, at this beautifully embellished pool area. And note that the lobby bar here serves a martini that ranks among the very best in town—down to the extra that comes to you in a very 1930s flask chilled to frosty perfection in an ice bucket.

Whether or not you dive into the pool (or into one of those martinis), you'll want to get started on sampling the riches of downtown. Again, the easiest way to be sure you won't miss anything major is to sign up for a Chicago Architecture Foundation (CAF) tour. Consider a Loop double header, "Early Skyscrapers" and "Modern and Beyond." Each is offered on a schedule that allows people to do both with a lunch break in between, although schedules vary enough that you'd best call for the times. Each tour is $10 per person, but buying both at one time is a bargain $15. For recorded information on tour schedules, call (312) 922–8687.

If you want a more in-depth look at some of the city's highlights, choose the appropriate CAF tour. Two Daniel Burnham buildings have tours of their own: the **Marshall Field and Co.** store (111 North State Street), which Burnham did from 1902 to 1907, and the 1888 **Rookery Building** (209 South La Salle Street), where the exterior was the work of Burnham's partner, John Root, and the stunning, light-filled interior—with a staircase that's pure poetry—was Burnham's plan (remodeled years later by none other than Frank Lloyd Wright!). Another Root building with its own tour is the 1891 **Monadnock** (53 West Jackson Boulevard), one of the last skyscrapers built without a steel frame; one thing you may not learn from a tour is that the the Monadnock is the professional home of V. I. Warshawski, the fictional detective heroine created by Sara Paretsky.

More greatness? Certainly. Learn about the work of Wright's mentor, Louis Sullivan, at his magnificent **Auditorium Building** (70 East Congress Boulevard). Historical sidelight: Here the city's first air-conditioning system blew air over blocks of ice to cool summertime theater-goers. Or explore Sullivan's **Carson Pirie Scott** (1 South State Street) store, where the master's more subtle ornament took a back seat to focusing shoppers' eyes on big windows showcasing merchandise. Each building is the subject of a CAF tour.

Or leap in the opposite direction, to the latter half of this century, with a look at the local masterpieces of Mies van der Rohe. Driven from Germany by the rise of the Nazis, Mies settled in Chicago and created the buildings of the South Side's Illinois Institute of Technology. His austere geometry can be seen in the **860–880 North Lake Shore Drive** apartment building, though it's not easy to get a good perspective on how the buildings' mass balances. Another downtown Mies building, done near the end of his career, is the grand **IBM Building** (North Wabash Avenue at the Chicago River). This imposing tower offers a good lesson in form following function. Its large, featureless plaza leaves pedestrians prey to Chicago's often savage weather, especially the sweeping winds that necessitate emergency ropes for passersby to cling to as they struggle through this impressively austere but impractical expanse.

And let's not forget some of the city's best-known landmarks. Architect Bruce Graham's 1969 **John Hancock Building** (875 North Michigan Avenue) was the city's first 1,000-foot-plus skyscraper and remains one of its most instantly recognizable buildings. Just as distinctive, and built just a few years earlier, is Bertrand Goldberg's **Marina City** (300 North State St.), the two cylindrical towers some call corncobs and others call great. And, of course, there's the

Sears Tower (a full city block, bounded by Adams Street, Franklin Street, Jackson Boulevard, and Wacker Drive), the 1974 behemoth that is still arguably the world's tallest (Chicagoans are tenacious; that building in Malaysia counts antennae, which we believe is cheating).

Lunch

The downtown area offers lots of good places for lunch, depending on where you find yourself. If you're in Sullivan's Carsons' Pirie Scott building or Burnham's Marshall Field and Co. building, eat at Field's seventh-floor restaurants. Farther south in the Loop, head for the **Berghoff** (17 West Adams Street; 312–427–3170), an institution since 1898 and one of the places where, not so long ago, women weren't allowed at the bar. In those days, the Berghoff's menu was strictly German; nowadays, there's pasta next to schnitzel, plus lighter fare for those who prefer it. Whatever you eat, though, don't skip the chance to try the restaurant's own beer. Figure about $20 to $30 total for lunch, and don't feel rushed if it's busy; the Berghoff is *always* busy.

DAY TWO: EVENING

Dinner

As you return to the Inter-Continental, think of that gorgeous pool to revive your weary feet. Then think about dinner—but, surprisingly, it's not so easy to get a nice dinner in an architecturally significant building. A happy exception is the John Hancock Building's **Signature Room on the Ninety-Fifth Floor** (875 North Michigan Avenue; 312–787–9596). The view, of course, is unbeatable; ask for a window table on arrival, if you're willing to wait.

The room has had its ups and downs over the years, but the current management is doing well with a health-conscious menu that offers fish, chicken, and vegetables alongside the power-lunch steaks and thick lamb chops you might expect. (A weekday lunch buffet is a fabulous bargain at $7.95 per person.) There's live music on Friday and Saturday evenings, and the lounge (one floor up) has jazz on other nights. Dinner entrees range from about $21.00 to about $30.00. Do note that you'll definitely need a reservation, and several weeks in advance is none too soon for a weekend evening. Sunday brunch is available here, too ($27.95), and it's a wonderful treat to come here in daylight when the weather is good. (On the other hand, I've been here during a thunderstorm and actually felt the building sway!)

To continue your appreciation of the city's architecture by using its beautiful spaces, cab south on Michigan Avenue to catch a play at Louis Sullivan's glorious Auditorium Theatre (50 East Congress Parkway; 312–902–1500). It's truly a beautiful place to see a show; the building's grandeur serves well whatever takes the stage. For up-to-date information, check the Friday or Sunday entertainment listings in the Chicago *Sun-Times* or *Tribune*.

DAY THREE: MORNING/AFTERNOON

Breakfast

Two full-tilt days, and you've barely scratched the surface of Chicago's architectural glories! Talk it all over over breakfast—maybe near your next destination, which is the Chicago River. You'll be within a couple of blocks if you have breakfast at **Primavera** (in the Fairmont Hotel, 200 North Columbus Drive; 312–565–6655). A full breakfast buffet is open from 6:30 to 11:30 A.M. daily, with eggs, meats, baked delicacies, and fruit. The buffet costs $16.50 per person. (Another time, consider dinner at Primavera, where the staff accents a mostly Italian menu with opera arias and show tunes every night. It's festive and fun; dinner runs about $35.00 per person.)

After breakfast, stroll downtown and pick out the buildings you've been studying, as well as some riverside notables—**333 West Wacker Drive,** for example, a glass-sheathed 1980s beauty whose curve seems to echo the river's own. Then put it all in perspective with one last tour, the **Chicago Architecture Foundation River Cruise,** a ninety-minute trip that spotlights fifty-three historic and/or architecturally important sights as you ply the Chicago River. The cruise takes place aboard *Chicago's First Lady* and commentary comes from (who else?) CAF guides. From late April through late October, three daily cruises are offered, departing at 9:30 A.M., noon, and 2:00 P.M. Tickets are about $16 per person on weekdays, somewhat higher on weekends, and a cash bar is open on board.

Now's the time to take your drink to a comfortable seat and relax while someone else does the talking. Hold hands as you let yourselves go with the flow, musing over what you've seen in the past few days—and how much more there is to do, another time, together.

WORDS OF LOVE

A LITERARY GETAWAY FOR LOVERS

*C*hicago has always loved writers, and the affection is mutual. It was our own Charles MacArthur, playwright and man-about-town, who, when he met the great actress Helen Hayes, offered her a handful of peanuts, saying he wished they were emeralds. We like to think of our town as Carl Sandburg's brawny "City of the Big Shoulders," but in fact Chicago is a very accommodating place for any wordsmith. Early in the century, *Poetry* magazine was born in a Michigan Avenue building, where its home remained for many years. More in the local image is another Chicago product, the poetry slam, in which poets read for tough, often raucous audiences.

The city's daily newspapers have nurtured countless writers, from Sandburg and Theodore Dreiser to early slammer Patricia Smith. Two daily papers remain. The *Chicago Tribune* carries the great curmudgeon, Mike Royko, while at the rival *Chicago Sun-Times,* film critic Roger Ebert turns his famous thumb to typing beautifully crafted essays disguised as routine movie reviews. Even Bill Zehme, who writes exquisite celebrity profiles for *Esquire* magazine, got his start at Loyola University's school paper.

We have other favorites, too: Sara Paretsky of Hyde Park, whose detective heroine V. I.

Romance at a Glance

♥ *Stay in a snug little European-style hotel.*

♥ *Talk for hours over a Savoy Truffle dinner.*

♥ *Visit the Newberry Library's splendid home and treasures.*

♥ *Explore the stunning Harold Washington Library.*

♥ *Lose yourselves in specialty bookstores and bibliophilic coffeehouses.*

♥ *Salute your sweetheart at a poetry slam.*

Warshawski is every inch a Chicagoan, and North Sider Nicole Hollander, whose opinionated comic strip, "Sylvia," appears daily in the *Tribune* and other newspapers all over the country.

If your romance rests on a passion for words, if you thrill together in a love of language, this is your city. Explore the downtown library, snuggle in wonderful bookstores, read (or gasp) at a poetry slam. In a word, wow!

Practical notes: This itinerary works at any time of year. You don't really need a car to reach these locations; impoverished writers travel by CTA bus or train. Also, if you want to seek out one of the city's many chain bookstores, such as Borders or Crown, just check the yellow pages.

DAY ONE: EVENING

Begin your rendezvous by checking into the **Claridge Hotel** (1244 North Dearborn Parkway; 312–787–4980), a small, 1920s-vintage Near North Side hideaway where you can snuggle by a fireplace while reading. A suite with a fireplace also offers a comfy sitting area and king-size bed.

The fireplace suites—there are three—command the Claridge's highest price of $180 per night, but you can get a nonfireplace suite for $129 per night. Or choose a room with a queen-size bed and a terrific city view for just $115 for a weekend night. All the suites and rooms come with some dandy amenities: free local phone calls, continental breakfast, limousine drop-off service within a couple of miles of the hotel (which includes downtown), *and* Starbucks coffee served gratis in the lobby round the clock (reason enough to stay, if you ask me).

Dinner

Naturally you've brought a book (maybe a few?), and you could get so comfortable, you don't even want to go out for dinner. No problem. The Claridge has a restaurant, but you also could use **Room Service,** a meals-on-wheels service that offers delivery from the menus of quite a few fine restaurants, including **Hat Dance** (which serves innovative Mexican food), **Scoozi!** (modern Italian), **Blackhawk Lodge** (smoked chicken, top-quality meats, salmon), and **Russian Palace** (herring, duck, stroganoff, quail). Ask the desk for more information and a menu.

If you prefer to go out for a dinner that takes a whole evening, head to the fashionable yet anti-chic Wicker Park/Bucktown neighborhood, which is loaded with artists who aren't all starving. Some are auteur chefs in small restaurants who serve up vision along with dinner. One of this breed is chef-owner Wendy Gilbert, whose **Savoy Truffle** (1466 North Ashland Avenue; 312–772–7530) is all for romance. "I've seen many a good date here," Gilbert declares. "It's intimate; I have little candles and great lighting, so everybody looks good here. Plus, I do all the cooking, and I don't have a liquor license, so what you do here is bring a bottle of wine and sit and talk."

Now there's an evening for lovers—and so much the better if you have Gilbert's cooking to keep you company. A world traveler who lived for several years in India, she brings an Eastern influence to her classical French training. Place your palates in her hands by asking what's great today, and she'll take great care of you. Prices are moderate, and Gilbert herself is a pleasure.

DAY TWO: MORNING/AFTERNOON

Just outside the Claridge is one of the city's most bustling neighborhoods, which makes its quiet oases all the sweeter. One such retreat is the **Newberry Library** (60 West Walton Street; 312–255–3510), an independent research institution whose strengths include cartography, Native American, and family and community history. The library supports a center for scholarly study in each of those specialties. It's also a second home for bookbinders, calligraphers, and genealogists from all over the world. But you don't have to have a Ph.D. to appreciate this stately, beautifully kept old building and the library's holdings of rare books, maps, and manuscripts. To get an overview, join the tour that's offered at 10:30 A.M. on Saturdays.

You'll get even more from the Newberry by perusing a schedule of its programs before you visit. Events at the library include stimulating exhibits, lectures, readings and performances by the resident Newberry Consort, which draws most of its thirteenth- to seventeenth-century music from the library's collections. Call well in advance and ask to have one sent to you. And if you happen to have a research interest that fits into the Newberry's collections—genealogy is the most common for nonscholars—you can gain a remarkable access to the collections by becoming a Newberry reader. All you have to do is bring a photo ID and register, although it's important to have your topic clearly defined for maximum help from the staff.

When you're ready for a breath of fresh air and respite from the Newberry's rarefied atmosphere, pause in the small park across the street to contemplate how the other half thinks. This is **Bughouse Square,** the time-honored free-speech space where, during the late nineteenth and early twentieth centuries, anyone could find an audience by mounting a soapbox (literally—they were bigger and studier then!) and offering opinions. Today it's almost as quiet as the Newberry itself.

Lunch

The area around the Newberry is loaded with restaurants, though not all are open for weekend lunches. You could walk a couple of blocks south and a couple of blocks west to **Cafe Iberico** (739 North La Salle Drive; 312–573–1510), a tapas bar that's as lively as the Newberry is staid, for a late lunch that can be as light or substantial as you wish. Excite your taste buds with the grilled wild mushrooms, tortilla espanola (an omelette with potatoes), and tender octopus. Nibbles do add up, but $20 will cover lunch for the two of you.

Double Word Score

Enjoy an indoor evening with the bibliophile's favorite game, which also makes a great gift for the two of you. Look wherever games are sold for a compact, traveling Scrabble set with tiles as magnetic as the game's appeal. Pack it for your weekend, and you'll be able to enjoy an evening of killer Scrabble. You might even want to award yourselves bonus points for words of love.

When you're ready to move on, walk or hop the El to one or more of the specialty bookstores that are all over town. Here are a few favorites:

- **Prairie Avenue Bookshop** (418 South Wabash Avenue; 312–922–8311), just a block east of the Harold Washington Library, is the nation's largest bookstore specializing in architecture.
- **Brent Books & Cards** (309 West Washington Street; 312–364–0126), north and west of the Washington library, is owned by the son of renowned bookseller Stuart Brent, whose Michigan Avenue shop now is closed and frequently lamented. Look here for fine fiction and nonfiction, and bring on the special orders.
- **Myopic Books** (1726 West Division Street; 312–862–4882), in the hip Wicker Park neighborhood, offers used books and tons of atmosphere.
- **Scenes Coffeehouse & Drama Bookstore** (3168 North Clark Street; 773–525–1007), specializes in books and magazines about the performing arts, plus scripts and an intense, flamboyant clientele.
- **The Stars Our Destination** (1021 West Belmont Avenue; 773–871–2722), around the corner and a few blocks west of Scenes, is a haven for fans of science fiction, horror, and fantasy.
- **People Like Us** (1115 West Belmont Avenue; 773–248–6363), a block west of Stars Our Destination, is devoted to gay and lesbian works.

- **The Emperor's Headquarters** (5744 West Irving Park Road; 773–777–7307), up on the far Northwest Side, carries books and magazines on military history as well as war games.
- **Women & Children First** (5233 North Clark Street; 773–769–9299) is a friendly North Side hangout in which to browse kids' and feminist books.
- **Centuries & Sleuths** (743 Garfield Street, Oak Park; 708–848–7243) is a happy home for mystery lovers like owners Augie and Tracy Alesky.
- **Transitions Bookplace/Cafe** (1000 West North Avenue; 312–951–7323). Personal growth is a full-time job at this serene, New Age-y store.
- **The Savvy Traveler** (310 South Michigan Avenue; 312–913–9800). Guides to everywhere are here, as are maps, language aids, and accessories to smooth your way.
- **Barbara's Bookstore** (five locations; call 312–624–5044 for information). The city's top indie, Barbara's offers a thoughtful stock and wonderful service.
- **Sandemeyer's Bookstore in Printer's Row** (714 South Dearborn Street; 312–922–2104). In the historic Printer's Row area, this quiet spot specializes in children's and grown-up literature.
- **Unabridged Books** (3251 North Broadway Avenue; 773–883–9119). Look for the staff's recommendations throughout this extensive store's shelves.
- **Ed & Fred—A Travelers' Store** (1007 West Webster Avenue; 773–447–6220). The Midwest's largest selection of outdoor books and maps in this Lincoln Park shop.

DAY TWO: EVENING

Where, oh where, have your bibliophilic wanderings led the two of you by nightfall?

Dinner

Let's assume you're back in the general neighborhood of Claridge's—and you're *hungry*. Make your reservations for **Mango** (712 North Clark Street; 312–337–5440), which is open for dinner seven nights a week and where the food makes you feel as though you are in Southern California—but the prices don't. One connoisseur friend calls the entire menu delicious, although you can't actually eat mango in every course. That's hardly a disappointment, especially when you're choosing from among such delights as pork chop with white beans, sausage, and mustard sauce. Or duck prosciutto with mango, lettuce, and chive. Or free-range chicken with lemon-raspberry sauce. You can see how the entire menu actually could be delicious. And at these moderate prices—entrees top out at $15—you'll be able to spring for dessert (mango sorbet, anyone?).

After dinner take a chance at the totally eclectic **Lunar Cabaret** (2827 North Lincoln Avenue; 773–327–6666), where artists are booked without regard to their particular style or even their medium. True, the Lunar does go mostly for music; you might hear avant-garde jazz, world music, folk, or pop. But the night's entertainment might instead be a local performing artist or, well, who knows what? Come and find out for an evening you'll remember. Note that Lunar Cabaret has no liquor license, but you're welcome to bring your own bottle.

DAY THREE: MORNING/AFTERNOON

Breakfast

Roll out of bed for a way-cool breakfast at **Wishbone** (two locations: 1800 West Grand Avenue, 312–829–3597; 1001 West Washington Street, 312–850–2663). The menu at both Wishbones is pure Southern comfort, from crab cakes to corn muffins to pecan pie. And the prices are comforting, too—breakfast isn't likely to set you back more than $10 or so for the two of you. The Grand Avenue site is smaller and very laid-back, about a mile west and another mile south of the Claridge; Washington Street is farther east, farther south, and places you a bit closer to your downtown destination, which is the pride of Chicago's populist-bibliophiles

❧❧❧

The **Harold Washington Library Center** (400 South State Street; 312–747–4300) is named for the city's first African-American mayor, elected in 1983, who succeeded the first woman mayor, Jane Byrne. This one-two punch of affirmative action greatly riled the City Council's powerful old-timers, who made Washington's initial four years in office a spectacle of continuous wrangling. The big, genial man known universally as Harold was hugely popular among the voters, however, and his second term followed a landslide electoral victory in 1987 that brought the City Council to its senses. Too late, however: Washington suffered a heart attack that year and died soon after, leaving the city bereaved and the aldermen in a state of bafflement that lasted pretty much until the present mayor, Richard M. Daley, took over in 1989.

Meanwhile, a suitable monument to Harold took shape. The new library opened in 1991, housing 1.6 million volumes. Get an eyeful of the gargoyle-like owls on the outer corners of the building, and then head inside. As you enter the library itself, pause to look at the wall exhibit of Chicago-related memorabilia. Inside ascend to the second-level balcony for a good view of the grand lobby's lovely mosaic floor, with its touching words from Washington about the city's many faces. Also off the first few floors' open stairways is a lovely tinkling fountain into which many visitors toss coins.

Guided tours of the building are given at noon and 2:00 P.M. Monday through Saturday and 2:00 P.M. Sunday, starting at the third-floor information theater. Meanwhile you can entertain yourselves by consulting wall directories for your own special interests. If you know anything about children's literature—even a rusty recall of nursery rhymes from your youth—be sure to stop in the kids' area and examine the librarians' dollhouse, which holds more than 70 references to fairy tales, Mother Goose classics, and modern works. Maybe you'll be inspired to share some pleasant childhood memories with your partner.

Also note that some half-dozen special exhibits are up at any given time throughout the library. "Preserving the Glory: The Grand Army of the Republic Collection" is an ongoing exhibit that changes periodically to display items from the library's Civil War collection, which includes such artifacts as battlefield musical instruments as well as writings and artworks. Other exhibits typically showcase Chicago topics, with photography and art by local talents. Take a stroll and see what you think.

If you want to catch an arts program here—they're free, of course—call before coming to find out what's happening when you plan to visit. Dance, theater, readings, music, and lectures are all represented in a brimming schedule you'll hear about, the number is (312) 747–4648.

To relax with a pair of books, head upstairs to the glorious **Wintergarden,** a sunny, skylit atrium where chairs and tables offer comfortable reading areas. Note, however, that you're not supposed to eat in the Wintergarden. For that there's the adjacent **Beyond Words Cafe** (312–747–4680), where renowned local caterer George Jewell provides a pair of buffets, hot and cold, that include sandwiches, soup, pastas, and salads. Choose the cold buffet for $6.00, the hot buffet for $8.75, or get both for $10.50: It's a bargain any way you go. Beer and wine are available, and there's even breakfast (muffins, Danish, quiche; $3.75) on Monday, Wednesday, Friday, and Saturday. The cafe's hours vary with those of the library, which is why tea is served only a couple of days a week, and unfortunately it's closed on Sunday.

Should you happen to come on a Sunday, stop at the **Uncommon Ground** coffeehouse in the library's lobby for a beverage and something to nibble. Maybe you'd like to take your refreshments outdoors, to the little park immediately north of the library, where you can sit and read near a fountain that helps muffle downtown noise.

If the two of you get tired of wallowing in words (impossible!), take a walk. If you thought to tuck in your neat little set, play Scrabble. Or write notes to the folks back home (who never have time to devote a day to books) or get one of those magnetic-poetry kits and amuse yourselves by assembling words at random.

Too Risky?

Remember the movie that made Tom Cruise a star? This is the El route that Cruise and Rebecca de Mornay rode in Risky Business. *If you haven't seen the movie, you'll have to guess at how they passed the night in their deserted El car.*

DAY THREE: EVENING

Dinner

Dinnertime already? You bet, and here's where you get your noses out of a book long enough to hop the El route that gave the Loop its name. The Brown Line (formerly known as the Ravenswood line) traces a rectangle bounded on the north by Lake Street, on the east by Wabash Avenue, on the south by Van Buren Street, and on the west by Wells Street. Leaving the library, get on the El a block north, along Van Buren, and enjoy the clackety din.

Back to reality! You're heading for the trendy River North area, where dozens of restaurants, clubs, and other festive possibilities await. One good bet is **La Locanda** (745 North La Salle Street; 312–335–9550), where Italian risotti are a specialty and the place is *not* closed on Sunday! Try a risotto with vegetables and white truffle oil, or a risotto paired with mushrooms or seafood. If entrees seem a bit high (maybe $30 for dinner), stick with pastas, which are also very good and less pricey.

After dinner, head north to the **Green Mill Jazz Club** (4802 North Broadway Avenue; 773–878–5552), a Prohibition-era club that now is the home of the poetry slam. Slams and other competitive poetry events are held all over town, but this regular Sunday-evening slam is reliably interesting and varied. Poet-ringmaster Marc Smith hosts an evening that combines performance art with pro wrestling as poets read their work in competition for audience approval. It's sport, but not blood sport; often exhilarating, never boring, a fascinating glimpse into a creators' culture of men and women, younger and older, office types and ex-hippies, WASPS and people of color, all propelled by an inner voice that makes them write and read out loud.

Come early—by 7:30 P.M. is smart—and if you *really* want to impress your sweetheart, slip a word to Smith that you'd like to read during the early open-mike part of the slam. Then get up there and address something to your beloved. You don't have to read your own work, although most do; if you choose someone else's piece, just acknowledge the poet and get on with the reading. They're kind to newcomers, but the audience *will* let you know if they don't like you. So be brief and be fearless. "Macho poet" is no oxymoron at a slam.

When you're finished, sit down, breathe deeply, and enjoy the rest of the slam, as well as the jazz that, if you're lucky, just might be scheduled for after. You can stay put for that after-dinner drink you've earned. Maybe your honey will buy it for you.

FOR MORE ROMANCE

Check out the terrific new regional library on the city's North Side. **Sulzer Regional Library** (4455 North Lincoln Avenue; 773–744–7616) was built to replace the old Hild Library down the street. Sulzer is a shiny new haven for book lovers, with row after row of English- and foreign-language newspapers, audio and video rentals, computer terminals, a great children's area—and that's just the first floor. Upstairs are the quiet stacks bibliophiles dream of, with plenty of seating and good librarians. And it's open seven days a week, the better to offer movies, speakers, and other programs in its auditorium. Sulzer's neighborhood, Lincoln Square, is a charming one to visit, too, an eclectic mix of ethnic influences that accommodates Greeks and Hispanics and Eastern Europeans along with the old German places.

Right across the street from the Sultzer library is **Welles Park** (2333 West Sunnyside Avenue; 312–742–7511), where you might catch a baseball or soccer game or, during the season, a kids' basketball game indoors. Or you can just stroll this spacious, well-kept park's inviting grounds. Going north on Lincoln Avenue brings you to the **Davis Theater** (4614

Book That Fair!

Every year, Chicagoans who love books flock to the **Printers' Row Book Fair,** *a celebration of the printed and spoken word that's mostly outdoors, mostly free, and totally fun for two. It's held on a June weekend, in a south-of-the-Loop neighborhood whose turn-of-the-century printing houses now are fashionable lofts with charming shops and restaurants galore. Prominent local authors appear at the fair to read from and/or sign their work. There's also performance by theater groups for kids and adults, plus music, refreshments, and general festivity. For more information, call (312) 987–9896.*

North Lincoln Avenue; 312–784–0893), a great spot to catch current movies for just a buck. There's also a time-suspended German institution, **Merz Apothecary** (4716 North Lincoln Avenue; 773–989–0900), an old-fashioned pharmacy where rows of herbs and curatives gleam on wooden shelves, right next to the toothpaste (also herbal).

For a delightful lunch or dinner, go a bit farther north to **Cafe Selmarie** (2327 West Giddings Street; 312–989–5595), a sweet little bakery-plus-restaurant that serves salads, sandwiches, and more substantial fare, all made from scratch on the premises. Prices are very moderate, although this is one spot where you can't help budgeting calories for dessert, since you have to pass the bakery cases on the way to your table. Many patrons plan dinner around what they've just perused!

Another local favorite is **La Bocca della Verita** (4618 North Lincoln Avenue; 312–784–6222), a snug *trattoria* that has become a word-of-mouth success among North Siders. You can cozy up at a little table while you enjoy well-prepared pastas—go for the salmon fettuccine with portobello mushrooms, if at all possible—or free-range chicken, or perhaps a whole fish, at prices as low as $12 for an entree. Do feel free to dress casually. La Bocca is open seven days a week from 5:00 to 11:00 P.M.

ITINERARY 15
One day and one evening

Art and Soul

The Art Institute and More

Truth, beauty, you and your sweetheart—what could be more romantic? It's all within easy reach when you devote a day to nourishing your souls as well as your relationship. The space of a few downtown-Chicago blocks holds a world-class art museum, two of the city's top-notch theater venues, sultry spots for late-night music—plus charming places for lunch, elegant dinner options, and just the right nightcap.

Practical notes: This day works at any time of year. Be sure to check on what's playing at the theaters mentioned; both are popular, and you may need to order tickets well in advance.

MORNING/AFTERNOON

Get in the mood for art over café au lait and a croissant at the nearby **Au Bon Pain** (122 South Michigan; 312–427–4070). As you cross Michigan Avenue and ascend the grand stone steps to the **Art Institute of Chicago** (Michigan Avenue at East Adams Street; 312–443–3600) you'll pass between the famous lion statues that "guard" the entrance. They're one of the city's favorite landmarks—part meeting place, part civic treasure, adorned with evergreen wreaths at Christmas, and, when a local team wins big, with the appropriate colors or logo. (Chicagoans still remember fondly the huge Bears helmets the lions wore for 1985's Super Bowl victors.)

Whether it's your first or your five-hundredth visit here, keep the map you'll receive as you enter; it offers a floor plan with photos of well-known works from each area. There's more information in the guides to the collections that you'll find at the entrance to each major area. For 25 cents, you get an illustrated discussion of major pieces and a preface explaining their context and importance.

Romance at a Glance

♥ *Spend an art-drenched day at the Art Institute of Chicago, with lunch in its garden cafe.*

♥ *Browse the museum gift shop.*

♥ *Dine at Prairie.*

♥ *See a play at the Goodman Theatre or Auditorium Theatre.*

♥ *Catch a late show at Buddy Guy's Legends.*

The Art Institute is best known for its magnificent collection of French Impressionist works. These include Georges Seurat's pointillist panorama, *Sunday Afternoon on the Island of La Grande Jatte,* and Pierre Auguste Renoir's *On the Terrace,* a glowing portrait of a beautiful woman and her daughter on a sunny afternoon. Renoir's *The Rowers' Lunch* is a don't-miss for lovers, as is Henri de Toulouse-Lautrec's famous *At the Moulin Rouge.* Claude Monet's *Irises* is glorious, but get a look at his luminous *Haystacks,* too. You'll want to jump right in—together.

There's also a glow to *The Place de l'Europe on a Rainy Day,* Gustave Caillebotte's precise and subtle marriage of geometry and mood, known to many simply as "the umbrella painting." And luminosity reaches new heights in Marc Chagall's stunning, exuberant stained glass windows. They're guaranteed to fill your hearts with love and joy, and if you remember that heartfelt moment in the movie *Ferris Bueller's Day Off,* you'll realize Ferris was kissing his girlfriend before these irresistible windows.

Two of the Art Insititute's most famous works are American, and you'll recognize them the moment you see them. Edward Hopper's *Nighthawks,* the shadowy late-night diner that is perhaps the quintessential picture of loneliness in America, will definitely make you appreciate your sweetheart. And the poker-faced farmers in Grant Wood's *American Gothic,* another instantly familiar work, just beg for mischief. If only you could put your own faces on their bodies to create one of those goofy fake photos.

Lunch

When it's time for lunch, you can stay right here and do very well. The **Garden Restaurant,** which is open during the summer, lets you relax over an inexpensive light lunch in a beautiful, relatively quiet outdoor courtyard. (You'll appreciate the quiet if you check out the overpriced, mediocre Court Cafeteria, which is likely to be crowded with school groups.) For a real treat, though, go upstairs to what a tuxedoed waiter calls "the best-kept secret in Chicago." The **Restaurant on the Park** is open to the public for lunch only, so don't make the mistake of expecting to return later for dinner. This white-tablecloth oasis of civility looks out over Grant Park toward the lake. (Although reservations are accepted, they won't promise a window table—but you can try!) The menu, whose elegant appetizers and entrees run from $4.50 to $12.75, features several dishes inspired by artist Claude Monet's cooking journals. Wine, beer, and luscious desserts are available, too.

You can also **picnic in the park** without having to pay a second museum admission, since your ticket is good for the day. All of Grant Park awaits you at the Art Institute's east end, although you'll have to leave your picnic backpack at the front entry and walk around the block after retrieving it. You might want to picnic near the Isamo Noguchi sculpture that many call "the fountain"; it's a horizontal, loglike piece with flowing water that calms the sound of traffic.

Later, when you've had your fill of gallery wandering, stop at the museum shop to browse through art books, souvenirs, jewelry, and gifts. Don't forget to choose a beautiful postcard and write a note of thanks to the person who introduced you to each other. As you leave at the main entrance, stop for a peek behind the northernmost lion. You'll find a staircase that's perfect for a secluded snuggle and a secret smooch.

Timeless Treasures: Eight Romantic Masterpieces

When you're looking through the eyes of love, just about everything is gorgeous. So you may need to pare down the possibilities of a day at the Art Institute. Here's a strictly subjective list of lesser-known works that speak of romance. Be on the lookout for others to call your own!

Are They Thinking of the Grape? *Francois Boucher. Probably not! A shepherd lolls at the knee of a shepherdess about to feed him a grape in this ripe, racy eighteenth-century painting.*

The Buddah God Ilevajra Embracing His Consort, Nairatmya. *The fierce yet joyful god wraps all sixteen arms around his love in this Nepalese gilt bronze statue from the sixteenth or seventeenth century.*

Venus and Cupid, *Luca Cambiaso. Love's favorite deities, in a sweet mother-and-child representation.*

Lovers, *Sugimura Jihei. A man, a woman, a couple of cats—all lying down, or about to, in this Japanese woodblock print.*

Solitaire, *Balthus. If you've ever agonized over a love letter, you know this painting's feeling.*

Veranda Post Representing an Enthroned King and His Senior Wife, *Olowe of Ise. Here's a power marriage. He's the king, but she brings the woman's ashe—"power and force in all things"—to their union in this Yoruba wood carving.*

Sky Above Clouds, *Georgia O'Keeffe. Hanging over a huge, circular double staircase, this massive canvas looks like a lovely brick walk straight to heaven.*

Uma Maheshvara. *Casual gods, indeed. Shiva caresses Uma's breast as the couple rides a bull, surrounded by their sons and other acolytes, in a ninth-century sandstone sculpture.*

EVENING

Dinner

A curtain-conscious early dinner is easy to find at restaurants near the Art Institute. One good choice is **Printer's Row** (550 South Dearborn Street; 312–461–0780), a dignified place where the fare is sophisticated *and* satisfying; foodies enjoy nouvelle-ish entrees, and guys rejoice in man-size portions of venison. Dinner ranges from about $60 to about $80 for two; it's served from 5:00 P.M., so you'll have plenty of time to make your show. Another good bet is **Russian Tea Time** (77 East Adams Street; 312–960–0000), a *very* popular spot where dinner is available early (from 4:00 P.M.!) and runs to about $60 per couple. Closing as late as midnight on weekends, the restaurant also is a good place for a drink after the show.

And which show will it be? Two outstanding possibilities are close by the Art Institute—in fact, one is right in the museum's backyard. The **Goodman Theatre** (200 South Columbus Avenue; 312–443–3800) is at the east side of the Art Institute, although the two are entirely separate enterprises. Goodman is known for its lavish annual staging of *A Christmas Carol,* and has an admirable record ranging from Shakespeare to Tom Stoppard. One felicitous pairing is the Goodman's productions of plays by Eugene O'Neill featuring the actor Brian Dennehy. Dennehy, the well-known television and movie actor with the canny Irish face, solidified his local reputation in *The Iceman Cometh* a few years back at Goodman; more recently he starred in *A Touch of the Poet* there. If you have the chance to see him, do. But anything on the Goodman's stage is worth taking a chance; I've seen a few clunkers, but many a mesmerizing show there.

Another good possibility nearby is the gorgeous **Auditorium Theatre** (50 East Congress Parkway; 312–902–1500) where the revival of *Show Boat* settled in for a long run in 1996. The show is richly Chicago-connected; novelist Edna Ferber loved the city and set much of the action of *Show Boat* here. Even if that ship has sailed by the time of your visit, the Auditorium may have another Broadway-style musical in its place; that's the kind of production the theater typically books. If a big show is a bit much, walk over to the **Fine Arts** (418 South Michigan Avenue; 312–939–3700), where foreign and other "art" films find their audience.

After the show, finish your evening with a dose of the famous Chicago blues at **Buddy Guy's Legends** (754 South Wabash Avenue; 312–427–0333), where the longtime bluesman books buddies and talented lesser-knowns. You might happen upon a recording session, like the recent live-album set that captured Son Seals. And if you're cosmically fortunate, you'll catch the likes of Eric Clapton, who played a three-night stand here not long ago. The location is perfect if you're downtown, and cover charges don't go over $10 or so. There's even a kitchen that serves up tasty Louisiana specialties, including red beans and rice, at inexpensive prices till midnight.

OPERA LOVERS' TRYST

*E*ven people who don't know aria from an airplane fall in love with the Lyric Opera, Chicago's world-class entry in this most rarefied stratum of show biz. Everything at Lyric is top-notch, from musicianship to set design to gracious ushers, so newcomers and old-timers alike are assured of an evening that's the best of its kind.

Many novices fear they'll spend an evening at the opera wondering what the heck everyone's singing about. That's not a problem at Lyric, where supertitles projected above the stage translate lyrics to help you track the onstage action. It's easy to see why this addition has contributed to opera's surging popularity in recent years; knowing what's going on *does* enhance your enjoyment of the music.

Realize, too, that at Lyric, what's onstage is definitely not the whole show. The company owns its home, the grand old Civic Opera House, an opulent fantasyland of marble and velvet and gilt, gilt, gilt. Better yet, your fellow operagoers make a fascinating pageant that you'll enjoy watching (and eavesdropping on!) before curtain, during intermissions, and as you depart.

Practical notes: Where to begin? You'll need two things to begin planning your night at the opera: a schedule and a head start. A season consists of eight different operas, with performances starting in September and finishing in March. Schedules are available early in the year for the shows starting in September, with season subscribers getting first pick of seats. A mailing that lists available single tickets goes out in July, and orders begin in August. Don't expect the selection to be plentiful.

Your first task, then, is to get a schedule from the Civic Opera House box office, which is open year-round at (312) 332–2244. When you've received it, you can begin deliberating on which production you'd like to see. Lyric publicity manager Danny Newman advises a little research to narrow down the possibilities. "Of our eight productions each year, six are tried-and-true, traditional works—Verdi, Puccini, Mozart, Richard Strauss," he says. "There are so many recordings of these operas; even the public library has them. Also, read the capsule descriptions of the operas in the schedule brochure. These give the essence of the opera, its mood. And ask your opera-wise friends—this is not such a rare thing anymore!"

You might even rent a video of a title you're considering. *Tosca,* for example, was filmed not long ago in Rome, in a real-time production that critics and fans loved. There are films of *Carmen, Madame Butterfly,* and many others. (*La Boheme* is the opera that moved Cher and Nicolas Cage to tears in *Moonstruck.*) All of these, by the way, are among the great romances of opera.

When you've chosen your title, be flexible on which performance you want. Getting tickets to a Lyric production is by no means a cinch, as its sellout rate of 107 percent attests. (Baffled about the math? They do it by getting season subscribers, as well as individual ticketholders, to notify the box office when they won't be using seats already bought. These turned-back seats give the ticketholder a tax break and Lyric a chance to sell the same ticket twice.)

As you might expect, opera tickets aren't cheap, but you won't go bankrupt, either. Tickets

Romance at a Glance

♥ *Tour the Civic Opera House to peek behind the scenes at one of the world's great opera companies.*

♥ *Enjoy a pretheater dinner at one of the city's finest, Everest.*

♥ *Hear a world-class production at Lyric Opera, and then have a nightcap at the Italian Village.*

for a single performance can be bought for as little as $25 or $30 apiece, although main-floor seats on a weekend evening can ascend well into three figures. Ask about sightlines when you buy; the box office personnel are patient and knowledgeable.

Be careful, though, to get seats together. (And if your definition of *together* is "side by side," specify that or you'll end up seated one in front of the other in consecutive rows or in the same row but separated by an aisle.) This is trickier than getting single tickets, but your first opera is no time to go it alone. Unlike airline passengers operagoers are not likely to trade seats so you can sit with your sweetheart.

AFTERNOON

If you really want to learn more about what goes into making an opera, plan to take in one of the afternoon tours of the Opera House that are offered from time to time during the season. Rehearsal rooms, dressing rooms, workshops, and the stage itself are included in the two-hour tours, which cost $17.50 per person. Ideally, you can choose a backstage tour that coincides with the performance you want to see; check with the box office when you buy tickets to arrange this.

This is one evening that demands attention to correct attire—but, happily, it's pretty simple to be correct at Lyric. Dressing up is always acceptable for the opera, although black tie and formal gowns are mostly seen at opening night and, sometimes, at Saturday evening performances. Weekends are dressier than weeknights, when many patrons come directly from work. Since you'll be appropriate in just about anything snazzier than blue jeans, feel free to get as gussied up as you wish.

Plan an early dinner before the opera, because the curtain goes up at 7:30 P.M. sharp and nobody is seated afterward. (Late arrivals are stuck watching the show on a television monitor in the lobby.) It's wise to arrive by 7:00 P.M., so you can check coats, find seats, locate restrooms, and get in a little people watching in the lobby before the performance begins.

Dinner

Several fine restaurants offer pretheater dinners that will send you on your way in good time. One of the city's very finest restaurants, **Everest** (440 South LaSalle Street; 312–663–8920), serves an early menu consisting of four courses of spectacular French food from 5:30 to 6:30 P.M., at the equally spectacular price of $39. You even get free parking, although it's a bit of a hike over to the Civic Opera House and back. A pleasant one, though, if the evening is mild and your shoes are comfortable.

Even closer to the Opera House is the charming **Yvette Wintergarden** (311 South Wacker Drive; 312–408–1242), where a pretheater menu offers such delectable choices as grilled salmon or tenderloin tips of beef. It's a bargain at about $20 per person, and here, too, there's the welcome opportunity to park the car and leave it during the opera.

EVENING

When you arrive at the Opera House, ushers will guide you in the right direction and, as you locate the right aisle, help you find your seats. If you aren't familiar with the opera, read the synopsis in your playbill to get the plot. And note, on the title page, how many intermissions you'll have. Usually there's one, but often there are two.

Once the music starts, strict silence is the norm; if you have a bit of a cold, bring cough drops, and if you have a beeper, turn it off! Don't fret about whether or when to applaud; take your cue from the people around you. And relax. Let the music embrace you.

At intermission you'll find refreshments ranging from champagne to coffee to chocolate-chip cookies at counters in the lobbies on almost every level. Lines are long, but you can pass the wait by observing your fellow culture vultures' appearance, conversation, and pick-me-up practices. Intermissions often are lengthy—fifteen to twenty minutes, but sometimes as long as half an hour—so you should have time for a snack *and* a visit to the washroom.

As the performance ends, stay in your seat long enough to applaud the conductor as well as

*If you don't have the stamina for a night at the opera, get a pleasant, undemanding taste of it by dining at **Rigoletto** (2478 North Lincoln Avenue; 773–348–8611), where the food is as exquisite as the music, which generally is opera or a classical cousin. The Rigoletto "theme" is carried out in photos of various productions of Verdi's romantic tragedy, and the menu is divided into acts. Try a pasta or chicken entree, or go for the hefty veal chop, which at $25 is the most expensive dish on the menu. The restaurant's contemporary decor is very tasteful, but patrons are welcome to come as they are. "We're not stuffy," a waitress told me, and she was right. Another big plus: Rigoletto offers valet parking in one of the city's most car-choked neighborhoods.*

the performers; he of she will come onstage after the first round or two of bows. Then head out into the night for a snack, a nightcap, and/or a postshow wrap-up. According to Lyric's Newman, the **Italian Village** (71 West Monroe Street; 312–332–1637) has been "our unofficial restaurant ever since Lyric began," more than forty years ago. The reason is simple: The kitchen serves up good Italian food and stays open late enough for operagoers.

You can walk there if the weather's reasonable (and since cabs are nearly impossible to get after the show, you may have to!). The building actually holds three Italian restaurants, each with its own identity and menu. At the main level, **Vivere** (312–332–4040) is a postmodern vision of swirling flourishes and startling colors, with a sophisticated Italian menu of pastas, fish, and some meat. It's a good place to wrap up your equally sophisticated night at the opera. Romantic in a very different way is the upstairs Italian Village, a Chicago favorite of such long standing that some of your fellow diners may be high-schoolers on the same post-prom trip downtown that their parents made. Get one of the room's little tucked-away nooks for two, and settle in to decide for yourselves whether those twinkling lights are charming or hokey. The menu is as reliable as the clientele, with filling pastas and traditional entrees. Downstairs, the pleasant **La Cantina** (312–332–7005) is decked out as a fishing village, suggesting its specialty of fine seafood.

Another wonderful post-opera spot is the older sibling of Yvette Wintergarden. At **Yvette** (1206 North State Parkway; 312–280–1700), about ten or fifteen minutes' drive from the Opera House, the kitchen is open until midnight weeknights, till 1:00 A.M. Friday and Saturday. In addition to dinner, on most nights there's live cabaret entertainment and dancing, too.

FOR MORE ROMANCE

A night at the opera is a late night; why not extend its pleasures by reserving a room at a downtown hotel? Lyric puts up its out-of-town singers at the Drake or the Four Seasons, Newman says, and both are ideal for continuing the evening's feeling of grandeur. If you'd like to rub some famous elbows in these elevators, call the Drake at (312) 787–8667 or the Four Seasons at (312) 280–8800 for reservations. (For a detailed description of the Four Seasons, see the earlier chapter "Let it Snow: A Cozy Winter Weekend.")

Another possibility, a brief cab ride from any of these restaurants, is the hotel many people think of immediately when they think of Chicago. Even after the feverish hotel-building boom of the 1980s, the decades-old **Chicago Hilton and Towers** (720 South Michigan Avenue; 312–922–4400), formerly the namesake Conrad Hilton, remains one of the city's premier hotels. Rooms—there are 1,543 of them—are decorated in pale peachy shades and warm cherrywood furnishings, and baths feature Italian marble and brass fixtures. In the Towers, a hotel within the hotel, guests enjoy their own concierge, a separate registration area, and lots of deluxe perks. A fully equipped fitness club offers plenty of machines, a spacious pool, and a sauna and whirlpool for working out and relaxing afterward. Rates for a double room start at $165 per night, but look for a weekend package to bring that down to $125 and include a continental breakfast, too. (Suites are pricey—$440 and up.)

Two of the Hilton's biggest attractions are **Buckingham's,** its top-of-the-line steak house (where entrees include plenty of fish and seafood, running from about $17 to about $35) and its pub, **Kitty O'Sheas,** which is among the most authentically Irish spots in this Eire-loving town. It's especially packed around St. Patrick's Day, but the Irish staff are here year-round and there's often Irish music performed by bands from the Auld Sod. The kitchen serves up corned beef and cabbage, fish and chips, shepherd's pie, and more from 11:00 A.M. till 9:00 P.M., so if you knock off that continental breakfast early, you're positioned for a hearty lunch. Best of all, nothing at Kitty's runs more than $10.

You'll be in town when Lyric's season is over? No problem: There are at least two other opera possibilities in Chicago during Lyric's downtime. **Chicago Opera Theater** (P.O. Box

39270; 773–292–7578) offers three productions every summer, all sung in English at the downtown Merle Reskin Theater (60 East Balbo Drive). Pre-show dinner packages are available at excellent restaurants including Printer's Row, Carlucci, Prairie, Moonraker, and the two restaurants in the Chicago Hilton and Towers. The Hilton and the Hyatt on Printer's Row even offer weekend opera getaways with special room rates; ask for more information on these when you call about tickets.

Another way to see opera here is in the first suburb north of Chicago at **Light Opera Works** (927 Noyes Street, Evanston, IL; 847–869–6300), which specializes in high-quality music that isn't heavy-duty—Gilbert and Sullivan rather than Richard Strauss, Leonard Bernstein rather than Philip Glass. Light Opera Works produces a couple of shows each summer and a holiday show as well; call for seasonal information.

ITINERARY 17
Three days and two nights

THE FOOD OF LOVE

MUSIC IN CHICAGO

*I*f Shakespeare was right in calling music "the food of love," then Chicago is an all-you-can-eat buffet! Feast on three courses—jazz, folk, and blues—on Friday. Make a double entree of rock and pop on Saturday. And on Sunday, brunch with gospel and go till teatime with the Chicago Symphony Orchestra. Here's a weekend that invites you to bop till you drop with three gluttonously, gloriously tuneful days—and nights.

DAY ONE: EVENING

Make a base for your musical explorations at a cozy, centrally located bed and breakfast in Old Town. Your hostess owns **Bed & Breakfast Chicago** (312–951–0085), so you can relax in the knowledge that you'll be well cared for during your stay! This B&B is a self-contained apartment within a larger home that has a lovely garden where you can enjoy your breakfast. The apartment's bedroom features a queen-size four-poster, plus your own full kitchen and private bath, as well as a living room area. At about $95, it's a spacious and comfortable bargain.

Lunch

Arriving on Friday means you can start taking in tunes as soon as you've unpacked! If you're *really* early, you can catch the lunchtime set at **Andy's** (11 East Hubbard Street; 312–642–6805), a friendly bar-restaurant where downtown workers recover from the morning with a burger and quality jazz from noon till 2:30 P.M. daily. Some even come back after work for more, though you'll find yourself sitting near jazz-loving out-of-towners as well as ad execs. In Chicago everyone who knows jazz comes to Andy's. There's no cover for the noon shows, and covers vary in the evening.

Dinner

Make your way north on the El, exiting at Armitage Avenue to stroll through some of the Lincoln Park neighborhood before dinner at **Carlucci** (2215 North Halsted Street; 773–281–1220). This Italian restaurant is a fashionable favorite that has endured in a super-trendy neighborhood. One fan says the polenta here is the best in town, and everybody loves the many pasta choices. Fish and meats are good, too, and if the weather cooperates, you can sit in a lovely, trellised little garden that truly makes you forget you're in the big city. Prices are somewhat expensive (perhaps $75 for both of you), but you won't need a cab to your next stop—the **Old Town School of Folk Music** (909 West Armitage Avenue; 773–525–7793).

An institution nationwide as well as in its hometown, the Old Town School has nurtured and hosted absolutely everyone in the folk world. That's partly because its definition of folk music embraces every sort of folk: African as well as Celtic, East European as well as all-American, joyful noise as well as angry protest, challenging rhythms as well as pretty voices.

And there's history as well as musical anthropology. Though plans are afoot to move the performances into a larger space north of the school's present location, I remember apartment-hunting many years ago for my very first place. I thought one building was just too rundown, but the neighborhood couldn't be *so* bad with the Old Town School right around the corner. And the neighborhood wasn't, as you can see from the fashionable company the school keeps now, in the very same home it's always had. When you call to ask who's playing during your weekend, be open-minded to anything they care to program here. You won't be sorry. Depending on the show, tickets usually run about $20, and shows usually are at 8:00 P.M.

That leaves you plenty of evening left to explore another Chicago specialty, the blues. If you want an authentic neighborhood to go with the music, cab down to the **Checkerboard Lounge** (423 East 43rd Street; 773–624-3240). This legendary name still attracts well-known players and fans from all over town and all over the world. Cover charges vary, but the music always starts after 9:30 P.M. If you come, realize that the neighborhood can be rough and don't go wandering. Close to the Old Town School is a pair of reliable blues bars. **B.L.U.E.S.** (2519 North Halsted Street; 773–528–1012) and its nearby sibling, **B.L.U.E.S. Et Cetera** (1124 West Belmont Avenue; 773–525–8989). Both offer high-quality local talent from about 9:30 P.M. at variable cover charges. Both *are* bars, though, and you might be looking for something a little quieter. In that case, head for **Lilly's** (2513 North Lincoln Avenue; 773–525–2422), a blessedly civilized haven for blues. Music starts at 9 P.M., and there's no weekend cover charge.

DAY TWO: MORNING/AFTERNOON

Sleep late, breakfast in your kitchen, and then take the El downtown for a free-form day. Don't neglect to tip the street-corner musicians you're sure to encounter as you make your way to the **Harold Washington Library Center** (400 South State Street; 312–747–4300). You may not think that this would be the natural place to look for music—but this is no ordinary library. (The library itself is described in more detail in the earlier chapter "Words of Love: A Literary Getaway for Lovers.") Be sure to call before coming and ask about the music programs scheduled during your stay. There are sure to be some. Among the library's most popular events are the sessions in which blues performers play and talk about their work and lives. Or you might catch a performance by an up-and-coming local classical artist. It's always worth a look.

Also worth checking out is the **Chicago Cultural Center** (78 East Washington Street; 312–346–3278), which used to be the city's main library. Outgrown but not outdated, the lovely building now serves as an exhibit and performance space for a wonderfully eclectic schedule of programs. You might catch a show by a resident company, such as the Chicago Children's Choir or City Lit Theater. On Wednesdays at 12:15 P.M., the Dame Myra Hess Memorial Concerts offer classical artists whose performances are broadcast live on WFMT radio, a station that calls itself "Chicago's fine arts station."

DAY TWO: EVENING

Dinner

Before heading into more music, stop for sustenance at the **Mashed Potato Club** (3914 North Clark Street; 773–871–4062), home of down-home dinners at down-to-earth prices. Chicken, fresh fish, meat loaf, and more come with a double scoop of silky spuds (oven-roasted or sweets, if you prefer), with entrees ranging from $9.95 to $17.95.

இஇஒ

Next up is a 7:00 P.M. all-ages show at **Metro** (3730 North Clark Street, 773–549–0203). Call it Metro or call it Cab Met, but don't ever call it boring. This longtime fixture on the city's rock/alternative scene is where you might have caught Smashing Pumpkins, Veruca Salt, or other big names before they were big, and the club's frequent all-ages shows let a younger crowd enjoy the music at a reasonable hour. The attraction for grown-ups is that there's no alcohol, so things are likely to be less rowdy than they will be later. The place is funky—and the washrooms are downright scary, but Metro has a vibe that can't be denied. Ticket prices vary, so be sure to call. And stop in at another fixture, the downstairs Smart Bar, before you leave.

The early hour leaves time for the two of you to see another set at another location. Good bets are the **Double Door** (1572 North Milwaukee Avenue; 312–489–3160), which books both local and national rock acts and keeps cover charges reasonable at $10 per person tops. Or visit the **Lounge Ax** (2438 North Lincoln Avenue; 773–525–6620), which brings very happening rockers to town, also at reasonable covers. Be warned, however, that the Ax is looking to relocate at this writing, so you may have to track down a new address.

If you aren't drawn to loud rock, put part of your leisurely day to use in choosing the evening's entertainment. The best source for complete music listings is the weekly Chicago *Reader*, a free paper that's available in stores, libraries, and other public places all over town. No matter what you choose, keep in mind that a great place to talk it over afterward is **Third Coast** (29 East Delaware Place; 312–664–7225), a cross between cafe and coffeehouse that's open till 3 A.M. Friday and Saturday nights. Open even later—though the neighborhood can be dicey—is the authentically Deco **Green Mill Jazz Club** (4802 North Broadway Avenue; 773–878–5552), where the crowds thin after a poetry slam or jazz show, and you can drink in a quieter atmosphere.

DAY THREE: MORNING

Brunch

It's worth getting out of bed to take in the unlikely but wonderful Sunday gospel brunch at **Dick's Last Resort** (435 East Illinois Street; 312–836–870). Like some reprobate hustled off to church every Sunday by a God-fearing wife, Dick's transforms itself weekly from a raucous good-time bar into a respectful home for soul-stirring gospel singers from all around the area. The food is almost as heavenly as the music, with dozens of entrees, any breakfast item you can conjure, and a sinful dessert table to tempt even the straight-and-narrow dieter. It's all here from 10:00 A.M. till 3:00 P.M. every Sunday, at moderate prices.

DAY THREE: AFTERNOON

When you're thoroughly redeemed, head west to Orchestra Hall (220 South Michigan Avenue; 312–435–6666) for a splendid finale to your musical weekend: a matinee by the **Chicago Symphony Orchestra.** One of the very top orchestras anywhere, the CSO has traveled the world to universal acclaim and given the city something to brag about besides Al Capone and Michael Jordan. Any program you happen to catch, it goes without saying, will be first-rate. Perhaps you'll even hear a performance of works by Romantic composers. Even if you're not a fan of classical music, taking your seat in this venerable house and listening to some of the world's best musicians warm up gives you the thrill that comes with knowing you're in the presence of greatness. Tickets are not as hard to get as you might expect, but it's always wise to plan ahead; and because prices vary widely, you'll need to pin down a date before ordering.

There are lots of other ways to enjoy classical music in Chicago. The most efficient approach is to consult *Chicago* magazine before you get to town, or the *Reader* weekly newspaper once you're here. Then get your dialing finger to work on tickets.

FOR MORE ROMANCE

There's yet another way to enjoy music on a late Saturday night: Join **Rosa's Blues Cruise.** Tony Mangiullo, the Italian-born owner of this friendly Northwest Side bar (it's named for his mom!), organizes a cruise or two every summer for regulars *and* people who've never set foot in the bar. He books top performers—Otis Clay, Syl Johnson, Melvin Taylor, and Sugar Blue are past cruise stars—and the fun runs into the night. "It's a nice combination of people," Mangiullo says. "We get lots of couples, and we get groups of five or eight or ten. Rarely does anyone buy only one ticket. We get tourists, too—I just got a fax from some Germans who are planning their trip to make it!"

Rosa's Blues Cruise sails on the *Spirit of Chicago,* so the ride is smooth and the engines don't drown out the tunes. Tickets, which include Italian submarine sandwiches and two free passes to visit Rosa's, are $39 per person (a cash bar is open throughout). The three-hour cruise boards at midnight, departs at 12:30 and returns at 3:30 A.M. To find out future dates and order tickets, call Mangiullo at Rosa's (3420 West Armitage Avenue; 773–342–0452).

If classical music isn't what you want on Sunday afternoon, hang loose till 4:00 P.M., when the **Jazz Showcase** (59 West Grand Avenue; 312–670–2473) presents its "matinee" show of the weekend's attraction. Don't even fret about who's appearing—it's certain to be a high-quality talent. Sunday afternoons are a relative bargain at $15 per person (other weekend shows are $20), and the bands are cooking.

SHALL WE DANCE?

*T*here's an ad around town at the moment for a flamenco show. "The vertical expression of horizontal desire," says the headline. Indeed, isn't that what much of dance—from ballet to salsa—really is about? And doesn't it make terrific sense to devote yourselves to pursuing it? The *vertical,* of course. The horizontal—well, there you're on your own.

As for *watching* dance, you'll find the best variety in town during the springtime Festival of Dance, usually held in May and offering everything from classical ballet to avant-garde dance. To find out what's shaking at any time of the year, call the Chicago Dance Coalition Hotline at (312) 419–8383 for a recorded list of scheduled performances. And if the groups mentioned below aren't on the performance list, don't despair. Take a chance on a different company— Ballet Chicago, Muntu Dance Theater, River North Dance Company, anything at Columbia College—all are good bets, and could be a dance experience you'll remember always.

Practical notes: Most of this weekend is within easy reach of the Ambassador West, but you'll need a car to get to Willowbrook. Here's how to go:

DAY ONE: EVENING

Make your headquarters for a romantic weekend in motion at a spot that just might make you feel like dancing right away. The **Ambassador West Hotel** (1300 North State Parkway;

312–787–3700) offers sumptuous surroundings, deluxe suites, and rooms for which "comfort" is an absurd understatement. Try to arrive in time for the delightful afternoon tea; and before you check in, do ask about the Fantasy Escape package. This offers a welcome bottle of champagne, two souvenir glasses, chocolate-dipped strawberries, and a gift certificate for Victoria's Secret—

all waiting when you arrive at your elegant suite with its king-size bed. The package also includes breakfast for two at the hotel's **Beau's Bistro**—but since the option of room service also is offered, surely you'll prefer *that*.

The Fantasy Escape goes for $185 per night, and if that's a bit too steep, scale down to the scarcely less enjoyable Gold Coast Escape, for $145 in a suite, $125 in a double room. The two of you will still be stretching out on a king-size bed and tucking into breakfast at Beau's Bistro. And maybe you don't really *need* anything else from Victoria's Secret.

Be sure to check on whether your visit will coincide with the monthly ballroom dances held in the hotel's **Guildhall,** which offers high steppers the largest wooden dance floor among the city's hotels. If you come an hour before the dancing begins, you can even take advantage of group dance instruction that's provided free with the $15 cover. Then you can swing to the big-band sound as performed by top local groups, such as Bobby Benson and his ten-piece orchestra.

Romance at a Glance

♥ *Take a whirl on the Pump Room's dance floor.*

♥ *Delight in the city's most popular movers and shakers, the Hubbard Street Dance Company.*

♥ *Browse through the Ann Barzel Dance Collection at the Newberry Library.*

♥ *See a breathtaking performance by the Joffrey Ballet in its new home— Chicago.*

♥ *Swing your sweetheart at the Cotton Club—or go for salsa at the Village Cafe.*

♥ *Dance by daylight at Willowbrook Ballroom.*

Dinner

In any case, bring something glamorous to wear to dinner. You're going right across the street to a Chicago icon, the **Pump**

Room (1301 North State Parkway; 312–266–0360), where generations of stars and star-gazers have dined and danced. Rescued some years back from a drift into downslide, the pricey Pump Room has returned to its former glory as a chic spot to meet and eat. The kitchen's all-American food ranges from salmon to duck to filet mignon, all served with delightful flourish; but it's the atmosphere that really draws people to this high-style room, with its hall-lining photos of glitzy Big Names, all shot on the premises. Past the pix there's the room's polished service and its posh booths—where *you* just might receive a phone call. I've interviewed several show-biz personalities here, and I can tell you that they love it every bit as much as the regular folks.

Everybody also loves the *intimate* dance floor, where you can get your evening off to the right start with a whirl or two—or maybe even a dip. Before you know it, though, you'll be off to a performance by the city's foremost nonclassical dance group. The **Hubbard Street Dance Theater,** led for years by their beloved teacher and choreographer Lou Conte, has developed into a versatile group of performers whose work is very accessible and wonderfully energetic. Beyond their hugely popular standards by Conte and others, Hubbard Street recently has broadened its horizons by creating a working relationship with the choreographer Twyla Tharp.

To find out when Hubbard Street is performing around town, call the company at (312) 663–0853. If possible, catch them at the Shubert Theater (22 West Monroe Street), a great old venue for a show. Tickets range from $12 to $40.

Leaving a Hubbard Street show, you'll probably have energy to burn! Luckily, the Shubert is a short cab ride away from a chic club where you, too, can dance the night away. The **Cotton Club** (1710 South Michigan Avenue; 312–341–9787) attracts a youngish professional crowd that divides its allegiance between the tasty jazz in one room and the heated disco in another. Take your pick and boogie. Cover charges range from $4 to $20 (for a well-known act), and the club is open till 3:00 A.M. on Friday and Saturday.

DAY TWO: MORNING/AFTERNOON

A night at the Cotton Club means a late morning after. When you've bestirred yourselves and breakfasted at Beau's, take a leisurely walk over to the **Newberry Library** (60 West Walton Street; 312–255–3510), where the history of dance in Chicago lies in some four hundred boxes. The **Ann Barzel Dance Collection** is the life's work of a passionate lover of dance—a tiny, omnipresent woman known to all as Miss Barzel. She is attending shows to this day, and you can bet that when you see her, she'll be clutching the evening's program to add to her collection. Her posters, books, programs, photos, films, and other items go all the way back to the Century of Progress Exposition of 1933.

Admission to this marvelous collection is free, but bring a a solid idea of what you'd like to see, plus a photo ID, when you come to the library's front desk. You'll receive a Newberry card and be guided to the Special Collections department, where librarians can help locate your chosen topics. Subjects are classified mostly by company or regional area, so think in those terms. The Newberry is open on Tuesday, Wednesday, and Thursday from 10:00 A.M. to 6:00 P.M., Friday and Saturday from 9:00 A.M. to 5:00 P.M.

Dinner

When you've feasted on Miss Barzel's collection, head back to the Ambassador West to change for the evening. Have an early dinner at **Gordon** (500 North Clark Street; 312–467–9780), where the food is eclectic and the atmosphere, utterly stylish and swell. From 5:30 till 6:30 P.M., the restaurant offers a pretheater dinner that will get you out, well-fed, in plenty of time and at a reasonable price (especially considering the sophisticated cooking here) of about $30 each. The signature appetizer is artichoke fritters, and anything fish is always delicious. And don't forget, if it's Saturday, you can come back *after* the show for an extra helping of cheek-to-cheek chic, with music provided by a trio that plays till midnight.

Then—it's off to the **Joffrey Ballet**. The former New York stalwarts have relocated to the Midwest, which is mighty glad to see them. Chicago's own ballet history has been difficult, with several companies starting in great promise and going through quantities of money before collapsing. The Joffrey comes established, and many local dance lovers are hoping the company's presence will help to build a stronger scene here.

Meanwhile you can enjoy the Joffrey in its new environment. If you visit during the springtime Dance Festival, you should be able to see them at the Shubert Theater, where they're likely to present a mix of old favorites from choreographer Gerald Arpino and others, plus newer pieces by up-and-coming choreographers. Tickets generally run from $10 to $45. Note that during the season, the Joffrey also performs at the **Rosemont Theater** (5400 River Road, Rosemont; 800–859–7469). For information, call the Chicago Dance Coalition Hotline number listed at the beginning of this chapter.

After the Joffrey, if you'd like to step to something more saucy than the trio at Gordon, make it the potent merengue-and-salsa mix at the **Village Cafe** (510 North Western Avenue; 312–278–5138). On Friday and Saturday nights, this little Puerto Rican restaurant metamorphoses into a hip, hot dance den where you'll find salsa upstairs and merengue downstairs. Be ready to party and you won't be disappointed.

DAY THREE: MORNING

Breakfast

Have a super morning—not too early, of course—at the **Breakfast Club** (1381 West Hubbard Street; 312–666–3166), where breakfast is served seven days a week from 6:00 A.M. till 3:00 P.M. This off-the-beaten-path spot offers everything you've ever wanted to start the day, from eggs Benedict to a chaste egg-white omelette. Pancakes and waffles are popular, too, as are

a huge variety of omelettes and frittatas. Breakfast for two will run you about $12 to $14—and the coffee's plentiful!

❧

DAY THREE: Afternoon

By about 1:00 P.M., you'll want to head for the suburbs, where a *very* special afternoon awaits. Out in west suburban Willowbrook, you'll find a haven for ballroom dancers in the **Willowbrook Ballroom** (8900 Archer Avenue; 630–839–1000). The ballroom brings in a ten-piece orchestra on Sundays, from 2:00 to 5:30 P.M., for the kind of dancing everyone did before the twist—the kind in which you actually touched your partner. Take Lake Shore Drive to Interstate 55, exiting I–55 at La Grange Road. Continue south on La Grange Road until you see a turn-off for Archer Avenue. Take this, and after about 2 miles, you'll see Willowbrook on the right side of the road.

Much of the Willowbrook crowd is over forty, but younger dancers sometimes come just to watch, often outfitted in vintage finery that fits the music to a T. And speaking of Ts, don't even think of wearing your jeans to Willowbrook. Women wear anything from 1930s frocks to nice pantsuits to after-five dresses; for men, a tie is optional but a jacket isn't. The cover charge for dancing is $10 per person, and if you work up an appetite, an a la carte buffet is open from 3:00 to 5:00 P.M., offering entrees, soups, salads, desserts, and coffee, all at modest prices.

FOR MORE ROMANCE

Are you one of those couples who dread weddings? For whom dancing is a divisive force, rather than a uniting one? Is your two-left-feet sweetheart slowing you down? Help him or her take the cure at **Dance Connection** (3047 North Lincoln Avenue; 773–404–0006). At just $7.00 per ninety-minute lesson, you needn't spend much for a gift series of sessions that will get your partner swinging. Instructor Howard Bergman emphasizes the versatile Lindy hop version of swing dancing, so you'll be able to take your newly nimble honey just about anywhere after a few lessons.

STAGES OF ROMANCE
A THEATER LOVERS' WEEKEND

*A*h, the stages of romance! Introduction, flirting, first kiss, commitment . . .

Whoa—not *those* stages! We're speaking here of the other stages. The ones on which our dreams, hopes, fears, and joys come to life. The ones where, whether you're on a first date or celebrating an umpteenth wedding anniversary, the show always gives you something to talk about. The ones that, to Shakespeare, were all the world—and the men and women on it all players.

In Chicago, one of the world's best cities for theater, there's always plenty to see onstage. To sort out the most romantic possibilities, I called on a good friend and foremost expert, Hedy Weiss. Hedy is theater critic for the *Chicago Sun-Times,* a woman who combines an optimistic outlook with a critic's omniscience. Most important, Hedy knows romantic when she sees it.

Here are her picks for the most romantic prospects on the stages around town, arranged into a fabulous, theater-hopping weekend for those who love "the theatah" *and* each other.

Practical notes: If you choose an in-town show over an excursion to the Candlelight, you really won't need a car. The best way to sort out theater options is to consult the *Reader,* a free weekly newspaper that offers extensive listings and reviews. Both the *Chicago Tribune* and the *Chicago Sun-Times* also carry theater listings in Friday's editions. And don't neglect Hot Tix!

DAY ONE: EVENING

When you're devoting yourselves to the theater, you won't want to spend a bundle on your hotel room. So consider a bed and breakfast location that lets you save the big bucks for theater tickets. One good choice, represented by Bed & Breakfast Chicago, is **Maud Travels,** a snug B&B in the hot Wicker Park/Bucktown neighborhood. Located on a quiet side street—so parking isn't a nightmare—this cozy home offers good access to expressways, yet it's close enough to Lakeview and downtown theaters that cab fares wouldn't be prohibitive. Maud Travels' accommodations run from $75 to $95 per night; make sure to get a queen-size bed, and try for the room with its own Jacuzzi.

Once you're settled in, start your theater getaway by getting away from the city! You'll probably want to drive to **Candlelight Dinner Playhouse** (5620 South Harlem Avenue, Summit; 708–496–3000); if you do, take Interstate 90-94 south to Interstate 55, then go west to the Harlem exit. (Depending on traffic, this may take anywhere from half an hour to quite a bit longer!)

When you arrive, don't be deceived by the suburban location, dinner-theater package, and in-the-round staging here. Those little candles on your table may be electric, but a Candlelight show is the real thing: smart staging, good acting, and fine singing in top-notch musicals.

"Musicals are great to do on a romantic date," notes Hedy, and a Candlelight musical is likely to contain some familiar tunes you already can hum in harmony. *Crazy for You, Carousel, Phantom of the Opera,* and *Brigadoon* are among its recent offerings. If you're here during the holiday season, be sure to check out Candlelight's special production; past favorites include *A*

Christmas Carol and *It's a Wonderful Life,* set to tunes. Better yet, the theater's Equity casts include many of the area's top names, most of whom are good enough to take on the coasts but prefer the steady work and relatively sane atmosphere Chicago offers its actors.

Dinner

It's possible to buy show-only tickets to a Candlelight production, but why not make an evening of it? Prices for both dinner and the show range from $36.50 to $47.50 per person (depending on the night of the week), which is reasonable indeed. Here's how the Candlelight arrangement goes: Dinner is served two hours before the show begins, which means arriving by 6:15 P.M. for an 8:15 curtain. Of course, it's fine to arrive a bit earlier to have a drink at the cash bar.

As you settle in at a table for two, giggle if you will at those little candle-like lamps. But, says Hedy, "they really do give you an intimacy," as well as plenty of illumination by which to consider dinner. The menu offers five entrees, always including meat and fish, a pasta dish, and—for the dedicated vegetarian who orders in advance—a big platter of steamed veggies with rice, potato, or both.

When dinner is cleared and the show begins, you'll appreciate Candlelight's careful floor plan, with tiered tables that don't obstruct vision. And as you applaud the cast's final bows and head out to the car, you'll have lots to talk about during your ride back to the city. It's bound to be quicker than the drive out, and when you get back to Bucktown, you'll find a bit of France at a little bistro that cooks till midnight. And a good thing it's late, because if you came at dinnertime you'd have quite a wait at **Le Bouchon** (1958 North Damen Avenue; 773–862–6600). At this hour, you might still be tempted by such classics as snails in garlic butter or steak frites, but dessert could be enough. In any case, you wouldn't spend more than $50 or so even for a full dinner for two. Dessert and coffee, of course, will run much less.

DAY TWO: MORNING

Rise and shine—you're off to glory in a doubleheader day of Chicago theater! Breakfast is whenever you want it in your little B&B kitchen. Your host makes morning coffee, and supplies everything from cereal to yogurt and muffins for guests; if you're in a cooking mood, check the refrigerator for eggs, too. (The kitchen is available to all three guest rooms, so dress before coming down!)

ⁿ⁓⊙⌐⌐

Head downtown to the **Hot Tix** booth at 108 North State Street or, near Water Tower Place, at 707 North Michigan Avenue. Both are open from 10:00 A.M. to 6:00 P.M. Monday through Saturday and noon to 5:00 P.M. Sunday. (A third Hot Tix is in north suburban Evanston, at 1616 Sherman Avenue.) Hot Tix information is at (312) 977–1755.

And what *is* Hot Tix? It's a service that offers half-price, day-of-show tickets to just about everything in town that isn't sold out. It's a perfect way to cut your ticket costs, if you're willing to make the trip and to be flexible in what you'll see. I recommend it strongly!

Unless you linger very late at your B& B, you'll have some time before a matinee curtain (generally between 2:00 and 3:00 P.M.). Why not visit the sparkling new **Museum of Contemporary Art** (22 East Chicago Avenue; 312–280–2660)? The museum even offers performance art, if you want to stick with your weekend theme. The MCA's new home, which at this writing was about to open, has plenty of space for its permanent collection and changing exhibits. Be adventurous; whatever's up is worth a look. When you've finished perusing the galleries, hit the street again. The neighborhood is prime for another secret pleasure of theater fans: people-watching.

Lunch

If you've become hungry again, the neighborhood is loaded with good places for lunch. Sample the all-American menu at the **Blackhawk Lodge** (41 East Superior Street;

312–280–4080), where everyone loves the corn muffins with honey, butter, and raspberry-pepper jam. Weekday lunch and weekend brunch are a good value that won't set you back more than $15 or so each.

DAY TWO: AFTERNOON

Consider making your matinee a show at **Court Theater** (5535 South Ellis Avenue; 773–753–4472). A 3:00 P.M. matinee here will let you get back downtown for an evening show, and coming during the day gives you the chance to stroll around the theater's beautiful Hyde Park location. You can simply drive south on Lake Shore Drive—a pleasure in itself!—and exit at 55th Street, then continue west and look for street signs. The trip is an easy twenty minutes or so from downtown.

Court does the classics with style and verve in a lovely theater that attracts lots of University of Chicago types as well as art-minded folks from all over the area. You'll find a more detailed description of Court in the "Hyde Park Honeymoon" chapter of this book. Whatever the show is, it's bound to be good—and the neighborhood is charming.

DAY TWO: EVENING

Dinner

As you return downtown from your matinee, you might want to park in the city lot across from your evening destination, the Auditorium Theater at 70 East Congress Street—on which more will come later! Before the show, however, walk a few blocks north on Michigan Avenue to Adams Street, then turn left and indulge yourselves at the chic, bustling **Russian Tea Time** (77 East Adams Street; 312–360–0000). Open from 11:00 A.M. daily, Russian Tea Time serves up a luscious lunch or dinner of borscht, piroshki, latkes, beef Stroganoff, and other Russian/Ukrainian specialties. Depending on the time you're here, lunch or dinner can cost as little as $40 for two.

Now, the centerpiece of your theater weekend: the **Auditorium Theater** (312–902–1500). This 1889 gem, designed by the great local architect Louis Sullivan, is "probably *the* most beautiful space in the city," according to critic Hedy Weiss, and there's no argument from me. The Auditorium is a classic lost-and-found story of urban architecture, a gorgeous building that fell on hard times and, at its nadir, saw its stage used as a bowling alley. Today, its upper floors are occupied mostly by a respectful Roosevelt University; the theater area, happily restored to its former glory, is the venue of choice for the biggest shows, from *Les Miserables* to *Miss Saigon*.

At this writing, *Show Boat* is playing to great reviews and full houses—so full, in fact, that you'll have to negotiate tickets months in advance. But no matter what's onstage—go! Just being in the Auditorium is an intoxication. I often remember seeing a show here not long after the theater's restoration and being far more entranced with the building than the program. I had never seen such splendor and sheen, such plush seats and lavish ornament. Even the lightbulbs, their tiny filaments glowing golden, were fascinating. Years later, at a high-society opening night of *Phantom of the Opera,* I looked around the lobby and concluded that the house itself was every bit as glamorous as this glittering A-list throng.

Especially if you and your sweetheart have never experienced this sort of splendid, old-fashioned theater, do your best to see a show here. Afterward, stay in the show's spell by wandering north on Michigan to the **Artists Cafe** (412 South Michigan Avenue; 312–939–7855). It's just a cut above a short-order spot, but the Artists is always full of, well, artists. Especially after a show, your fellow diners are sure to be interesting in this inexpensive place for a drink and/or dessert.

You can alternatively head back to Bucktown and talk over the evening in one of that neighborhood's many late-night spots. A good choice is the **Bop Shop** (1807 West Division Street; 312–235– 3232), a local stalwart where jazz rules (and you might catch part of a poetry slam—see "Words of Love" for more on this form of stand-up art). Open until 2:00 A.M. nightly, and 3:00 A.M. on Saturday, the Bop Shop may be crowded—but it's never boring. Give it a try if you're still buzzed.

DAY THREE: MORNING

Brunch

Are we awake yet? If so, head for brunch at the friendly, trendy **Eat Your Hearts Out!** (1835 West North Avenue; 773–235–6361), where the kitchen is hopping from 10:00 A.M. to 3:00 P.M. on Saturday and Sunday. The food is resolutely healthful but creatively eclectic, which means there *is* meat, along with lots of imaginative vegetarian choices; at dinner, for example, the most popular vegetarian entree is black bean ravioli in chipolte sauce (yum!). Prices are friendly, too, and brunch won't set you back more than $25 or so for two.

DAY THREE: AFTERNOON

For a convenient (2:30 P.M.) matinee, challenge yourselves at **Steppenwolf Studio** (1650 North Halsted Street; 773–335–1650). The space itself is an offshoot of the famous Steppenwolf, built by the now-prosperous company where stars including John Malkovich, Joan Allen, Terry Kinney, Laurie Metcalf, and Gary Sinise got their start as writers and directors. Unlike the high-profile Steppenwolf, however, the Studio stages "more experimental works," critic Hedy Weiss says. Give whatever's here a try, especially if you came to see theater beyond the mainstream.

DAY THREE: EVENING

Dinner

Stay in the neighborhod for dinner at **Vinci** (1732 North Halsted Street; 773–266–1199), a casual but spiffy Italian spot. The delicious *nuovo* menu offers a wonderful polenta, as well as lots of grilled selections and, for dessert, homemade gelato. Sunday also brings a brunch, so think of that, too. Dinner will run about $60 for two.

An even better bargain is **Blue Mesa** (1729 North Halsted Street; 773–944–5990), where you can eat terrific Southwestern food in a setting of turquoise and terra cotta while holding the bill to about $45 for both of you. Among the favorites here are guacamole, chicken fajita salad, cheesy pizza, and lots of blue corn everywhere.

∽◦◦∾

Still up for something offbeat? Check out the **Goodman Studio** (20 South Columbus

Drive; 312–443–3800). "It's very intimate, a bit more funky than the mainstage Goodman," Hedy says, "and really kind of exciting, because you're so close to the action." Another plus: Goodman's 7:30 P.M. curtain fits neatly with the Steppenwolf Studio's 2:30 P.M. matinee.

Of course, there are countless other theaters where you can be thrilled by productions of new works or classics. Hedy recommends, in the Wicker Park/Bucktown neighborhood near Maud Travels, **Latino Chicago** (1625 North Damen Avenue; 773–486–5120). Its works address the concerns of Hispanics here, and, Hedy says, it's a good choice for its "younger, chicer appeal."

Also making a stir well beyond its Pilsen neighborhood is **The Blue Rider** (1822 South Halsted Street; 312–733–4668). Artistic director Donna Blue Lachman, a woman of vision and energy, does everything from write to act to direct. Her work never fails to attract attention, and praise usually follows right behind the spotlight.

Among established companies, consider anything from **Shakespeare Repertory** (generally at Ruth Page Auditorium, 1016 North Dearborn Street; 312–642–2273); **Victory Gardens** (2257 North Lincoln Avenue; 773–671–3000), the merged **Organic Touchstone** (3319 North Clark Street; 773–327–5588) or **Northlight** (at this writing, without a permanent home; call 847–869–7278).

Above all, don't get hung up on what to see. Just go together and share an experience. I've seen some unforgettable shows—and some terrible ones—at the city's best theaters and at its small, struggling ones. I always remember who was with me. Good or bad, going live creates a bond that lasts.

ITINERARY 20
One day and one evening

Small Pleasures

*W*hen you're in love, there's nothing nicer than taking a day off together. A day without responsibilities, chores, or entanglements; a day whose only goal is to revel in each other, enjoying whatever comes your way. It's the sort of break that makes people fall in love all over again.

These things don't just happen, of course; so it's smart to lay some plans, and that's just what this itinerary does for you. Starting from the assumption that your love is bigger than life, why not devote your lazy day to the appreciation of the *little* things? From train sets to tapas, dollhouses to dim sum, here's a collection of good things painstakingly placed in small packages, the better for you to enjoy them together. And if it all sounds a tiny bit precious, set your sights on ending the day at one of the city's best piano bars—a great spot that's so small, it's called the Sardine.

All you need is each other and a car (hey, make it a compact!) to make your way through this collection of small pleasures. They'll add up to a big day to remember.

Practical notes: This itinerary goes from the South Side to downtown to the North Side, so driving is the most practical way to go.

Romance at a Glance

♥ See the Santa Fe Model Railway and Colleen Moore's Fairy Castle at the Museum of Science and Industry.

♥ Have a dim sum lunch at Hong Min.

♥ View the miniatures in Art Institute of Chicago's Thorne Rooms.

♥ See the Chicago history dioramas at the Chicago Historical Society.

♥ Nibble tapas for dinner at Cafe Ba-Ba-Ree-Ba!

♥ Examine tiny treasures at Think Small . . . or squeeze into the Gold Star Sardine Bar for drinks.

MORNING

Breakfast

A romance without a sense of humor is no romance at all. So start your day at any Dunkin' Donuts, where a breakfast of Munchkins miniature pastries will get you feeling small.

Then proceed to the **Museum of Science and Industry** (Fifty-seventh Street and South Lake Shore Drive; 773–684–1414), where people who love tiny things could spend hours enthralled at two spectacular permanent exhibits. Choosing which one to begin with is up to you.

For the train enthusiast, there's the ultimate basement layout. The **Santa Fe Model Railway** is a sprawling, bustling maze totaling 1,200 feet of track on which dozens—no, surely hundreds—of Santa Fe locomotives, boxcars, flatcars, sleepers, and cabooses travel endlessly along a desert landscape. A few years back, the museum got a fast reminder of how much the trains are loved when it closed the exhibit. The immediate outcry brought hasty assurance that the closing was merely a break for renovation, and the spiffed-up spread now appears to be safe in its popularity.

You can watch the trains as long as you like, and that's likely to be a long time. Be prepared to discuss them with fellow buffs who gather and linger around the exhibit. Then, when you're ready to move on, you can head for the museum's other monument to smallness: **Colleen Moore's Fairy Castle.** Moore was something of a fairy tale herself: a movie star in the silent era who left Hollywood to become the socialite wife of a wealthy Chicagoan. Over the years, she indulged her love for miniatures with the construction and fitting of this dreamlike palace. The Fairy Castle now lives in a velvety darkened room, the better to heighten its dramatic splendor. Lit so that it seems to sparkle, the castle is surrounded by a ramp along which visitors move—never very fast—to view its many rooms, its grounds, even its exquisite little lightbulbs. A guidebook to the castle is imperative and may be bought in the museum shop—perhaps on the way in, rather than as you leave, so you can use it as you look at the castle.

Lunch

Leaving the museum, take Lake Shore Drive to Thirty-first Street, then go west to State Street. Heading north on State, you'll soon reach Chinatown and a lunch of yummy little dim sum—bite-size portions of egg roll, wonton, and more—at **Hong Min** (221 West Cermak Road,; 312–842–5026). It's not the prettiest place in Chinatown, but Hong Min is famous for its weekend dim sum brunches, when servers roll wheeled carts to your table for grazing. Prices are low, too; a bountiful lunch won't set you back more than $25 altogether.

AFTERNOON

From Chinatown, you can drive right up Michigan Avenue to downtown, and when you reach the entrance to the Grant Park underground parking lot, drive right in. Then head for the **Art Institute of Chicago** (South Michigan Avenue at Adams Street; 312–443–3600), where the legacy of Narcissa (Mrs. James W.) Thorne is a breathtaking collection of sixty-eight miniature rooms, each decorated with scrupulous accuracy in a period style, like tiny models for stage sets. Like her friend Colleen Moore, Mrs. Thorne was a wealthy, socially prominent Chicagoan whose fondness for miniatures developed into a full-scale passion. The ambitious goal Mrs. Thorne set was creating and furnishing rooms that would constitute a history of European and American interior design from the sixteenth to the early twentieth century. To carry out her mission, she employed Old World artisans and top-notch architects (many of them available only because of the Great Depression); one of these likened her to Walt Disney in her vision and personal presence in every detail. The Thorne Rooms are known all over the world—one depicting a library at Windsor Castle is in London's Victoria & Albert Museum—and it's easy to see why when you devote to looking the merest fraction of the time it took to create them.

The museum shop has a good guide to the Thorne Rooms, and again, it's smart to buy it on the way in. It's impossible to take in all the pleasures and subtleties of the rooms in one visit, so you can enjoy the guide as a souvenir and in future visits.

If you're in the mood for an antidote to the painstaking prettiness of Mrs. Thorne's tasteful rooms, search out the museum's collection of works by another sort of miniaturist. Joseph Cornell is as modern as Mrs. Thorne was classical; his boxes and small houselike structures carry an air of mystery, sometimes menace, that's fascinating. Cornell's pieces are in the twentieth-century area, upstairs from the Thorne Rooms; museum guides can show you the way.

Now head north on Lake Shore Drive, exiting at North Avenue, for the **Chicago Historical Society** (North Clark Street and North Avenue; 312–642–4600). Here you'll find another small-scale exhibit that has entranced generations of Chicagoans, young and old. In their own darkened room, eight dioramas re-create moments from the city's history in a collection of miniatures more in sync with model trains than French salons or fairy castles. The leaping "flames" of the Great Chicago Fire are the favorite of many children, but others love the soldiers meeting Indians in the very first installment. There are also a sweet, snowy scene depicting the city's earliest hotel and another showing the leisure class out for a day at the races in a turn-of-the-century glimpse at Washington Race Track.

EVENING

Dinner

The Historical Society closes at 4:30 P.M., which leaves time for a leisurely stroll over to North Halsted Street. (Load up the meter before leaving; you could drive, but parking is even tighter on Halsted.) More small pleasures await you at dinner, courtesy of a cuisine that appreciates nibbles and is enjoying great popularity these days. Little bits of many delicacies constitute a tapas evening at **Cafe Ba-Ba-Ree-Ba!** (2024 North Halsted Street; 773–935–5000), a shrine to the appealing Spanish custom of whiling away the hours over drinks and appetizers. Tangy Spanish ham is de rigeur, but be sure to consider the daily specials and remember that even little bits add up; decide at the outset to save a little room to split dessert. Depending on how much you drink, dinner can be as inexpensive as $30 for the two of you. And remember to make reservations; Ba-Ba-Ree-Ba! is a *very* popular place.

If walking back to the car revives you enough to stop at one more small world, make it **Think Small by Rosebud** (3209 North Clark Street; 773–477–1920). This shop carries supplies for enthusiasts who build their own dollhouses. The folks at the store may let you take a look at the houses in progress in their downstairs workroom, and they'll get you started if the day has inspired you to tackle a tiny project together.

Or end your small-scale day in upscale way at the **Gold Star Sardine Bar** (680 North Lake Shore Drive; 312–664–4215), the snuggest little spot in town for a chic drink and even chic-er cabaret music. The Gold Star is no bigger than a minute; its seating capacity hovers in double digits, changing according to how much room the performer needs. Part-owner Bobby Short is a compact act, but singer Pia Zadora brought a thirty-four-piece orchestra. No matter who's playing, the atmosphere and entertainment are wonderful here, especially considering that cover charges rarely top $10. And if you're peckish, look for another little giggle on the Gold Star's menu: Where else does a swanky place offer those small but powerful White Castle sliders?

THE SPORTING LIFE

FOOTBALL FANTASIES

"*Football*" and "romance" may not seem like a perfect fit, but many couples eagerly anticipate the season, both for the sport itself and for the companionship afforded on a crisp, fall day, walking into the stadium arm in arm, carrying a warm woolen balnket. Even when you're half of a couple in which your other half lives and dies by the sport, love will find a way for both of you to revel in the glory of the gridiron. Beyond the NFL razzmatazz of the downtown Soldier Field crowds supporting the Chicago Bears, you can enjoy a rousing college game in Evanston, the first lakeside suburb north of the city limits. The most famous local heroes her are the Northwestern University Wildcats, who climbed from the bottom of the Big Ten barrel all the way to the Rose Bowl itself in 1996. Even though they lost that last big one, the winning season left a warm glow around the entire campus.

Northwestern's campus is pretty much aglow year-round anyway. It's a woodsy sprawl of lovely old buildings and spiffy new ones that occupies a good stretch of Evanston's northern lakeshore area. The town of Evanston is a leafy, liberal enclave of gracious old homes and even older trees. Altogether, it's a charming setting in which to enjoy a slice of collegiate life during an autumn weekend.

Practical notes: Of course you'll have to plan ahead for tickets to a Northwestern game—although it wasn't long ago that you could have wandered in and bought tickets an hour before kickoff. Those days may be gone, but non-Northwestern folks can still come by tickets. Start in the spring by calling the university's athletic department at (847) 491–2287. Ask to have a schedule for the upcoming season sent to you. Then, when you've chosen the game you want, wait for individual tickets to go on sale (after the season ticket holders order theirs). This happens early in June for the following fall, and tickets cost about $22 each.

DAY ONE: EVENING

When your weekend arrives, get comfortable in style at the **Omni Orrington** (1710 Orrington Avenue; 847–866–8700). Checking in at the Orrington on Friday night means more than a good night's sleep; it means you can mention casually (to everyone) that you stayed at Princess Diana's hotel—well, technically. During her 1996 charity fundraising visit to Northwestern, the Orrington provided the Princess of Wales a stopping-off place where she freshened up. (She actually slept at the Drake Hotel in downtown Chicago, if you must know.) In any case, it seems safe to say that if it's good enough for Di, it's good enough for you and the one who rules your heart.

The Orrington even has something of an English look, with a chandelier-and-staircase lobby to greet you and rooms decorated in soothing pastels. Georgian-style furniture, built-in bookshelves, and pretty fireplaces add to the cozy but elegant ambience. If you need more space, minisuites and one-bedroom suites are available, too, with fall-season rates ranging from $119 per night for the double room to $179 for a suite.

Romance at a Glance

♥ *Enjoy a classic fall weekend in quiet, charming Evanston.*

♥ *Savor an extraordinary dinner at the North Shore's most romantic spot, Carlos'.*

♥ *Snuggle under a cozy blanket as you cheer the Northwestern Wildcats.*

♥ *Linger in a serene garden around the corner from heavenly Va Pensiero.*

♥ *Stroll or stride along the lakefront park and beach.*

Dinner

Once you're on the North Shore—which is what the well-to-do suburbs hugging the lakefront are called—a glamorous dinner a deux awaits in one of the Chicago area's finest restaurants. Voted their area's most romantic restaurant by the moneyed readers of *North Shore* magazine, **Carlos'** (429 Temple, Highland Park; 847–432–0770), is a top-of-the-line spot blending French, Italian, and nouvelle cuisine influences into a personality all its own. This is the place to pop for things you wouldn't consider elsewhere—foie gras, for instance, which here comes in a crust of crunchy sesame and poppy seeds, all sauced in an unlikely but heavenly pool of vanilla. For maximum sampling, choose the degustation menu (it's $70, or $100 with wines included). A vegetarian degustation is available, too, by advance arrangement.

Carlos' is north of Evanston; the drive isn't a long one, but do ask at the desk for directions and allow extra time if you're unfamiliar with the area. Consider driving north along Sheridan Road, the closest road to Lake Michigan. Its twists and turns force drivers to slow down and enjoy the view of lush vegetation and glacier-carved ravines that makes this some of the nation's priciest real estate. On the way back to Evanston, you'll probably prefer Green Bay Road, a more straightforward route that also winds through such picturesque, wealthy enclaves as Kenilworth and Winnetka.

If you're not in the mood for a drive up to Carlos', you're certain to be fed just as glamorously at **Trio** (1625 Hinman Avenue, Evanston; 847–733–8746). This very sophisticated spot caught a lot of eyes when it first opened because of the chef's penchant for putting things in and on interesting surfaces, from a slick white painter's palette holding a selection of caviars to a mirror reflecting sushi-style vegetable rolls. Trio's kitchen also pioneered the trendy art of vertical presentation, which means arranging food up as well as around on a plate (or whatever). For all this glitz, however, the bottom line is that Trio serves up a really good, really interesting dinner. Like Carlos', Trio samples from Italian and French cuisines, with some Asian thrown in. The best way to get to know Trio is with a degustation menu, which brings you eight to ten mini-courses at a price of $75 per person (or go vegetarian for $55 each).

DAY TWO: Morning/Afternoon

You can spend the morning luxuriating in your room, or you can get outdoors and stroll around the Northwestern campus, which is just to the Orrington's north and is the perfect place for a pleasant morning ramble. If you head in this direction, you'll be able to get Starbucks coffee at every turn *and* have no trouble spotting the crowds to follow to the Saturday afternoon game.

Also near the hotel are some of Evanston's shopping areas, with the quaint boutiques the town treasures alongside such chain giants as the Gap and Barnes & Noble. And just to the east of the Orrington is Lake Michigan and a lovely public park along the shore. The beach is great, too, and though you may think football season isn't ideal for a dip, late summer and even early fall often are surprisingly steamy here. In any case, try to find time to enjoy a visit to the lake during your stay.

You can get a pregame snack at the Orrington's own **Huddle Sports Bar.** Weekdays it's mostly business-type lunching, but evenings and weekends it becomes a student spot. Just make sure you're at Dyche Stadium (1501 Central Street) before game time. It's a very do-able walk from the Orrington, so the inevitable dense traffic needn't bother you. And don't forget to pack something purple if you're cheering on the 'Cats!

Even approaching Dyche is a little spine-tingling, with flags flying and the band playing and throngs on their way in. No matter how you feel about football, once you're here, you're sure to be caught up in the mood of the day.

"Going to a game is a great date," says Northwestern alum Fern Schumer Chapman, whose husband, Steve, adores college football. "Until the '95 season, you never expected the team to win, so we would just go for the spirit of it. And you do get the goosebumps when they play the Northwestern 'fight song'!"

If you find your goosebumps are weather-induced, snuggle under a cozy blanket and sip some hot chocolate together as you watch the action, which even in the 'Cats worst doldrums

The Bridges of Cook County

As you drive north along Sheridan Road, watch for a succession of lovely little stone bridges that you'll see toward northern Wilmette and as far north as Highland Park. Many bridges don't actually cross anything, and the road is too narrow to be conducive to pulling over and taking a moment to smooch. No matter—these bridges are so sweet and scenic, you'll be glad you kept an eye out.

always included some fine plays. And get with the crowd, clapping and cheering and stomping. "It's really exuberant," says Fern. "Believe me, you don't have to know much about football to have a good time."

DAY TWO: EVENING

Dinner

After the game, make your way back to the Orrington and get ready for a swell evening at **Va Pensiero** (1566 Oak Avenue, in the Margarita Inn, Evanston; 847–475–7779). Ask for recommendations of romantic restaurants on the North Shore, and Va Pensiero is one you'll hear frequently. (*I* certainly did!) This small room is housed in a pensione-style hotel that originated as a home away from home for young women who went to work during the late nineteenth century and, naturally, needed a respectable place to stay and a chaperone to look out for them.

Today, its first floor holds a restaurant decorated in soothing shades of peach; do ask for a cozy booth when you reserve. The menu is Italian, but with an eye toward lightness and beautiful presentation. And you'll notice some dishes that incorporate *agrodolce* (sweet-sour) flavors and Asian influences. Chef Peggy Ryan's kitchen is attentive to the smallest detail, as you'll see from the butter that comes with your predinner bread. A touch of cream cheese and some subtle seasoning elevate this spread from tasty butterfat to true ambrosia.

Entrees at Va Pensiero include wonderful pastas and expertly prepared fish, seafood, and meats. It's also a good place to make your dinner from a half order of pasta and an appetizer or two—but don't forget to save room for a cappuccino custard. Va Pensiero's dinner tab should weigh in at perhaps $60 to $80 for the two of you.

DAY THREE: MORNING/AFTERNOON

Breakfast

Here's a dilemma: If you start the day with a brisk walk along the lakefront, or a stroll through Evanston's beautiful residential areas, you'll feel virtuous and entitled to the whipping cream you'll get with your coffee at **Walker Bros. Original Pancake House** (153 Green Bay Road, Wilmette; 847–251–6000). On the other hand, if you eat first and walk later, you're likely to arrive earlier and thus have a shorter wait for your table at this densely populated spot. Whatever your decision, it's true you'll have to cool your heels before placing an order at this North Shore landmark. But who else gives you a gorgeous array of elaborate stained-glass windows to contemplate in the meantime? Bring the Sunday paper and exchange sections while you're not discussing the windows, and before long you'll be glad you were patient. Pancakes and waffles are the favorites in this family-friendly restaurant (it's just down the block from the popular Kohl Children's Museum), but everything else here is delicious, too. It's a lip-smacking way to blow the final whistle on your Wildcats weekend.

FOR MORE ROMANCE

The true-blue football fanatic is sure to swoon for a weekend that also includes a **Chicago Bears** game. Season ticket holders have a lock on home-game tickets, but a ticket broker can

Let Your Love Blossom

*As you leave Va Pensiero, ask the staff to head you in the right direction for a visit to **Merrick Park** (at the corner of Lake Street and Oak Avenue in Evanston). This lovely haven is a riot of roses in season, but even when the blooms are faded, its graceful fountain and shady benches offer a serene spot to sit or wander. The only note of civic sternness is a posted sign informing you that ceremonies are allowed only by permit—so if you're choosing the perfect spot for a wedding, be sure your papers are in order!*

help, especially when chilly weather is forecast and/or the Bears aren't playing as well as Chicago fans wish they would (which is usually—it's been mostly downhill since they won Super Bowl XX in 1986). Try for tickets through the Bears office (847–615–2327). If you have no luck, call a bonded, licensed ticket broker, such as Looks Like the Front Row (800–525–3380), which is run by former White Sox baseball player Eric Soderholm.

When your tickets are set, arrange a tailgate party for two from **A La Carte** (111 Green Bay Road, Wilmette; 847–256–4102), a charming take-out place located a few doors south of Walker Bros. They'll create a yummy, sturdy feast that stands up to the journey to Soldier Field, which is most easily reached by car. Drive south on Green Bay Road to Chicago, where the street's name changes to Ridge Avenue, and stick with its twists and turns—including another name change, to Bryn Mawr Avenue, just before you reach Lake Shore Drive. The Drive, as locals call it, takes you directly to Soldier Field, where there's plenty of parking and you can enjoy your repast before the game.

ITINERARY 22
Three days and two nights

WRIGLEYVILLE WEEKEND

*T*here are lifelong Chicagoans who don't care a bit about sports but love to go to a baseball game at Wrigley Field. And Wrigley is ideal for romance. "It's perfect for a date," explains a fan of the park (not necessarily the game). "The game's going on, so you have something to talk about. And you *can* talk, unlike a movie, or pay attention to the game when you don't feel like talking. Plus, if you don't know much about baseball, fans love to explain things."

Whether you're getting acquainted or long past dating, you'll love relaxing in the verdant, venerable "friendly confines." And even if you're not a baseball fan, you probably know that the Chicago Cubs are baseball's perennial—there's no nice way to say it—losers. But Chicago loves them anyway, partly because their home field is a baseball legend. Wrigley Field is small and comfortable in an old-shoe way. Its outfield walls are covered with lush ivy, and its scoreboard has the distinction of being the last one in which humans post the numbers by hand. After a game ends, a W or L flag (telling whether the Cubs won or lost) flies above the park for the benefit of commuters passing by on the El train.

Another secret of Wrigley Field's charm is that it's in one of the city's hottest residential-plus-entertainment neighborhoods. Most of its homes and apartment buildings are as old as the park (which dates to 1914) but beautifully restored. And its nightlife is superb: good restaurants, lots of music, and plenty of coffeehouses for the morning after.

Romance at a Glance

♥ *Snuggle up in a cozy neighborhood hotel.*

♥ *Walk to "the friendly confines" of Wrigley Field for an afternoon in the famous bleachers.*

♥ *Be daring for dinner at the Afghan restaurant Helmand.*

♥ *Dance at the Cubby Bear; try a chocolate cocktail at the Pepper Lounge.*

♥ *Lose yourselves in an old-fashioned Saturday movie matinee at the Music Box.*

♥ *Dine on Japanese or Mexican fare, then laugh at the Improv Olympics.*

♥ *Wrap it up with another Cubs game.*

So join the fabled Bleacher Bums for a weekend that starts and ends with the Cubbies, packing tons of fun in between. Go Cubs!

Practical notes: This weekend can and should be done on foot. Wrigleyville is relatively safe and friendly, and destinations are close enough to walk to everything.

DAY ONE: AFTERNOON

Check into a great little neighborhood hotel. The hard part is choosing between a pair, both under the same ownership and with identical rates (rooms start at $85; suites are $99). The **Park Brompton** (528 West Brompton Place; 773–404–3499) nestles on a quiet little block, all its neighbors residential; yet it's only steps from the lakefront and Lincoln Park and just about 6 blocks east of Wrigley Field. Decorated to resemble an English inn, the Park Brompton boasts a large lobby that's really more a clubby sitting room, with comfy chairs, built-in bookshelves, and a gorgeous pink marble fireplace. It's an excellent place to linger over the complimentary morning coffee and cinnamon rolls (from Ann Sather, yum). Plans are underway to add an afternoon tea, so be sure to ask about it.

Rooms and suites at the Park Brompton are big enough to be comfortable but small enough to be cozy, with pastel shades, queen-size beds, and huge old mirrors in the bathrooms. Try to get the Sunroom Suite, one of the most inviting I've seen: Its sunroom area is all windows, looking out onto leafy trees and, to the east, Lincoln Park. Suites offer kitchenette convenience, with microwaves, minifridges, and place settings. For maximum romance ask about the bridal suite.

If the Park Brompton is quiet and English, the **City Suites** (933 West Belmont Avenue; 773–404–3405) is Roaring Twenties and all-American. Opened in the 1920s as a hotel for vaudeville performers, the hotel is on a busy thoroughfare, just 4 blocks south of Wrigley Field and a few doors down from a major stop on the elevated rapid-transit system. You might find the block slightly seedy, with its tattoo parlor across the street and foot traffic that isn't all yuppies—but other neighbors include very respectable Japanese shops and restaurants, so don't be intimidated.

Besides the atmosphere changes immediately as you step into the front hallway and look to your left, where a huge black-and-white photo of a citified smooching couple titled *Romance Circa 1930s* meets your eye. The lobby is all soft lighting and soothing, green-and-burgundy decor highlighted by a beautiful green marble fireplace. A lovely antique sideboard holds complimentary morning coffee and delicious cinnamon rolls (Ann Sather is next door; its full menu is available through room service), which you can sink into a comfy chair to enjoy.

Rooms aren't much for views, but who cares when they're so nicely renovated and offer such a comfortable sofa in which to cuddle and channel-surf? Try to get the largest suite, with its two full rooms separated by doors and double-size living area with a big dining-room table.

Once you're settled in, head for **Wrigley Field** (1060 West Addison Street). It scarcely need be said that you want an afternoon game. After a major battle to install lights in 1988, the Cubs have played a minimum of night games, and, anyway, you can't beat baseball in the sunshine. Tickets often are available on game day, but it's safer to order in advance by calling (773) 831–2827 (or, outside of Illinois, 800–347–2827), starting in late February for the season. Bleacher seats—which offer no cover from the sun, but give a good view and are the home of the legendary Bleacher Bums (on whom more below)—are $10.00, or $6.00 for weekday games in April, May, and September. Terrace and upper-deck boxes are $15.00 but are available only for weekday games. Reserved terrace seats are $12.00, and upper-deck reserved seats $9.00; all these also are cheaper for spring and fall weekdays.

Come to Wrigley before game time so you can stroll hand in hand throughout this venerable old park as you find your seats. Bleacher seats are unnumbered, so you may want to arrive well before the first pitch to stake out a spot you like. In years past bleacher seats never were sold until game day and cost just a few bucks. This policy allowed maximum flexibility for the persons of leisure known as the Bleacher Bums—retired folks, night-shift waitresses or factory workers, and codgers of every stripe who were immortalized by the Organic Theatre's long-running hit play named for them. Today's "bums" are a little more upscale, but there's still no shortage of opinion in the bleachers, which will you give you plenty to talk about later.

DAY ONE: Evening

Dinner

Of course you'll have eaten lunch at Wrigley—a hot dog and beer, naturally—and you'll probably be ready for a walk as you leave. Clark Street is a major entertainment strip, so it's easy to stay right here for dinner, music, dancing, or whatever. For an inexpensive dinner, consider **Matsuya** (3469 North Clark; 773–248–2677), a local fixture where the sushi was great before most Americans ever heard of it. Squid, chicken, and beef teriyaki are tasty, too, and you really ought to try the ginger ice cream. Prices at Matsuya are low—probably not more than $15 or so per person. Similarly inexpensive Thai food is at **PS Bangkok** (3345 North Clark; 773–871–7777), which makes an excellent satay (plain grilled meat or chicken on a skewer) as well as more complex, authentic dishes. Or line up at **Mia Francesca** (3311 North Clark; 773–281–3310), where people don't mind waiting for pastas, pizzas, and specials that rarely cost more than $20 per person at dinner. It tends to be noisy and busy, but this restaurant's fans are as devoted as they are numerous.

☙◦❧

If you've both got a rock 'n' roll heart, dance the night away at **Metro** (3730 North Clark

Street; 773–549–0203), where the audience and the bands are pretty black-leather. But this is where you'll hear some of the best rock around, and at low rates—generally not more than $15 admission for the two of you—and this could let you experience a very happening band *before* their record deal. Call beforehand to find out who's booked. Also, don't overlook the **Cubby Bear** (1059 West Addison Street; 773–327–1662), kitty-corner from Wrigley and home of an incredibly eclectic booking policy that runs from jazz performers to country stars to rock bands.

Or yuck it up at **Improv Olympic** (3541 North Clark; 773–880–0199), home of the Harold. What's the Harold? Funny you should ask, although the answer turns out to be even funnier. It's a uniquely Chicago theater game involving comic improvisation on the Second City model, which requires audience participation to "feed" the onstage proceedings. Tickets are $7.00, and Friday and Saturday shows are at 8.00 and 10:30 P.M.. In the Second City tradition, the later show tends to be more freewheeling. To the north on the strip are two of the younger generations of Chicago theaters that offer provocative shows, sometimes comic, sometimes serious. **Annoyance Theater** (3747 North Clark; 773–929–6200) originated the hugely popular *Real Live Brady Bunch* show and the long-running and hilarious *Coed Prison Sluts*. **Live Bait** (3914 North Clark Street; 773–871–1212) is a staging ground for avant–garde shows by various companies, including the performance art group Loofah Method. There's even a militantly *non*-sports bar, **Ginger Man** (3740 North Clark; 773–549–2050) a bit to the north; you'll recognize it by its pub-like outdoor sign.

Maybe you'd like to venture from Clark Street. Do so for dinner, and you can sample a cuisine you won't find on every corner. Walk east to Halsted and south to Belmont. Here you'll find the **Helmand** (3201 North Halsted Street; 773–935–2447), a white-tablecloth storefront that offers the exotic food of Afghanistan. Afghan turns out to be surprisingly familiar to fans of Middle Eastern fare: lamb, grains, yogurt, and even the Greek dessert baklava are all here. It's unusual but not weird, so give it a try for an experience you'll both remember. Prices are moderate—maybe $15 each for dinner. Note that this heavily gay area (basically Halsted Street, to the north and south) is nicknamed "Boys' Town," but lesbians and straights are much in evidence, too. The important thing is that nobody is bothering anybody.

For after-dinner entertainment, a stroll few blocks to the west to one of Chicago's better blues clubs, **B.L.U.E.S. Etcetera** (1124 West Belmont Avenue; 773–525–8989), which books the city's top bands regularly and sometimes features out-of-town acts, too. There's a dance floor and cover charges are moderate—no more than $10 or so per person—even for the best bands. And the club is especially convenient if you're staying at the City Suites, a couple of blocks to its east.

DAY TWO: MORNING/AFTERNOON

After enjoying your hotel's complimentary continental breakfast, get ready for an old-fashioned treat: the Saturday movie matinee. It's alive and well at the **Music Box** (3733 North Southport Avenue; 773–871–6604), a neighborhood theater lovingly renovated and intelligently booked by a movie-loving management. Saturday matinees start at 11:30 A.M. and include short subjects before a double feature that pairs a great oldie with something contemporary—anything from the classic *Citizen Kane* plus the supermodel saga *Catwalk,* to the definitive Western, *The Searchers,* plus the Oscar-winning *Anne Frank Remembered.* (Lighter titles have included *Breakfast at Tiffany's* and the Carmen Miranda epic, *The Gang's All Here.*)

Admission is $7.50 per person (not bad for two movies), and if you might be back, pick up a five-admission card for $25. For a schedule that covers thirteen weeks of programs, call the theater. And to hear an old-fashioned movie organist hold forth on the Music Box instrument, come on a weekend evening, when Dennis Scott plays during intermissions.

The Music Box area is, again, a very congenial place for strolling and chatting, with lots of little shops to browse. Vintage clothes are worth a look at **Wisteria** (3715 North Southport Avenue; 773–880–5868), and **Fourth World Artisans** (3453 North Southport Avenue; 773–404–5200) offers gifts aplenty for the folks back home. As you stroll, notice this area's

Classic Chicago Couples: Siskel and Ebert

Well, let's call them a classic Chicago duo. *Gene Siskel (the balding one) and Roger Ebert (the heavy one) have been professional rivals for longer than most folks stay married. Years before starting the television show that became "Siskel and Ebert at the Movies," Gene was reviewing movies at the* Chicago Tribune *while Roger did the same at the* Chicago Sun-Times. *They were intensely competitive, and though Roger's Pulitzer Prize gave him a leg up at work, Gene beat Roger to marriage and fatherhood. As their relationship stretches into a ripe old age, both are happily married, fabulously successful, still writing for the rival papers, and carefully keeping up the bickering image that made them famous.*

many examples of new homes (lots of townhouses) that are being built with an eye toward fitting gracefully in with the existing older buildings.

Dinner

When you're ready for dinner, stay on the street and go Italian. Reservations aren't accepted at the **Red Tomato** (3417 North Southport Avenue; 773–472–5300), so if you're hungry early, go on over. You can relax with a drink while looking forward to rigatoni in Gorgonzola sauce, or fettucine carbonara, or one of the weekly specials (which might include game). Prices hover in the $9.00-to-$14.00 range for entrees.

Or try pasta with a sense of humor at **Strega Nona** (3747 North Southport; 773–244–0990). Named for the wise witch of children's literature, Strega Nona calls its menu "global Italian," which means the cheese on your fettucine with veggies might be feta. Or try the popular penne-veggies combination under a creamy garlic sauce. You shouldn't miss the bruschettone (looks like bread, tastes like a million lira). Dinner here should come in under $50 total. Again, reservations aren't accepted, but appetizers and drinks are available while you wait. If the weather cooperates, there's a nice outdoor area, too.

Not up for noodles? Try **Dish** (3651 North Southport Avenue; 773–549–8614), the droll "home of the Margatini," where the menu features thirty tequilas and "pan-Southern" food. Lines are common here, too (this casual neighborhood seems to have a bias against reservations), but the buzz on Dish is very positive, and dinner for two is about $40. Chef-owner Patrick O'Dea, in only a couple of years, already knows of two couples whose first date at Dish led to a wedding!

After dinner ramble back east to Clark Street and make another choice from yesterday's array (above). Later stop in at the **Pepper Lounge** (3441 North Sheffield Avenue; 773–665–7377), where you can sip a chocolate martini.

DAY THREE: Morning

Breakfast

For an unusual breakfast alternative, walk over to **Uncommon Ground** (1214 West Grace Street; 773–929–3680), which offers the genuine Chicago dish of steamed eggs. Said to have originated in the coffeehouses of Hyde Park (home of the University of Chicago), steamed eggs are made in an espresso machine. They're a creamier, smoother version of scrambled and well worth a try; many fans feel they can never go back to the old frying pan. Uncommon Ground's coffee is fine, too, and a huge cup of mocha and a chocolate croissant provide a sweet wake-me-up.

Or check out **Deleece** (4004 North Southport; 773–325–1710), where Sunday brunch offers such treats as a breakfast pasta tossed with tomatoes, goat cheese, scrambled eggs, garlic, and herbs. Wow!

A Little Taste of London

Amaze your sweetheart by finding a little bit of London tucked in the hustle and bustle of Wrigleyville. Go to the corner of Grace Street (3800 north, two blocks from the ballpark) and Seminary Street (1100 west, just east of Clark Street). Walk a block north on Seminary to Byron Street, then east on Byron to **Alta Vista Terrace.**

This quite residential street exists for exactly one block—and a beautiful one it is. Lined up along its narrow length are beautiful brick rowhouses that mimic those of London's nicer neighborhoods. They're so lovely, yet so un-Wrigleyville, that a stroll on Alta Vista makes a wonderful mini-getaway in the middle of your weekend escapes.

Alta Vista is nicknamed "the street of forty doors," and if you look carefully, you'll see that each door has a twin, across the street and at the other end. The houses come honestly by their turn-of-the-century look, having been built between 1900 and 1904—and it's a hint of their original character that, in some, the third floor was a ballroom. Their lovingly kept exteriors have changed little since then, and in the early 1970s, the entire street was named one of Chicago's very first official landmarks.

If you happen to be here at Christmas, your consolation prize for missing baseball could be a visit to Alta Vista Terrace. Beautifully decorated individually to a harmonious whole, these lovely homes are one of my favorite things about Christmas in Chicago.

Wherever you eat get a couple of fat Sunday papers to linger over. Then stroll back to Wrigley Field for the second part of your doubleheader weekend. As you cheer on the Cubbies, remember that we love 'em, win or lose. And don't forget to look for the scoreboard flag, W or L, as you head for home.

FOR MORE ROMANCE

Another baseball game? Absolutely, and especially if you're an American League fan. The

Chicago White Sox (333 West 35th Street; 773–924–1000) are the pride of the South Side, now playing in a shiny new stadium. I've been to the new Comiskey Park twice, and here's my advice: Stay low. The lower your seat, the closer you are to the action and the less likely you are to suffer the vertigo that afflicts poor souls in the park's upper reaches. Adding insult to that injury is the amazing fact that *you can't even follow the ball from up there.*

On the new park's plus side are creature comforts: clean washrooms and plenty of 'em; lots of snack stands; secure and abundant parking, and even reasonably safe public transportation to and from the Loop. Just be sure your tickets place you well below the nosebleed section, where you'll pay a bargain $4. Top price is $25, but there's plenty in between. And note that the trip from the North Side Wrigleyville to South Side Comiskey will take some time—a solid hour if traffic snarls—so you'll be able to quiz each other on sports trivia at length!

HOOP LOVERS' HOLIDAY

When Chicagoans talk about romance, about love and devotion and putting someone on a pedestal, they are just as likely to be discussing Michael Jordan and the Chicago Bulls as any personal relationships. The city has been lucky in love during this long-running infatuation with Chicago Bulls star Michael Jordan, also known as MJ, His Airness, the greatest basketball player ever, or simply Michael.

Basketball is a team effort, of course, but MJ is first among equals. Beyond his superhuman skills, Chicagoans love him as a gentleman—polite with fans and media, generous to charities (especially for children), and patient about the relentless attention he attracts. When not burning up the court, he lives quietly in a northern suburb with his wife, Juanita, and their three rarely photographed children.

Even among folks who don't know a thing about sports, no visit to Chicago is complete without a nod to the Bulls. Why not make it a full bow and spend a day following the bigger-than-big footsteps of MJ, Scottie Pippen, that wicked Dennis Rodman, and everybody's favorite Zen coach, Phil(osopher) Jackson?

Practical notes: The basketball season starts in October and runs into April, with playoffs in May and June. Bulls tickets go on sale in September (Chicago Bulls: 312–955–4000) but season-ticket holders generally clean out the entire supply, and playoff tickets require divine in-

Romance at a Glance

♥ *Savor a Michael-icious meal at Michael Jordan's Restaurant.*

♥ *Visit two Bulls "shrines"—Michael Jordan Golf and Nike Town.*

♥ *Enjoy a pregame dinner (and chauffeur service to the action) at the Como Inn.*

♥ *Cheer the greatest team ever—your Chicago Bulls!*

♥ *Stargaze at a postgame Bulls hangout: Paladino's, or maybe Michael Jordan's.*

tervention. Thus, your planning should include contacting a reputable broker, such as **Looks Like the Front Row,** which is run by former White Sox player baseball Eric Soderholm (800–525–3380). Note, too, that you'll want good weather for this itinerary's downtown walks.

MORNING/AFTERNOON

Lunch

Start your Bulls bash with an early lunch at **Michael Jordan's Restaurant** (500 North LaSalle Street; 312–644–3865), where every kid goes home with a basketball-size children's menu sporting a picture of MJ's huge right hand.

Lunch is preferable to dinner here for one simple reason: reservations. They're not accepted for dinner, when the wait for a table can stretch to three hours and beyond. (Going on a weeknight helps; one Monday at about 5:30 P.M., I was seated with a party of four within ten minutes of arriving.) Most of the waiting area is a massive, multiscreen bar where videotapes showcase the amazing feats of His Airness. There's some nonbar seating for the wait, but where another restaurant might provide more, this one has "Michael Jordan's The Store." Here you'll find tons of MJ stuff, including one fun item that, at $27, would make a great gift to ship back home. It's a life-size cardboard cutout of MJ that fans of the Chicago-made movie *Home Alone* will recognize as the "guest" who tootled through the party scene on a toy train.

If you're saving your shopping for later, instead peruse the hundreds of framed magazine covers, book jackets, photos, and memorabilia that leave no wall bare. There's also lots of kids' art culled from the mountains of mail MJ receives from admiring children. This isn't a bad spot for celebrity spotting, as team members come in from time to time. MJ himself visits a couple of times a week when the team is in town—but he eats in a private room, so don't count on actually seeing His Airness.

Happily, the menu, service, and ambience all are better than they have to be. White tablecloths and plenty of booths provide a more intimate feeling than you might expect. Foodwise, a pasta with chicken, pesto, and mushrooms ($10.00) is especially tasty, and Juanita's macaroni and cheese ($3.50 as a side) is comfort food in all its gooey glory. The Big Mike burger ($8.50) comes with two all-beef patties, special sauce, and a big grin; skin-on fries are a good addition. Even a side dish of broccoli ($3.50) is generously sized and perfectly cooked. As for service, this is one spot where you'll have to tell them to slow down. Everyone is friendly and polite and breathtakingly efficient—but if you're *not* in a rush, say so.

⟨∘⊙∘⟩

After lunch you can discuss the philosophical and financial ramifications of superstardom—or the beauty of the game of basketball—during a stroll over to the Magnificent Mile, where you'll find a tourist attraction that's something of a temple to the commercial aspects of modern sports. You might think of **Nike Town** (669 North Michigan Avenue; 312–642–6363) as the house that Michael built. Indeed, at its entrance you'll see a replica of the Jordan statue whose original, a tourist attraction itself, stands outside the Bulls' home, the United Center. Inside Nike Town there's even more Michael, along with other Nike-identified star names such as Spike Lee, to promote the label's shoes and gear.

When the multimedia Nike bombardment palls, pause across the street to refresh yourselves in the lovely little courtyard garden at the **Fourth Presbyterian Church** (866 North Michigan Avenue; 312–787–4570). A pleasant fountain helps muffle traffic noise, and you can sit together on any of several sets of steps to rest up for the next stop on your basketball pilgrimage.

Back on the Jordan trail, you'll find two different sports associated with His Airness at **Michael Jordan Golf** (835 North Michigan Avenue; 312–944–4545). This boutique at the posh Water Tower Place shopping mall attests to the proprietor's other passions, golf and baseball. Be sure to compare your footprints with Michael's, which are preserved in cement near the entrance. The shop's mix of memorabilia and merchandise from three sports offers plenty to browse through, and duffers can take advantage of a miniature putting green (fake turf, of course) in the rear of the store. Three television screens broadcast Bulls highlights—thankfully, all in unison. The stock is heavy on souvenirs, such as caps, shirts, keychains, golf balls, and trading cards. A big wall poster reminds shoppers that one of the star's pet projects is the Michael Jordan Golf Club, where disadvantaged kids can learn the game with MJ footing the bill.

Maxed out on Mike? Chill at a Chicago institution, the clothing store where Jordan, coach Phil Jackson, Bears coach Dave Wannstedt, and Chicago-rooted actors Dennis Franz and Joe Mantegna outfit themselves from a natty selection of top-quality menswear. Many other well-dressed public figures also favor **Bigsby & Kruthers** (605 North Michigan Avenue; 312–944–6955), and everyone enjoys the company's huge mural of its famous customers on the B&K warehouse building along the busy Kennedy Expressway. During the 1995–96 basketball season, adding bad-boy Bull Dennis Rodman to the mural created such a constant gapers' block that his likeness was finally removed. Look for a smaller replica at the store: Rodman's straight-on gaze, white shirt, tie—and a suit whose sleeves are ripped off to showcase his muscular, tattooed arms. You can see how it stopped traffic.

Things inside the store are much more sedate, with tasteful suits, casual attire, and accessories at reasonable prices. There are comfy chairs, a wide-screen television, a bar, even a special smoking room where you can enjoy a cigar from a private humidor, if you're so inclined.

EVENING

Dinner

By now it's time for a pregame dinner, and for a good meal plus maximum convenience, there's no better place than the **Como Inn** (546 North Milwaukee Avenue; 312–421–5222). This wonderfully old-fashioned Italian restaurant is perfect for a couple's dinner, with its dim lighting and rambling warren of cozy little rooms. Best of all, the restaurant offers service to and from the United Center via its own minibus, relieving you of the driving, parking, and aggravation. This wonderful perk is just $3.50 per person, round-trip, but remember that reservations are essential.

Naturally, the staff at Como will also get you through dinner in time to catch the bus. So sit back and relax with an Italian specialty of pasta, veal, or perhaps fish. There's plenty of marinara sauce, but the kitchen is thoroughly versed in lighter, modern fare as well. Dinner for two can easily be held to about $40.

⌁⌁⌁

When you reach the **United Center** (1901 West Madison Street; 312–455–4500), be sure to get a good look at the famous statue of Michael Jordan that went up after he returned to the Bulls from his foray into pro baseball. It's the sort of landmark people love to have their pictures taken in front of, so go ahead and bring the camera.

After a day on the Bulls beat, you might think you're jaded. But just wait and see: When the stadium lights go down, you'll fall for the thrill of the deep organ music, swinging spotlights, and Bulls announcer Ray Clay's tension-filled voice heralding *"your* Chicago Bulls!" The two of you are sure to feel a chill as the starting lineup is introduced, especially when the crowd goes wild for Jordan.

Even the completely ignorant can follow the basic action in basketball and get caught up in the excitement of the game. The show that accompanies the game is just as eye-catching, too,

Classic Chicago Couples: MJ and JJ

They met when he was practically unknown, a tall young athlete who still recalls how this attractive young woman impressed him by paying her own way at the restaurant where her bunch of friends ran into his.

Today, the restaurant they go to is the one bearing his name. Happily married and the parents of three, Juanita and Michael Jordan live a remarkably low-key life in the suburbs, where they've built a big house with plenty of room for extended family. And if we know everything we want to know about Michael, here's a telling story about Juanita: On the day the entire country watched her husband make his hugely hyped comeback to the Chicago Bulls, she skipped the game. It was out of town, and she had promised the kids they'd go see "Disney on Ice."

First things first. You can see why Michael married her.

what with wacky fans, cheerleaders, team mascots, and whatever else the marketing mavens have concocted. At half-time you can browse the lobby souvenir stands for a keepsake. (Your ticket stub would do, too, of course.)

Win or lose, Bulls fans—and many of the players—like to party after a game. Sometimes they go to Michael Jordan's, but often they wind up at one of the fashionable restaurants on West Randolph Street, an old warehouse district that's rehabbing as fast as building permits can be procured. (It's also near Oprah Winfrey's offices and studio, Harpo Inc., which improves the stargazing prospects.)

One good Bulls bet is **Paladino's** (832 West Randolph Street; 312–455–1400), a trendy spot where everything—chairs, tables, plates, portions—is a little larger than life, making things comfortable for those very tall guys. Even when crowded, it's a welcoming place for drinks, dinner, or dessert. The menu is mostly Italian, but there's plenty of variety. The house pizza is highly regarded; or, if you're not terribly hungry, split the platter of varied vegetables, all cooked imaginatively, presented beautifully, and priced moderately. Even a cappuccino has panache here and offers a perfect finish to your Bulls bash.

Another hot spot is **Adagio** (923 West Weed Street; 312–787–0400), where the food is also Italian and the crowd is fast and fashionable. Dennis Rodman has made it a hangout, as have other sports figures who are ever in search of the new. You won't have to spend much here if you come after a game; you might stop in for a drink and stay to eat, or you might decide it's too crowded and noisy for romance, even if you *would* love to get a close-up look at a local celebrity.

You might also consider a different Bulls finale that has nothing to do with basketball. **The Bulls** (1916 North Lincoln Park West; 773–337–3000), a venerable jazz club in the always-fashionable Lincoln Park neighborhood on the Near North Side, offers quality live music nightly from 9:30 P.M. It's a good place to wind down.

ITINERARY 24
One day and one evening

ROMANTIC HOLIDAY ON ICE

*W*hat could be more romantic than gliding on the ice, smooth and graceful, almost floating as you go? Cold and discomfort fade away as you zip along, and the only thing that could make it all even better is doing it with your sweetheart.

In Chicago, you can—right in the middle of the Loop, or along the lakefront, or at the Navy Pier recreation center. We're lucky to have three excellent ice rinks downtown, and hockey fans are even luckier: Chicago also has not one, but two pro hockey teams. The veteran Blackhawks of the National Hockey League trade time with the basketball Bulls in the United Center, while the upstart Chicago Wolves play at the northwest suburban Rosemont Horizon.

All in all, you're looking at a slippin', slidin' day of fun on ice. And it's a good chance to surprise your significant other with a mystery date: Get hockey tickets, make sure your companion knows how to stay up on ice, and then announce an expedition to a secret destination where you'll pull the laces tight and glide away together.

Practical notes: It's absolutely essential to call and check on whether outdoor ice is thick enough for skating. Also find out whether group lessons or an entertainment program is scheduled for the day and time you plan to skate.

Tickets to a Chicago Blackhawks game are easiest to get by mail. Get a schedule by calling (312) 943–7000 and choose the game you want to attend. Send the team office a note with a

Romance at a Glance

♥ *Take your skates downtown (or rent 'em) to Skate on State.*

♥ *Warm up at Heaven on Seven or Marshall Field's Walnut Room.*

♥ *Peruse another kind of ice at Mallers Building jewelers.*

♥ *Skate some more at Navy Pier or the lakefront's Daley Bicentennial Plaza.*

♥ *Watch the pros at a Chicago Blackhawks or Chicago Wolves game.*

check, and your tickets will be set aside *before* single-ticket sales begin. Prices range from $15 to $75, and sales start in September for the upcoming six games; as each cycle of six sells out, another begins. Tickets also are available through Ticketron (312–559–1212), whose service charges can really add up.

Tickets to a Chicago Wolves hockey game range in price from about $8.00 to $30.00 and are available at the Rosemont Horizon box office or through Ticketron (312–559–1212). Plans are underway for a dinner-game package that would include transportation to and from the game; for more information, call the Wolves at (847) 390–0404.

Most of this winter itinerary is easy to negotiate, even without a car. If you're staying downtown, you can walk to some destinations; others are an easy cab ride. And note that it's hardly necessary to skate in all three locations if you'd rather spend some of the day elsewhere.

MORNING

Your first challenge is choosing where to start the day. All three skating rinks offer their own pleasures, so let's compare and contrast. The one that's most likely to amaze the folks back home is **Skate on State** (North State Street at Randolph Street; 312–744–3315), which makes a delectable frozen lemonade of that common city citrus, a full-block vacant lot with no immediate development plans. This former eyesore is flooded as soon as weather permits (likely by December) and thereafter is open for skating from 9:00 A.M. till 7:15 P.M. daily. And open is the operative word: There's no admission fee, and skate rental is just $3.00 for adults. A warming trailer is available for periodic thawing, and the rink is lit when you're here in the evening.

Lunch

If you come on a weekday, don't be surprised at seeing office and retail-store workers flock to the ice for a lunch-hour spin. They can even grab a bite before heading back to work, since McDonald's is nearby. You can warm yourselves at a better place for lunch, though, by taking off your skates and going across the street to **Marshall Field and Co.** (111 North State Street; 312–781–1000), where lunch is more than a meal; it's a Chicago tradition. The Walnut Room has been favored by generations of hungry shoppers, especially for its famous chicken pot pie. The turkey club is good, too, and no matter what you have, save room for a dessert made with the store's signature Frango mints. Prices run from about $7.00 to about $12.00, and you can even get a glass of wine. *Caution:* Reservations are accepted only for groups of five or more, so you may have a wait. Try to come early or late; hours are 11:00 A.M. to 3:30 P.M. daily (noon to 3:00 P.M. on Sunday). Extra caution: If you're here around Christmas, the wait is interminable because of another tradition of lunch around the massive, beautiful Christmas tree.

You might prefer to go a block east to **Heaven on Seven** (111 North Wabash Avenue; 312–263–6443), a Cajun enclave in an otherwise nondescript office building. Two menus list "normal" food and such Cajun standards as red beans and rice as well as po' boy sandwiches. Regulars always check out the daily specials. Best of all, no item costs more than $9.95. Heaven is open from 7:00 A.M. till 5:00 P.M. weekdays, and from 10:00 A.M. till 3:00 P.M. Saturdays.

AFTERNOON

Once you're on Wabash Avenue, it's tough not to notice its abundance of great shopping. If you want to join the Chicago cognoscenti in searching out exquisite jewelry, stroll a little south to the **Jeweler's Center at the Mallers Building** (5 South Wabash Avenue; 312–739–1606). This Art Deco building, recently renovated to its original burnished splendor, is home to dozens of jewelers, importers, and dealers in gems and metals. From Shalom Wholesale Jewelry to Korea Gems to Bobby Precious Metals, someone here speaks your language. And they'll be happy to design your own piece, repair your watch, appraise a family heirloom, or sell you the engagement ring you thought you couldn't afford. Go ahead—it can't hurt to look.

Ready to return to the other kind of ice? Downtown's two other outdoor skating rinks are not far from each other, but they're very different in their surroundings. The larger is **Daley Bicentennial Plaza Ice Rink** (337 East Randolph Street; 312–742–7648). It's actually the flat top of the underground Grant Park parking garage, and its lakefront location gives you a wonderful view of Lake Michigan, Grant Park, and the city skyline. The rink is open from 10:00 A.M. to 10:00 P.M. weekdays; weekend hours are 10:00 A.M. to noon, 12:30 to 2:30 P.M., and 3:00 to 5:00 P.M. Admission is $1.50, which covers the whole day during the week or one of the two-hour sessions on Saturday or Sunday. (Senior citizens get in free!) Skate rental is $1.50 for adults, and the rink's amenities include music, a warm-up area, and vending machines for sustenance.

Also on the lakefront—practically in the lake, as a matter of fact, and rather breezy sometimes—is the **Navy Pier Skating Rink** (600 East Grand Avenue, in the Navy Pier entertainment complex; 312–595–7437), a charmingly small rink that's quite a contrast to the adjacent Crystal Gardens, a plant-filled atrium complete with trick fountains. The rink is open from 10:00 A.M. to 8:00 P.M. daily, and skating is free. Skate rental is $3.00, and you can get your skates sharpened for $5.00.

The appealing thing about skating at Navy Pier, apart from the pleasure of being on the lake and the cozy quality of this little rink, is that there's so much to do when you finish skating. The pier, once a collection of run-down warehouses, is now a beautifully renovated tourist destination with its own landmarks. They're a pair of carnival beauties: a grand merry-go-round and a tall, tall Ferris wheel that, when lit during the warmer months, suggests a faraway wistfulness.

On a more practical note, remember that Navy Pier is home to the **Chicago Children's Museum** (312–527–1000). This is a terrific place to visit even if you're not a kid, and its presence means that Navy Pier is a consciously family-friendly place. (In other words, if you're kid-phobic, be forewarned!)

Tub for Two

For couples who need a rest after ice-skating—and who doesn't?—here's a midday break your honey will never forget. Pamper your aching leg muscles, along with the rest of you, in a luxurious private hot tub at **Great Lakes Spa Suites** *(15 West Hubbard Street; 312–527–1311). This very clean, perfectly respectable operation offers patrons a cozy little suite of their own in which to soak in a hot tub and shower afterward. Bathing suits are optional, and towel service is available from the spa. Rates are $28 per hour for two, with VIP or presidential suites that also have a sauna at $33 or $38 per hour. Reservations are recommended, and there are special rates for weekday visits.*

EVENING

The pier also is loaded with pleasant little shops, plus an IMAX theater if you'd like to experience a slam-bang film—perhaps on space travel, volcanoes, or the Rolling Stones. The pier's food court has deli, Chinese, hot dogs, and the like; for a more upscale meal, wander down to **Widow Newton's Tavern** (312–595–5500), where a window table overlooks Navy Pier's entrance (where, if it were spring, you could enjoy a delightful fountain). This pleasant jumble of English decor holds everything from old church pews to stained-glass windows. The food includes such standards as prime rib and broiled whitefish. Figure about $50 total for dinner, and be sure to eat early enough to get to the game on time.

If you're going to a Blackhawks game, consider taking the bus to the United Center (1900 West Madison Street). The Grand Avenue bus will take you west to Damen Avenue, where you can ride south to Madison Street. You'll want to cab back afterward, though, perhaps stopping to line up with other fans at **Cheli's Chili Bar** (1137 West Madison Street; 312–455–1237), a sports bar owned by Hawks Chris Chelios that serves up a very warming bowl of red for only $3.50. (It's open late after Hawks, and Bulls home games, and Chelios is said to visit after almost every game.)

The CTA also can get you to Rosemont for a Chicago Wolves game. Take the Grand Avenue bus to the rapid-transit station at Grand and Dearborn, where you can catch the train that connects with the O'Hare line. Get off at River Road, then take the Pace bus to the Horizon. This may sound complicated, but, honestly, it's simple.

But enough about transportation: Let's talk about the game! We all know hockey is rough and prone to violence, but there's no denying the excitement of its fast-moving action and the players' spectacular skills. If the fights and fairly routine bloodshed brings on a squeamish spell, keep in mind that these guys are padded for protection and looking to win. Meanwhile, appreciate the speed and dexterity that are even more essential to hockey than strategy. Add the electricity of an intensely partisan crowd, and you've got yourselves a thrilling spectacle.

The crowd makes it easy to get caught up in the game, and you'll find yourselves hollering with abandon. Between periods, take a welcome break from screaming to browse the souvenir stands and maybe buy a keepsake. At the United Center, you'll find a good one that's not expensive if you pick up a Hawks puck (about $7.00).

Whether the home team wins or loses, you're both likely to feel exhausted from shouting and sweating. As you head homeward, devote your last bit of energy to cuddling up against the cold and enjoying some instant-replay reminiscence about your holiday on ice.

For More Romance

If you'd like to surprise your sweetie with ice skating in July, head for the Chicago Park District's own **McFetridge Sports Center** (3843 North California Avenue; 312–742–7585), where year-round skating is interrupted only at the end of summer for refurbishing the ice. Open-skate sessions are usually held from 4:30 to 6:00 P.M. on Saturday and Sunday (for all ages); from 9:15 to 10:45 P.M. on Tuesday and Friday (adults only), and 3:30 to 5:00 P.M. Friday (all ages). Admission is $2.50 for adults; skates rent for $2.00, and the skate shop will sharpen your blades for only $3.00.

OUT OF THIS WORLD

ITINERARY 25
Two days and one night

STEALING AWAY AT STARVED ROCK

$\mathcal{S}$ometimes leaving the city is the most romantic way for you to make time for each other. When you're interested in someone and want to know more; when you're in love and looking for a special interlude together—these are moments when you should consider getting out of town.

The area offers lots of getaway places, but not many of these lie in close proximity to the city. And you certainly don't want to spend half your time behind the wheel. So pick up the phone and start planning your escape to Starved Rock.

Practical notes: You'll need to drive to Starved Rock State Park. And remember to look ahead as you consider a Starved Rock getaway. If you have the flexibility, make it a midweek interlude; bookings are much more sparse at that time and the cabin you want more likely available. Also try for an off-season period; summer is the most popular, but the fall leaf-watching season is huge, too. Come in spring when it's muddy or in winter when it's snowy. The park is beautiful anytime. Don't forget to book dinner reservations at the Red Door Inn (815–223–2500) in Peru when you book at Starved Rock.

DAY ONE: MORNING/AFTERNOON

Before you even hit the road, you'll have reserved a room or cabin at **Starved Rock State**

Park Lodge. Plan well in advance; the lodge is very popular, especially in the summer and fall months, so you'll need to work ahead. Reservations are accepted two years in advance, and the most popular rooms are snapped up earliest.

To avoid such a wait, why not consider a getaway when you *really* need it—in the dead of winter? That's the time to rent cross-country skis by day and sink into a comfy couch by night. Or come in the spring, when early wildflowers bloom—as early as March, if the weather cooperates.

When you reserve, be aware that there's quite a bit of variation in accommodations. Romantically inclined visitors often like one of the lodge's private cabins, which feature their very own fireplaces and super-comfortable king-size beds. At $78 a night, they're an incredible bargain (subsidized by Illinois residents' tax dollars, so if you live in-state, don't be *too* grateful). They are on the small side, however—basically a comfortable, self-contained hotel room—so if you want to spread out, try to get what many consider the best quarters in the place: a lovely room whose bay window looks out over the park (excellent for a *rainy* weekend!) and whose sitting area offers a couch that's just right for two.

The lodge's other rooms are wonderful, too, although they don't offer the degree of privacy you'll have in your own cabin. But at $60 per night for a double, not many guests are complaining—even though meals are separate. Soothing green and mauve tones are featured in all the rooms' decor, and each room and cabin has a television and VCR if you want to while away a couple of hours in seclusion.

To arrive at Starved Rock, you'll drive about 90 miles from downtown along Interstate 80, out into the cornfields that tell you you've left the city behind. As you arrive and check in, be sure to make reservations at the lodge restaurant for lunch, dinner, and tomorrow's breakfast and lunch.

Take a moment to notice the lodge's classic woodsy look. In fact, if you've ever stayed in a rustic, northwoods lodge, you're likely to be struck by déjà vu. Unlike the many deluxe hotels and citified bed and breakfast homes elsewhere in this book, Starved Rock State Park Lodge offers the timeless "lodge" look of a rugged 1930s building—appropriately, since the lodge was a product of the Depression-era Civilian Conservation Corps, which put jobless men to work on public projects. Half a century later, a late–1980s renovation brought updating and the addition of more rooms to the main wing.

An excellent result of the renovation is the lodge's terrific swimming pool, complete with sauna and whirlpool, to let you take a delightful dip even in the midst of winter. Better yet, it's open until 9:00 P.M., so you don't have to swim in daylight hours.

And there's the Great Room, which is just what a lodge should be: roomy yet cozy, welcoming guests to its central feature—a huge, double-sided stone fireplace that's the very image of outdoorsy. It's the kind of place that looks as if an out-of-the-way table ought to be devoted to the jigsaw puzzle everyone's been working on. (Well, why not bring your own?)

The Great Room can be a tad crowded on busy weekends; the Starved Rock lodge has a total of ninety-four rooms and cabins and is a family-friendly place. Again, that suggests an offpeak getaway if you want to be sure of getting one of those comfy Great Room couches to yourselves.

Depending on the weather, your mood, and your energy level, you'll want to settle into your cabin before choosing an activity. A swim might be inviting, or maybe you'd rather stroll the grounds for as long as it takes both of you to unwind. Or you could just warm up your cabin—maybe with the bottle of champagne you cleverly thought to pack!

In any case, you're sure to wonder about the park's name. It comes from a tall sandstone butte

that, according to legend, was the last stronghold of an Indian band at war with another tribe during the eighteenth century. Surrounded by their enemies, the group starved rather than surrender.

But that's the only grim note to this getaway! Your time at Starved Rock will be filled with outdoor fun or indoor relaxation. Ask at the desk for details on fishing, canoe rental, cross-country skiing in season, or going into the park on horseback. Tennis is an option in summer, and don't overlook the park's status as a naturalist's haven. With hundreds of species of plants and plentiful birds and other wildlife, the park is a joy for those who always pack their nature guides.

DAY ONE: EVENING

Dinner

Like its accommodations, Starved Rock's restaurant is a bargain you'd be happy to get at a much higher price. Prime rib tops the menu at $13.95, but fried chicken, fish, and other selections are less. And for vegetarians, lots of salads and a veggie stir fry are a nice accommodation. At these prices, your budget won't notice if you pop for one of the kitchen's excellent desserts at every meal.

Walk off the calories with an evening stroll or swim, then retire to the privacy of your cabin, where you don't need any hints on how to entertain yourselves!

DAY TWO: MORNING/AFTERNOON

Breakfast

Breakfast in the lodge restaurant is an event in itself, especially for busy people who rarely enjoy a full spread of eggs, meats, and all the old-fashioned trimmings. And at $10 or less for both of you, it's tempting to indulge!

⟪⊙⟫

No matter what you choose for breakfast, be ready to walk it off as you explore the countryside. A stop at the park's Visitors' Center will get you oriented, with take-along brochures showing the park's trails and highlights. Marked trails total about 12 miles, with some trails as short as three-quarters of a mile. Most of the trails cover easy ground, with sand surfaces and even a bit that's paved. The park's terrain makes stairs inevitable, but if you prefer to skip the strain, trails make it easy to arrange your walk so you'll arrive at stairs to go down instead of up.

Visitors are allowed just about everywhere in the park, so you can get up close to the park's namesake, as well as its canyons and rock formations. Hiking trails are so clearly marked, you won't get lost unless you want to be alone together. Do try the one that leads to Lovers' Leap! It goes from the top of Starved Rock, down stairs, and through a left fork at a four-way intersection of trails. You'll zig-zag through woods, climbing gradually to a T-intersection where you turn left and walk another 30 yards or so to another left fork. Down this way is Lovers' Leap, a good spot for smooching and schmoozing.

Eventually you'll make your way back to the lodge for lunch in the restaurant. Spend the afternoon outdoors again, or make it a sinfully lazy spell of doing absolutely nothing. You wouldn't be the first high-powered couple to come all the way to Starved Rock and spend most of your weekend sleeping, relaxing, or otherwise using your quarters

DAY TWO: EVENING

Dinner

By dinnertime, maybe you're ready to stir. Take a drive—half an hour or so—to the little town of Peru, where the beautiful, quaint **Red Door Inn** (1701 Water Street; 815- 223-2500) is the nicest restaurant around. Dating to 1850, the Red Door was built along the Illinois River, then as now a thriving commercial route. Today, restored by the charming local couple who run it, the Red Door serves informal lunches and elegant dinners to customers who come from many miles around.

The restaurant's choicest seating is its lovely new atrium, which overlooks the river (and makes a fine haven for non-smokers). It's a wonderful spot to sip a before- or after-dinner drink together. The dinner menu is strictly fine-dining, with seafood, chicken and many other entrees—but the house specialty, well worth trying, is a posh steak Diane cooked tableside. Best of all, the Red Door's prices leave Chicagoans smiling in relief—about $45 for both of you. Remember to make reservations, and to ask for specific directions at the Starved Rock Lodge desk.

DAY THREE: MORNING/AFTERNOON

Enjoy another hearty breakfast in the lodge restaurant, then decide how much time you can devote to another hike before heading back to the city. You can also explore the neighboring **Mathiessen State Park,** just southeast of Starved Rock, where waterfalls tumble into the Vermilion River. Mathiessen's trails tend to be more challenging than those at Starved Rock. And Mathiessen is where you'll go during a winter visit to rent cross-country skis or ice skates—or even snowshoes, if you're really adventurous!

As you head for home, savoring the Midwestern landscape, detour about 20 miles to the west and look for the town of Princeton. Here, at 1863 Highway 26, is a sweet reminder of nineteenth-century Illinois: a red covered bridge that's the last one in the state still open to traffic. Whether or not you're fans of *The Bridges of Madison County,* there's no denying the romance of this simple, sturdy structure.

FOR MORE ROMANCE

Look for farmers' markets or roadside stands as you make your way back to the city. Often, there's more for sale than fresh fruits and vegetables. If you run across one that offers such other items as jams and jellies or handicrafts, make these your souvenirs of the weekend. Every time you butter your toast and open that jam, you'll think of each other—not to mention the warm feeling of curling up close under an afghan you bought together.

ITINERARY 26
One day and one evening

ROMANCE AND THE BUSINESS TRAVELER
HOW TO SAVOR THE O'HARE AREA

*S*ome visitors to Chicago see no more of the city than can be glimpsed from a taxicab window. Technically, of course, they're *in* Chicago as soon as they land at O'Hare International Airport—but they get off the plane, check in at a hotel, and plunge into a round of meetings or presentations or sales calls. When it's finished, these all-work, no-play travelers turn around and fly back out again.

Not a bit of local color in the picture, and not a bit romantic—but it *could* be! Many business travelers have the clout and/or the frequent-flier miles to bring a sweetheart if they want to. Trouble is, they know in advance that there won't be time for a fun trip downtown, and why bother traveling with a cherished partner if you're certain business won't leave you a moment alone together?

Here's why: because it's *very* romantic to jet off anywhere with your partner. Because it's *very* romantic to plan a special evening together that will bring a sweet and soothing end to a hard day's work. Because it's *very* romantic to share a fabulous dinner and see a memorable show in the most pedestrian of places—Rosemont, Illinois, the community surrounding O'Hare. (Note to Chicagoans: Couples seeking weekend getaways could go here, too!) Although all the

Romance at a Glance

♥ *Book a swanky suite at Marriott Suites or Rosemont Suite Hotel at O'Hare.*

♥ *Play golf at the Ramada O'Hare course.*

♥ *Travel in style via limousine.*

♥ *Dine sumptuously at Nick's, Carlucci, or Morton's, the Steakhouse.*

♥ *Take in a musical at the Rosemont Theater or a "big show" at the Rosemont Horizon.*

activity takes place in the course of one day and one evening, you and your partner presumably are already checked in at a hotel because of the business that brought you here, and you will probably return to the hotel to sleep rather than catching the red-eye out of town.

Practical notes: Plan, plan, plan! And note that while this itinerary covers an entire day and evening, you may take advantage of only parts.

Many business travelers are able to choose their own hotels. If you can, consider a suite for maximum comfort when you work. Two good choices in Rosemont are the Rosemont Suite Hotel at O'Hare and the Marriott Suites-O'Hare.

If business takes you to the Rosemont Convention Center, the connecting walkway from the **Rosemont Suite Hotel** (5500 North River Road; 847–678–4000 or 800–333–3333) will keep you out of the elements. Each suite opens onto a bright, art-filled central atrium where breakfast and a complimentary cocktail hour are offered daily. The hotel is decorated in Frank Lloyd Wright's Prairie style, which carries over into the suites' squared stained-glass lamps and muted green-and-burgundy colors. Living rooms are smallish but somehow fit in a refrigerator, coffeemaker, microwave oven, and minibar. And the television is situated so that you can cuddle up on a comfy couch to watch. Beds are king size, but be sure to specify that (rather than two separate beds!) when you reserve. A machine-equipped exercise area overlooks the indoor pool. The hotel's fairly formal restaurant, the **American Grille and Bar,** has plush booths; choosing a corner booth makes you feel quite private. Suites start at about $99 nightly for weekend packages.

At the **Marriott Suites** (6155 North River Road; 847–696–4400 or 800–228–9290) light fills the large rooms of a suite when the elegant French doors separating bedroom (with king-size bed) from living room are opened. A writing table has its own little nook for quiet; baths are downright luxurious, and a refrigerator and coffeemaker are provided. Downstairs, a sunny outdoor deck extends the indoor pool's recreational space during summer. The hotel's restaurant, Allie's, is informal and pleasant; and one of the area's best restaurants, Carlucci, is next door in a connected building. Marriott rates vary, with weekend packages available for as little as $99 per night.

Another O'Hare area hotel that's worthy of special note is the **Ramada Hotel O'Hare** (6600 North Mannheim Road, Rosemont; 847–827–5131). Right in the heart of airport country, this foresightful hotel put in a nine-hole golf course. It's open when the weather is favorable (unfortunately, there's no planning for *that!*) and is available exclusively to the hotel's guests. Ask about tee times and other information when you call to book a room.

MORNING/AFTERNOON

Making your romantic getaway as posh as possible is likely to mean a limousine. One reliable company is **Ace Limousine** (773–549–5550), which specializes in chauffering people around the O'Hare area. Available cars range from a Lincoln Town Car to a full-blown stretch limousine, and the wheels can meet you at the airport or hotel on as little as a couple of hours' notice. Charges are calculated on a trip-by-trip basis, which means that each time you're transported from one point to another, a separate trip is counted at $30. For a special touch (and an extra $15), they'll arrange to have a bottle of champagne waiting for you in the limousine.

Before you pop the cork, however, at least one of you has some work to do. How to pass that time comes down to what the non-working partner feels like doing solo. If you're limo-happy or are renting a car, you might want to spend the day shopping at one of the area's major malls. **Woodfield Mall** (at Golf Road [Highway 58] and Highway 53 in the farther-northwest suburb of Schaumburg; 847–330–1537 or 800–332–1537) is one of the world's largest, with hundreds of stores under one roof. **Oakbrook Center** is in the tony suburb of Oakbrook (at Highway 83 and Twenty-second Street; 630–573–1300), and its outdoor grounds are as beautifully kept as its upscale shops. Hotel staff can guide you to either mall, and both offer first-run movies as well as shopping.

One unusual attraction in Rosemont is the **Donald E. Stephens Museum of Hummels.** Named for the village mayor, this museum features more than one thousand of the little ceramic figures in the world's largest public display. Housed in the Rosemont Convention Center (5555 North River Road, Rosemont; 847–692–4000), the museum is open daily except Sunday, and admission is free.

Don't neglect the pleasures of a lazy day spent working out, swimming or just catching a cable movie at the hotel. All the better to help your hard-working honey relax when the day ends!

EVENING

Dinner

As befits an airport-centered town, Rosemont offers a wide range of restaurants, so you'll be able to choose a cuisine (and an atmosphere) you both enjoy. Just remember: Many restaurants are accustomed to serving businesspeople, so you should mention when reserving that your focus is romantic. Let the restaurateur help you make the evening magical.

Romantic is just the word that comes to mind when people suggest **Cafe La Cave** (2777 Mannheim Road, Des Plaines; 847–827–7818), where the continental menu goes for the kind of old-fashioned opulence that follows rack of lamb with a rich dessert. The big, formal dining room aspires to the Palace of Versailles, but the smaller "cave" room is where you'll find your own little world at an intimate corner table. (Mention "romantic" when you reserve and they'll take care of it!)

Several of Rosemont's nicest fine-dining restaurants—Nick's Fishmarket, Carlucci, and Morton's, the Steakhouse—are suburban siblings of big names in the city. At **Nick's Fishmarket** (10275 West Higgins Road, at Mannheim Road; 847–298–8200), fish and seafood are obviously the order of the day, as suggested by the big, beautiful saltwater aquariums (which some might feel bring dinner rather close while it's still swimming). Snuggle into one of those broad booths and feel the day's work drift away. When you get around to ordering, consider some of the Hawaiian specialties that are favorites of owner Nick Nickolas. If you're not the fishy type, you'll be pleased with chicken, steak, or pasta. Dinner for two will total about $80 to $100.

The rustic cooking of Tuscany is the basis for the menu at **Carlucci** (6111 North River Road; 847–518–0990), where there's a bottle of olive oil on each table for dipping the delicious bread that will come your way as you're seated (again, mention when you reserve that you're looking for cozy; this room doesn't have many nooks). The delicious scent of a wood-burning fireplace in the open kitchen should put you in the mood for something roasted—maybe chicken, maybe mushrooms or other veggies—and of course there are pastas, too. Dinner should total less than $80.

Morton's, The Steakhouse (9525 West Bryn Mawr Avenue, Rosemont; 847–678–5155) is located a short stroll from the Rosemont Suites hotel, and it's where *Home Improvement* dad Tim Allen might take his sons to study the art of manly dining. (Fresh fish and good service would appeal to wife Jill.) Thick, toothsome steaks are the big draw, with prime rib and lobster also popular. Depending on the size of your steaks—they range from reasonable to cardiac alert—dinner may cost anywhere from $60 to $100 for the two of you.

For your postdinner pleasure, Rosemont has two large-scale entertainment venues that are worth checking for the dates of your visit. The giant one is the **Rosemont Horizon** (6920 North Mannheim Road, Rosemont; 847–635–6601), which seats 18,500 people and holds the very biggest acts, from Bruce Springsteen to Luciano Pavarotti. Obviously this is not the place for an intimate romantic experience, but it may be a great opportunity to see a show you'd never be able to catch back home. The Horizon schedule also is of interest to sports fans, since it provides the home court for DePaul University's Blue Demons basketball team and the home ice for hockey's bad boys, the Chicago Wolves.

If you decide to take in a concert or other event at the Horizon, expect the attire and attitudes to be casual, and you should be prepared for lines at every turn (especially the women's bathrooms). On the other hand, the facility is clean and well-kept, and people generally are polite, so a show here can make for a pleasant or even outstanding evening. Ticket prices vary enormously, from $10.00 for a college basketball game to $39.50 for "Stars on Ice." Service charges will be added, too, although there is a box office from which to buy to minimize add-on charges.

The cozier—and, let's face it, much classier—of this area's venues is the **Rosemont Theater** (5400 River Road, Rosemont; 800–859–7469), which seats 4,200 and is elegantly decorated with glass, marble, and lots of shine. The theater opened in late 1995 with a lavish Barry Manilow show and has leaned almost exclusively toward musical offerings, including traveling productions of such Broadway favorites as *Ain't Misbehavin', Cats,* and *Carousel.* Popular music bookings range from the Righteous Brothers to John Denver, and the Chicago-based Joffrey Ballet calls this stage home as well. Again, ticket prices vary greatly, topping at $50 per person for chanteuse k.d. lang or weekend performances of the big musicals.

Rosemont probably has as many bars as it has restaurants, but the most satisfying spot for an after-show drink is likely to be your hotel bar—or even the cute little minibar up in your room, where dress is casual or even optional. It's the surest way to give your fellow businesspeople the slip and keep the end of the evening to yourselves.

UN-CONVENTIONAL

A CHANCE FOR ROMANCE AT MCCORMICK PLACE

*E*very year millions of people come to Chicago for conventions or meetings at McCormick Place. It's big, it's sterile, it's crowded, and it's busy. It's built for hordes, not for couples. Yet many of these visitors are in desperate need of a romantic break. Maybe they've just met someone and hit it off—or they *would,* if they could just get away for a moment to focus on each other. Then there are couples who are partners in work as well as love and who find their only respite from glad-handing and deal-doing at McCormick Place comes when they're too exhausted to notice. Believe it or not, however, even the vast indifference of McCormick Place can provide stolen moments that lovers treasure. Romance in the face of adversity is perhaps the truest romance—so indulge yourselves.

TAKING A BREAK AT MCCORMICK PLACE

When you're in the thick of doing business at McCormick Place, a quick break may be the best one you'll get. So stop for coffee in the **Chicago Room** restaurant, which is on the East Building's mezzanine level, near the entrance from the Soldier Field parking lot. It's off the beaten path. "Most people don't find us right away," said the friendly woman who rang up my order ($2.45 for a twelve-ounce bottle of spring water; bring plenty of money when you visit

McCormick Place). Better yet, this restaurant's walls are *not* glass; get a back corner booth or rear-wall banquette for privacy.

If you must get something done while making time for your beloved, head for the same East Building mezzanine area, opposite the escalators, or for the North Building's first-floor escalator area, around the corner from Gold Coast Dogs and across from the Visitors' Information area. In both these locations, you'll find **shoeshine stands** where you can sit comfortably, hold hands, and whisper to each other as experts spiff up your footwear. (Remember to tip generously; a stingy sweetheart is a former sweetheart.)

The best way to escape the peculiarly time-suspended feeling at McCormick Place is to go outdoors. At the far south end of the East Building, look for the ramp to the underground garage and exit through the glass doors beyond it. (Don't go down; you'll wind up among the cars.) Just to your left is a grassy area set with rustic stone benches and circles of various sizes that look as if they're waiting for modern-day Druids—or modern-day lovers. They seem to invite you to sit down and enjoy the lake, which is practically at your feet. There's a sidewalk for strolling next to the water and a thicket of trees for atmosphere. Even the dim buzz of Lake Shore Drive's traffic sounds has a lulling effect.

It's also possible to get close to the lake upstairs in the East Building. Doors in the building's east wall of windows open to loading docks that overlook the lake. Usually a couple of chairs happen to be out there, too. It's worth slipping out if you can.

One other way to enjoy some of your time at McCormick Place is to take in a show at the

East Building's **Arie Crown Theater** (312–791–6000). When the Arie Crown isn't booked for convention-related programs, it often hosts popular-music programs and touring companies of Broadway shows, as well as the holiday season's annual production of *The Nutcracker*. Do check before you come to find out if there will be a show here that you'd like to see together.

GETTING OUT

Perhaps the greatest challenge of McCormick Place is leaving it. Avoid deadly cab lines—and impress your sweetheart—by arranging beforehand to be whisked away by limousine! Both the East and North buildings provide a separate entrance for limos to pick up their passengers, and it's worth every penny to get out that easily. Remember, you don't need a giant stretch limo for just the two of you, which means you needn't spend a fortune; check on whether your company has a recommendation on which service to use. A good one is **Ace Limousine** (773–549–5550), which charges $30 to zip from McCormick Place to your chosen destination.

Whether you leave by taxi or limo, you can avoid construction tie-ups on Lake Shore Drive by *not* going north on the Drive. Instead take time to visit the nearby **Prairie Avenue Historic District,** where the city's oldest building, the Greek Revival Widow Clarke House, stands. Here, too, the Pullman, Armour, and Field families built opulent nineteenth-century mansions, including noted architect H. H. Richardson's 1887 Glessner House. Regular tours are available Wednesday through Sunday, and you can arrange custom tours, too; call (312) 326–1480 for information.

Near both McCormick Place and Prairie Avenue is **Chinatown,** with its abundance of shops and restaurants. Perhaps the most romantic place to dine is the **Emperor's Choice** (2238 South Wentworth; 312–225–8800), with linen tablecloths and napkins, soft lighting, and a tank of tropical fish for serenity. Seafood entrees are popular here, and prices are low—less than $20 per person for dinner.

Another way to make a quick exit from McCormick Place is to take the South Shore Metra train to Van Buren Street and Michigan Avenue or to its terminus, at Randolph Street

It can—and should!—be done. In the North Building look into the telephone area just beyond the Level 2 Business Center. The corner at the outside door is relatively secluded. Catercorner to this, all the way across the lobby and just behind Gold Coast Dogs, is a little nook holding nothing but a few soda-pop vending machines. Upstairs, overlooking the North Building's main convention floor, a deck is accessible by stairs on either side; more than a few conventioneers have strolled up there for a little light necking.

Between the North and East Buildings, a long corridor offers some cozy corners. One is at the exit to the Soldier Field parking lot; another comes at the angle where eastbound turns to southbound, near one of the picturesque blow-ups of Illinois scenes. Or gaze out the window walls at Lake Shore Drive traffic and, when you're sufficiently oblivious, kiss right in front of passers-by.

As you enter the East Building from the North Building, notice the secluded nook under the escalator you just got off. A little beyond that check out the locker area, where low walls can provide privacy. On the mezzanine level, just to the left of the escalators, an area of phone facilities offers some semibooths just big enough for two. Upstairs, at the east end of the building, there's a low-walled area with change machines, pop machines, and padded benches, as well as doors on the east wall that, if unlocked, will let you sneak outdoors. Best of all is this area's stretch of small meeting rooms, many of which usually are open and often are empty. Dim lighting and soft carpeting are a welcome change.

There. That's eleven *places. Enjoy them!*

and Michigan. The train platform is at the North Building; go to the escalator area and look for signs to the platform. Signs may be makeshift due to construction, but pay attention and they'll direct you there. The platform is outdoors, at the bottom of a steep stairway, and a must to avoid if it is deserted.

Leaving the train at Van Buren places you a couple of blocks south of the **Art Institute of Chicago** (Michigan Avenue at Adams Street; 312–443–3600). Stop in if there's time for a visit. (The Art Institute is described in greater detail in the earlier chapter "Art and Soul: The Art Institute and More.") Or stay on the train to Randolph Street, and you'll emerge at the **Chicago Cultural Center** (78 East Washington Street; 312–346–3278). This civic treasure, noted for its Tiffany light fixtures, once was the downtown library; now it holds a daily schedule of programs and exhibits and is home to the **Museum of Broadcast Communications** (open from 10:00 A.M. to 4:30 P.M. Monday through Saturday, and noon to 5:00 P.M. Sunday; 312–629–6000).

DINNER

If you're in the mood for dinner, right across Michigan Avenue is **La Strada Ristorante** (151 North Michigan Avenue; 312–565–2200), an elegant, New York–style Italian restaurant where reservations are a must, and entrees range from about $12 to about $28. Or you might prefer to cab about a mile north on Michigan to such top-of-the-line spots as the seafood lovers' **Cape Cod Room** (140 East Walton Place, in the Drake Hotel; 312–787–2200) or the **Ritz-Carlton** (160 East Pearson, in the Ritz-Carlton Hotel; 312–266–1000). There's even a bargain to be had at the **Ritz-Carlton Cafe,** which offers a daily three-course menu for an amazing $21 per person.

Still have some energy left? Take the El or a cab up to **Pops for Champagne** (2934 North Sheffield Avenue; 773–472–1000), a delightful wine bar that offers dinner by appetizer and, most nights, live jazz. You needn't spend much here to have a great time, especially if the weather is conducive to sitting outdoors in the garden. If the weather's that friendly, you may want to take an after-dinner stroll in the neighborhood as well.

Classic Chicago Couples: Oprah and Steadman

Talk about broadcast communications: Here's a power couple. Oprah Winfrey, of course, is one of the nation's richest women, wildly successful in her television talk show and Harpo production company. Her fiancé, sports promoter Steadman Graham, is a terrifically handsome former athlete who is pretty darn successful himself. There is no rush to the altar for these two grown-ups, nicknamed "steady-as-you-go" for their long, long courtship and engagement. It works for them—so here's to love before marriage.

ASIAN APPRECIATION WEEKEND

If you and your companion love the thrill of travel, you're in the right place. One of the wonderful things about Chicago is its incredible ethnic diversity. While this is more and more true of other cities nationwide, Chicago's ethnic angle is special. Here, there's some sort of critical mass that allows immigrants from all over the world to thrive while retaining their identities, customs, and languages. I've seen it among Poles, Hispanics, Chinese, Italians—you name it, there's a neighborhood grocery catering to it and parents praying that their children will continue to treasure it.

The Asian portion of this ethnic territory is especially fascinating because it's more than immigrants clinging to home. It's Japanese businessmen who crave the familiar and have the means to pay for it. It's generations of Chinese who have created a community so independent and successful, its firehouse and banks and street signs carry Chinese characters as well as English. It's Vietnamese, Thais, Laotians, Koreans, and others pursuing the American dream by way of little restaurants where one family member—the one waiting tables—speaks English.

Asian Chicago is a great place to visit and to share the excitement of exploring another culture together. Here's how to go about it.

Practical notes: Although this itinerary's destinations are accessible by public transportation and cabs, it's more practical to use a car to reach the Chicago Botanic Garden in Glencoe and the two Evanston locations. And it should be pointed out that the exoticness of Asian

Chicago is as seen through the eyes of a couple who are not of Asian descent.

DAY ONE: AFTERNOON/EVENING

Give your Asian "travels" authenticity by booking a suite at the downtown **Hotel Nikko Chicago** (320 North Dearborn Street; 312–744–1900). Located on the north bank of the Chicago River, the Nikko is a lovely outpost of non-Western civilization—although with a thoroughly Western respect for creature comforts and such amenities as a fully equipped fitness center that even provides workout wear. The hotel's public space includes a lovely traditional garden to help you unwind, and its Japanese suite will make you feel as if you're in the hotel's namesake, the city of Nikko. Designed by a Japanese architect, the suite opens to a traditional foot-bathing space to use after you've removed your shoes. A rock garden in the hall complements the earth-tone decor and light wood throughout.

A Western-style living area is separated by sliding glass doors from a traditional, tatami-matted sitting room, where you can enjoy a private dinner or tea ceremony. Later, a Japanese housekeeper will come to the room with a futon to transform it into a bedroom. In this suite, even the bathroom is different, with a bathing and rinsing area separate from a soaking tub.

Although the suite is definitely an exotic way to leave home, hotel staff say it's almost never used by Westerners. Price could have something to do with that; the Japanese suite goes for a cool $750 a night, although the Nikko's $2,500 presidential suite makes its

Romance at a Glance

♥ *Book a posh Japanese suite at the Hotel Nikko.*

♥ *Visit the hotel's sake bar; go Vietnamese or Chinese for dinner, or relax in your own private tea room.*

♥ *Stroll through the Chicago Botanic Garden's Japanese Garden.*

♥ *Enjoy a sushi lunch at Kuni.*

♥ *Relax with a ohashiatsu massage.*

♥ *Try Thai food at Arun, one of the city's finest restaurants.*

♥ *Get mellow with the Nikko's jazz brunch.*

♥ *Visit a Buddhist Sunday-morning service.*

♥ *Browse Belmont Avenue's Asian shops.*

Japanese counterpart look like a bargain. But weekend packages should allow you to spend the night for as little as $239, so be sure to check on this.

Once you're settled, make a predinner visit to **Benkay's Sake Bar** (312–836–5490), a new addition to the Nikko's dining room. This unique spot offers a couple dozen variations on Japan's ancient rice wine, and the staff is very nice about helping you choose what to sample. These little glasses do add up—in their effect as well as their prices, which range from about $8.00 to about $24.00—but you can stave off that woozy feeling with fortification grilled right before your eyes. Small portions of fish, meat, and vegetables run about $4.00 to $8.00 a la carte, or you can spend $21.00 to $46.00 for a full meal.

Dinner—Option 1

Another way to eat authentically at the Nikko is in **Benkay** itself, where you can book your very own private tearoom. Here, you'll be served by a waitress in a kimono, bringing one artful plateful after another. If you don't exactly recognize everything, be brave; this is what you came for. You'll never know whether you *really* like sushi until you try it!

After dinner, you might feel like getting out and about. You're in a great location to stroll along the riverbank, and a couple of blocks west of the Nikko, you'll find one of the best spots around to steal a kiss—at 321 North La Salle Street, immediately north and east of the bridge spanning the river at La Salle.

Staying at the Nikko places you near plenty of nightlife, in which you can give yourselves over to the appreciation of American music that flourishes all over the world, including Asia. There's jazz at **Andy's** (11 East Hubbard Street; 312–642–6805), an institution among those who work in the area. Weekend evenings, the crowd comes in especially for the music, which goes on till after midnight at a modest cover charge (and a two-drink minimum on Saturday). Or go a little north to **Blue Chicago** (736 North Clark Street; 312–751–2433), a slice of the South Side where many local veterans perform. Despite its location, Blue Chicago doesn't feel like uptown, which is its appeal. Music starts at 9:00 P.M.; again, cover charges vary.

Dinner—Option 2

A completely different way to spend your evening is exploring one of Asian Chicago's ethnic enclaves, the area that has evolved into Little Vietnam. This stretch of several blocks along Argyle Street, right in the middle of the tough Uptown neighborhood, is a brightly lit, reasonably safe, bustling oasis of restaurants, grocers, and little storefront businesses. One of the best restaurants is **Hau Giang** (1104-06 West Argyle Street; 312–275–8691), where the decor is minimal, the better to focus on the food, and you'll have to bring your own beer or wine (from the liquor store down the block). If you're familiar with Vietnamese food, you know your hotness tolerance; if not, try spring rolls, satays, and a low-intensity beef, shrimp, or chicken entree. Or ask your server for help; their English is fine and they're very pleasant, although the efficiency level varies from speedy to snail-like. Relax and concentrate on Hau Giang's oh-so-reasonable prices, which make it difficult to hit $50 for two.

My own favorite Vietnamese restaurant is a bit north of the Little Vietnam neighborhood. **Song-Huong** (5424 North Broadway Avenue; 773–271–6702), another storefront that lacks a liquor license (there's a big Jewel-Osco grocery store across Broadway and a block or so south) as well as Western-style speedy service. But it's a family place, and the people are nice, so get a cozy table near the wall and spend your down time chatting. A thorough reading of the menu will take awhile, with its many selections of fish, seafood, and meats. One surefire choice is catfish in a clay pot—and you won't find curried frog legs everywhere. Even if you go with more conventional choices, get some lime iced tea to wash it down. Dinner probably won't top $40 for the two of you.

For a Chinese dinner, try **Mei Shung** (5511 North Broadway Avenue; 773–728–5778), where the menu encompasses Taiwanese specialties as well as the more familiar Mandarin dishes. This is the place to try tofu (c'mon, park your attitude at the door), which is prepared with coriander and a zippy oyster sauce. I like the basil chicken, always a safe choice, but why not enlist your server's help in exploring the menu's more exotic selections? Mei Shung, like the Vietnamese places described here, has no liquor license but you're welcome to bring your own bottle. Here, again, prices are relatively low at about $30 or $40 for two, and you'll do well to take a patient attitude toward leisurely paced service.

Wherever you go for dinner, allow some time to browse through the grocery stores on Argyle Street. They're full of foodstuffs you probably never heard of; my Vietnamese sister-in-law makes a beeline here whenever she visits from her Florida home. Afterward, head back toward the Nikko and, perhaps, one of the nightlife spots mentioned earlier.

DAY TWO: MORNING/AFTERNOON

Breakfast at the Nikko's **Celebrity Cafe** (312–836–5499) can be as Western as you want to be, so stop in for fortification as you head out for a day at the **Chicago Botanic Garden** (Lake-Cook Road at Interstate 94, Glencoe; 847–835–5440). About 30 miles and a world away from downtown, this serene expanse of flora is a wonderful way to escape whatever you want to escape. In keeping with the weekend's Asian theme, you'll find a true respite in its Sansho-En garden, a three-island Japanese enclave.

Briefly, here's a bit of the garden's symbolism. Its pine trees represent long life, its lanterns represent water, and the rounded lines of its sculpted bushes stand in for hills and mountains. Even the rocks and gravel have meaning: Boulders represent islands, and gravel is arranged around them to suggest the motion of waves breaking on shore. And one of the islands represents Horaijima, the island of everlasting happiness reserved for the immortals. (Including you and your sweetheart, of course!)

There's much more at the Botanic Garden, including a lovely English garden. But don't feel you must come during the summer. The Japanese garden keeps its character year-round, its evergreens pruned for winter with an eye to helping them catch falling snow. I've been here on bleak fall days, when there's neither foliage nor snow, and still felt much better for it. Admission is free, but parking is $4.00; the garden is open from 10:00 A.M. to 5:00 P.M. Saturday and

Sunday, 8:00 A.M. till sunset on weekdays. You needn't leave the garden to get some lunch, although the Gateway Center is more gift shop than gourmet haven.

Lunch

If you prefer to eat Asian, head back south from Glencoe toward Evanston, the first suburb north of Chicago, where several Chinese and Japanese restaurants can give you a dandy lunch. **Kuni's** (511 Main Street, Evanston; 847–328–2004) offers some of the area's best sushi, sashimi, and maki. Noodle dishes are good, too, if you're not up to speed on the raw stuff. For maximum variety, order an assortment plate and share. Kuni's is open for lunch every day except Sunday and Tuesday (although dinner is available on Sunday), and prices, again, are reasonable: definitely less than $40 total for a very substantial lunch for the two of you.

❧❧

Evanston also is the home of **Ohashiatsu Chicago** (825 Chicago Avenue, Evanston; 847-864-1130), where you can experience another Asian pleasure—the ohashiatsu massage. Combining Asian medicine with a gentle touch, this technique aims to achieve balance among body, mind, and spirit while tuning up your energy flow and balance. To schedule an appointment and learn more about ohashiatsu, call and leave your telephone number, your call will be returned.

When all your kinks are worked out, head back into the city and a dress-for-dinner stop at your room before dinner. In fact, now that you're practically stress-free, a nap might even be in order before you strike out for the North Side, where an out-of-the-way Albany Park restaurant will give you a memorable Thai meal.

Dinner

Arun's (4156 North Kedzie Avenue; 773–539–1909) isn't just a local favorite. It's one of the nation's finest Thai restaurants, offering regional specialties that go way beyond the satay circuit. Ask for help in putting together a dinner of compatible choices, but do include the wonderful crepes and consider a curry. (I'm not a big curry fan, but here, it's great.) If you like hot, try one of my favorite Thai dishes, chicken soup made with coconut milk and lemongrass; or stay on the mild side with fish or seafood. Even the rice is special here, its jasmine scent giving another note to everything. You *won't* have to bring your own liquor here; try the Singha beer, which goes beautifully with this complex food.

Like any fine restaurant, Arun's is pricey—dinner could creep into three digits, depending on how much you order—but it's one of a kind. Monday is the day off here, and make sure you reserve well in advance.

DAY THREE: MORNING

Brunch

Roll out of bed for brunch at the hotel's Celebrity Cafe, where smooth jazz will wake you gently. Chicago's foremost New Age radio station broadcasts live from here on Sunday mornings, and the food is dandy, too. A fixed price of $36 per person covers an extensive selection of appetizers, breads, desserts, and (starting from 11:00 A.M., and if you're not sushi-ed out) a sushi buffet where you can sample many varieties. An entree is included, too. Even if you're staying at the hotel, you'll want to make a reservation for the brunch, which is popular among the public as well as Nikko guests.

A different Sunday morning option—and a good choice if you'd like to go deeper into the Asian spirit than a surface-skimming weekend—is joining the nonmembers who are welcome to visit Sunday services at the **Midwest Buddhist Temple** (435 West Menomonee Street; 773–943–7801). The morning starts early, with a meditation service at 8:00 A.M. The service contains several sections, with sitting, walking, and a brief talk, then a question-and-answer period. At 10:00 A.M., there's a service proper in English, which is followed by a Japanese-language service at 11:00 A.M. Be sure to dress appropriately—a skirt, dress, or nice-looking slacks for women, neat slacks for men. Shorts, sport shirts, and similarly casual attire are out.

Afterward, continue a couple of miles farther north to visit the Asian shops along Belmont Avenue. (If you want to take the El, the Fullerton stop is a few blocks west and north of the temple, and you'll be right where you want to be when you exit at Belmont.) The largest is **Toguri Gifts and Mercantile Co.** (851 West Belmont Avenue; 773–929–3500), where the staff is friendly and chatty, and the merchandise is authentic. Check out various kinds of Japanese slippers, including the ones that you wear anchored between second and third toes. They're actually comfortable, and you can get special cotton socks to accommodate them. One item to check out is a Salux "beauty skin cloth," a yard of textured nylon that seems expensive at $4.95. But take a chance and take it home. It's the greatest for scrubbing your back in the shower, as you'll learn if you buy one and try it on each other.

Other intriguing stuff: beautiful paper kites in many sizes, all brightly decorated and ready to fly; delicate porcelain tea sets and sake sets; all sorts of incense; pretty wrapping paper and stationery; exotic candies and cookies; and all sorts of children's accessories decorated with Hello Kitty, the wide-eyed feline that's more insipid than Barney. It's all pretty cool and fun to look at.

Lunch

When you get hungry, stroll north on Clark Street for lunch at **Noodle Noodle** (3475 North Clark Street; 773–871–2312), where what you get is in the name. Ramen soup is delicious, as are soba and udon noodles in soup or sauce. Grilled fish and curries are good, too, and again, the price is right—no more than $20 for a two-person lunch. Note that Noodle Noodle is closed on Monday and doesn't serve lunch on Saturday.

To sample yet another Asian cuisine, and take in another experience that lets you know you're not in Kansas any more, go west to the major intersection of Lawrence Avenue and Western Avenue, which is in the Lincoln Square neighborhood. Then go a few blocks farther

China in Chicago

If you only have time for a brief visit to Chicago's Asian community, head for the Near South Side corner of Cermak Road and Wentworth Avenue. You'll know you've found Chinatown when you see the pagoda-like buildings and huge, red and green gate spanning Wentworth. Prepare to be startled by the feeling that you've suddenly landed in another country. From street signs to restaurant menus, architecture to ambient music, absolutely everything here is Chinese.

You'll enjoy strolling south on Wentworth, browsing through souvenir shops and comparing restaurant menus posted in windows. As you explore, you'll realize that Chinatown is more than a tourist destination. This compact, self-contained neighborhood holds banks, schools, grocery stores, churches, a firehouse, dozen of businesses, and hundred of homes. Sure, it's touristy—but it's also a genuine community in which you can live long and comfortably without speaking English.

*Restaurants are Chinatown's major attraction, so arrive hungry if possible! The most spiffy restaurant here is **Emperor's Choice** (2238 South Wentworth Street, 312–225–8800), where the table linens are linen and the service is pleasant. Try the lobster-centered dinner for two, which will make you feel quite sumptuous for a thrifty $40.*

If you'd like souvenirs that outclass T-shirts, look for jade. There's plenty here, in designs you might not see anywhere else, and the prices are good. Coolest souvenir: If each of you has at least one pierced ear, buy and split a pair of jade earrings!

west to the **Korean Restaurant** (2659 West Lawrence Avenue; 773–878–2095), a nondescript spot where decor is hardly the point. This round-the-clock restaurant serves a huge variety of Korean specialties, from grilled meats and fish to still more selections you won't know how to pronounce. But try anyway, especially if you notice something you'd like that can be cooked at your table on a gas grill. You'll get plenty of food at a minimal price—not more than $20 or so total—but remember, the Korean Restaurant doesn't take credit cards.

Three days and two evenings

LOVE IN THE HOT ZONE

A TROPICS-INSPIRED WEEKEND

*W*hether you do it in the heat of summer or the chill of winter, a warmed-up weekend in Chicago is the next best thing to visiting the tropics—on four continents! The city's Hispanic and Indian populations each support a vibrant cultural life that welcomes others to join in; so does a sizable community of islanders, Jamaican and others, whose special foods and hypnotic music have seduced many a Northerner. Chicago has Turkish steam baths, Middle Eastern nightclubs, Ethiopian restaurants, and more. It's a melting pot indeed, one in which each ingredient retains its own zesty flavor. Whether you revel in your own ethnic link to one of these cultures or delight in the exploration of ethnicities outside your own, this round-the-world, all-over-town weekend will heat up your all-American love life.

Practical notes: This itinerary takes in some far-flung destinations, so it's most practical to drive. If you prefer cabs, they should be plentiful.

DAY ONE: EVENING

Stay in one of the city's hottest areas, Wicker Park/Bucktown, at the bed and breakfast favored by many regulars. **Maud Travels** (book through Bed & Breakfast Chicago, 312–951–0080) consists of several snug rooms in a building that dates from shortly after the Great Chicago Fire of

Romance at a Glance

♥ *Check into a cozy bed and breakfast.*

♥ *Nibble predinner Mediter-ranean tapas; dance the night away at Tania's.*

♥ *Check out a Caribbean bakery for breakfast.*

♥ *Luxuriate in a Turkish steam bath; enjoy the hot Wicker Park/Bucktown area (or a siesta!).*

♥ *Eat dinner with your fingers at Addis Abeba Ethiopian restaurant.*

♥ *"Lively up yourself" with reggae at the Wild Hare; then applaud Al Khayam's belly dancers.*

♥ *Sample South Asian specialties at the India House brunch.*

1871. Even older is the owner's frame cottage, immediately behind the B&B building. "The folks at the Chicago Historical Society tell me this house went up the weekend after the fire," chuckles Bob, who is his own "secret weapon" for attracting and keeping repeat visitors. He's a genial guy who works with wayward kids, knows the neighborhood inside out, and loves to help his guests plan their vacation. Be sure to ask for the room with a Jacuzzi; you're going to need it after all the dancing you'll do!

Dinner

Head out to begin the evening with a drink and a nibble at **Tuttaposto** (646 North Franklin Street; 312–943–6262), where the food is healthful, yet so delicious that a confirmed carnivore couldn't complain. (Trust me, it's true; I've eaten here with one!) Even the smell is enticing, with wood-burning grills going strong to turn out flavor-packed meats and veggies. Split an antipasto platter, wash it down with a drink or two, and your appetite will be whetted for the night ahead at a very modest price (maybe $10, plus drinks, total).

When you're ready to move on to a late dinner—in the tropic-zone manner, surely not before nine—head for **Tania's** (2659 North Milwaukee Avenue; 773–235–7120), a pan-Hispanic, white-tablecloth restaurant that's not too stuck-up to get down and dance. The mostly Cuban menu is large and varied, with excellent, familiar steaks and fish as well as authentic dishes, and dinner is served with considerable flourish on oversize plates. Expect to spend about $80 total for a full meal for two.

✺✺✺

Then work it off on the dance floor! This is the sort of place Hispanic families might choose for a celebration that will last into the night. Salsa, merengue, tango—you name it, someone's ready to do it, perhaps inspired by the bright neon signs suggesting dances by name. Of course, the live band that plays most nights might have something to do with the dancers' enthusiasm. The enticing thing about Tania's is its seamless blend of sophisticated service and uninhibited fun. Jump in and dance; you'll be glad you did.

DAY TWO: MORNING

Breakfast

Start the day—not too early, of course—with coffee at your B&B kitchen, then, if you're feeling energetic, hop in the car and head for the border. The northern border, that is, where the **Caribbean American Baking Company** (1539 West Howard Street; 773–761–0700) welcomes the area's islanders and mainlanders alike with Jamaican breads and pastries. Guava tarts are a yummy breakfast, or for something more substantial, try the hugely popular beef patties. They're a heavier, spicier version of the more familiar Cornish pasty—a thick dough encasing a pungent ground-beef or vegetarian filling. At just a little more than a dollar each, they're worth a try and potentially addictive.

✺✺✺

You might enjoy exploring this polyglot area, where practically everyone seems to be from an exotic homeland—Pakistan, Africa, Haiti, or somewhere you can only guess at. Keep in mind that it's off the beaten track for out-of-towners who *don't* live here, so you'll want to be big-city careful.

Back south, prepare to relax at **Division Street Russian Baths** (1916 West Division Street; 773 384 9671), where men have gone to escape home and hearth since 1906. Happily, the baths have moved into the twentieth century with the addition of facilities and hours for women, who are welcome on Wednesday, Friday, Saturday, and Sunday from 8:00 A.M. till 10:00 P.M. In the only "hot room" of its kind in the city, a large granite stone keeps dry heat going; there's a vapor room to improve the skin, a whirlpool for tired muscles, and massages (from masseuse or masseur) to promote relaxation.

Visitors pay $13.00, which includes a refundable $1.00 deposit on a lock for the locker where you'll store your clothes. Two towels, a sheet, and soap are provided. You'll find diversity aplenty in your fellow bathers, who may be Russian, Hispanic, African-American, or young Americans who live in Ukrainian Village, the regentrifying neighborhood you're in.

The only drawback is that men and women are separated while in the baths, so you'll have some time apart. When you get back together, you might want to spend some time exploring the area around your B&B, which is its own kind of "hot zone"—a neighborhood where relatively cheap housing has attracted the artists who then attract other, more moneyed residents. If you happen to come during September, try to catch the Around the Coyote festival of local art and artists.

DAY TWO: EVENING

Dinner

Or maybe you'd like to follow the time-honored tradition of hot countries everywhere by taking an afternoon siesta. Either way, when it gets to be dinnertime, tackle a new kind of dining at **Addis Abeba** (3521 North Clark Street; 773–929–9383), where Ethiopian food offers both new flavors and the delightful experience of eating with your fingers. People often try to come here with a group, the better to sample as much as possible, but don't hesitate to be adventurous in a group of just the two of you. If more exotic selections seem a trifle too offbeat, stick with vegetarian entrees from the inexpensive-to-moderate menu.

⋘⊙⋙

To dance another night away, stroll down the block to the **Wild Hare & Singing Armadillo Frog Sanctuary** (3530 North Clark Street; 773–327–4273), a Chicago institution for folks who love reggae—and that's not just Jamaicans. The Wild Hare is crowded nightly with fans of this hypnotic, languid beat that's perhaps the easiest in the world to dance to. Cover charges vary, depending on the entertainment; weekend evenings there's usually a band. Let your bodies sway to the rhythms of the islands. (Don't be surprised if you notice the distinct aroma of Jamaica's most famous—if illicit—cash crop.)

To wrap up your evening in astonishing style, head a little north and west to **Al Khayam** (2326 West Foster Avenue; 773–334–0000), where things don't really get going until after midnight. When they do, your senses will be awakened by a Middle Eastern mix of music, dance, and drink, highlighted by a belly dancer and singing that might be in Arabic, Hindi, Kurdish, Greek, or Assyrian. You can join in the dancing if you like; don't bother being self-conscious, but don't feel you have to dance, either.

DAY THREE: MORNING/AFTERNOON

Brunch

Do you have to be told to sleep in today? Probably not, so brunch is a natural instead of breakfast. Sample one more exotic region by driving to the Devon Avenue Indian neighborhood, a center of Indian and Pakistani life for the entire city. At **India House** (2548 West Devon Avenue; 773–338–2929), Sunday brunch is served from 11:30 A.M. till 3:00 P.M. and includes food and drink you may not be able to pronounce, let alone recognize—so feel free to ask the staff for guidance. Plenty of vegetarian dishes are available, as are mango shakes (yum!) and the yogurt drink, *lassi,* for the health-conscious. There's also chicken, seafood, and meat if you're up for a full meal.

Suit Up

*Sure, you adore your sweetheart's bod—but chances are, he or she is acutely aware of some ghastly flaws that are (the thinking goes) all too obvious in swimwear. Soothe that sensitive self-image with a super hot-zone gift: a custom-made bathing suit. Custom suits are available from the **Beach Club Ltd.** (15 East Chestnut Street; 312–654–8766), and the cost isn't as steep as you might expect. To arrange a gift certificate or a fitting appointment, call the shop.*

After brunch step outside, look around, and you'll see that once again, you're in a fascinating neighborhood. Venture into a "sari palace" and look through the hundreds of bolts of exquisite fabrics, perhaps choosing something irresistible for yourself or your partner. Get yourselves buzzed into a jewelry store and find stunning necklaces, ankle bracelets, and earrings, intricately worked in twenty-two-karat gold and precious stones. And don't miss **Patel Bros.** (2610 West Devon Avenue; 773–262–7777), a grocery that could change your life in the kitchen. Floor-to-ceiling shelves in an entire wall hold neat stocks of so many spices, your nose will spin. More varieties of rice and lentils than you ever dreamed possible are here, too, as well as canned goods you won't find at the supermarket back home. If you enjoy cooking together, be sure to look through an Indian cookbook before you come, and bring a shopping list. On the way out, be sure to pick up a purple can of delicious passion-fruit soda.

FOR MORE ROMANCE

Back in the 1950s and 1960s, the only "hot zone" *most* Americans knew was Polynesian—not the South Sea islands themselves, but a playful blend of Hawaiian and South Pacific influences that you could visit in stateside restaurants and nightclubs. The theme still has enough fans to keep a few Polynesian places thriving, including a couple in the Chicago area. One is about 40 minutes from downtown—**Kona Kai** (at the Marriott O'Hare, 8535 West Higgins Road, Rosemont; 847–693–4444), is a restaurant whose basically Chinese menu is upstaged by wicked tropical cocktails and a hula-dancing, fire-tossing floor show featuring the Barefoot Hawaiians and Sonny Kuni and his Polynesian Revue. Sure, it's hokey, but where else around Chicagoland are you going to wear your matching Hawaiian shirts in February?

ITINERARY 30
Three days and two nights

CITY SLICKERS' WESTERN WEEKEND

Yee-ha! Chicago's a big city, but it's got a country heart—if you know where to look. And the funny thing is, you'll find it all over town.

A friend once told me that she liked Chicago because it's a place where you can re-invent yourself without having to leave town. If you've ever harbored a secret wish to be a cowpoke (and what red-blooded kid didn't?), this here's the place, right now's the time, and look who you've got to ride with!

So git along and saddle up for a weekend that a little bit country, a little bit Western, a little bit Mexican, and a whole lotta fun. Bring your drawl, if you have one. If not, just bring the sweetheart of your personal rodeo. Y'all are all you need anyway.

Practical Notes: You'll need a car for some of this weekend's stops, most notably the rides to Fitzgerald's and South Forty. City destinations can be reached by cab, but not those two.

DAY ONE: EVENING

Luckily for all us comfort-lovin' city folk, this countrified weekend doesn't mean tossing the ol' bedroll on the ground in Grant Park. You can keep to the Western theme (at least nominally) at the **Best Western Inn of Chicago** (162 East Ohio; 312–787–3100). Located in the heart of city-slicker land on the posh Gold Coast, just off Michigan Avenue—the Best

Western dates back to the early years of the century, when it was the St. Clair, one of those independent little hotels that regular guests treasure. Refurbished for today, with cool grays, glowing greens, and health-club facilities next door, it retains a friendly ambience and even friendlier rates (starting around $85, or $140 for a suite). A sibling hotel, **Best Western River North Hotel** (125 West Ohio; 312–467–0800), is just west of State Street in the fashionable district from which it takes its name. With similar rates and accommodations (River North does boast its own indoor pool), either offers a comfortable, reasonably priced home from which to explore the West—Chicago style.

Romance at a Glance

♥ *Stay on the Gold Coast—at the Best Western.*

♥ *Dine at Bub City Crabshack; line-dance at Whiskey River.*

♥ *Try a Mexican brunch at Frontera.*

♥ *Pick up some new duds at Alcala Western Wear.*

♥ *Catch a country crooner at Schubas.*

♥ *Chow down at Brother Jimmy's barbecue brunch.*

♥ *Go riding at South Forty.*

Dinner

Once you're settled into your accommodations, head out for a night on the town—in this case, in the fashionable yet varied Clybourn Corridor neighborhood. Dinner is a casual affair at **Bub City Crabshack & Bar BQ** (901 West Weed Street; 312–266–1200), but don't be fooled by the funky affectations— this is first-rate grub. Shellfish and seafood with a Southern drawl are a big draw, but give some thought to the highly regarded Texas-style barbecue, too. Prices are moderate, so dinner shouldn't total more than $50 for both of you.

Proceed to work off that barbecue in style at **Whiskey River** (1997 North Clybourn Avenue; 773–528–3400), which calls itself "Chicago's authentic country nightclub." Two-stepping is a way of life here, so if you know your stuff, prepare to show it. Lessons are offered, too, so even novices can jump in and give those fancy steps a whirl. The club presents live music several times a month, occasionally a well-known name such as Jerry Jeff Walker, and it's worth checking on whether a show is booked during the spell when you're planning to visit.

DAY TWO: MORNING

Brunch

Start your day with a brunch to tell the folks back home about. As you'll learn at the **Frontera Grill** (445 North Clark Street; 312–661–1434), Mexican food is much more than margaritas and mole. Chef-owner Rick Bayless is a former student of anthropology who lost his objectivity by falling in love with the food of the nation he studied. With his wife, Deann, Bayless has become one of the nation's most accomplished students of Mexican food; the couple have made Frontera and its fine-dining sibling, Topolobambo, destinations for serious connoisseurs from all over.

Saturday brunch goes on from 10:30 A.M. till 2:30 P.M., and since Frontera accepts reservations only for groups of five or more, you may find a wait. Be cheerful about it and your reward will be subtle, delicious dishes you'll never even hear of beyond the villages of Mexico. Frontera is one of those restaurants you can tell friends back home about, and if they know anything about restaurants, they'll be impressed with your sophisticated selection. Better yet is the modest price: Expect brunch for two to run about $30.

DAY TWO: AFTERNOON

Even the roughest rider gets a kick out of approaching **Alcala Western Wear** (1733 West Armitage Avenue; 773–226–0152), where the full-size horse out front lets you know this is the place. Browsing indoors, you'll find absolutely everything for the well-dressed cowpoke of either sex. The aisles are filled with boots and hats, fancy shirts and real jeans, silver accessories, and leather everything. There's genuine riding gear, too, and it's Western, not English—chaps,

Potter and Bertha Palmer: Chicago was not long past its own days as a wild, woolly Western outpost when Mr. and Mrs. Potter Palmer became its first and perhaps finest "power" couple. Potter was an enormously influential real estate baron; his Palmer House hotel carries on today, and he was the first to build a palatial home on what eventually became Lake Shore Drive—still the finest address in town. His equal in moving and shaking was Bertha Honore Palmer, who was one of the prime organizers of the World's Columbian Exposition in 1893 and an early fan of French Impressionism, especially the work of Claude Monet and of her own friend, Mary Cassatt. If you go to the Art Institute (one of her great beneficiaries), look for the portrait of her that I always think of as "the fairy princess." And by the way, in the twenty years between her husband's death and her own, this twinkling beauty more than doubled the fortune Potter had left.

spurs, short crops, saddles, and more. Don't miss the toreador outfits in the rear and the glass display cases throughout the store, in which turquoise jewelry and elaborate belt buckles are artfully arranged around real rattlesnakes (dead, thank you).

Another authentic aspect to this Tex-Mex haven is its bilingual whoopin' and hollerin'. There's no problem if you speak only English, but Spanish is at home here, too. And nobody minds if you want to spend your time just looking.

As you head back to the Best Western temporary homestead, you might take some time to enjoy all-American art at the **Terra Museum of American Art** (664 North Michigan Avenue; 312–664–3939). Or check out the hallway near the lower-level cafeteria at the **Art Institute of Chicago** (Michigan Avenue at Adams Street; 312–443–3500), where several examples of Frederic Remington's Western work are on display.

DAY TWO: EVENING

Dinner

This is a day whose only appropriate dinner is a succulent steak, and Chicago—a meat-and-potatoes town if ever there was one—does not disappoint. There are several top-notch steakhouses not far from the hotel, and your main decision is likely to be based on atmosphere.

The traditional steak house is a rowdy place, so if you prefer somewhat quieter surroundings, make reservations at **Eli's the Place for Steak** (215 East Chicago Avenue; 312–642–1393). Eli's is a Chicago institution, the kind of place that pops up regularly in the newspaper gossip columns. From local socialites to Sinatra himself, it's a favorite among discerning carnivores. Prices are reasonable: a sirloin will run about $28, and many a regular wouldn't dream of skipping a side of potato pancakes. Save room for dessert, too; Eli's cheesecake is famous all over town.

Another institution is **Morton's of Chicago** (1050 North State Street; 312–266–4820), where part of the draw is maître d' Raki Mehra, a smooth professional who, when asked, can help assure your evening will be special. The steaks alone would do it, of course; Morton's stood fast during the lean years when steaks were out of fashion (actually, the Morton's crowd never noticed steaks were out of fashion), and its gigantic double porterhouse is still a standard. This forty-eight-ounce stunner costs about $60 and, need it be mentioned, definitely will feed both of you.

A newer spot that's favored by the stretch-limo set (meaning you just might spot a hungry celeb) is **Gibsons Bar & Steak House** (1028 North Rush Street; 312–266–8999). While hardly a soothing experience, the hustling, bustling Gibsons delivers a superb sirloin at about $60 for two. If your romance is rock-solid, get a side order of garlicky sauteed spinach.

❧

With a belly-bustin' steak dinner finished, your major decision for the remainder of the evening is whether you're up for a drive. If so, go west on Interstate 290 about 20 minutes to the suburb of Berwyn—the home of one of the area's very best music clubs. **Fitzgerald's** (6615 Roosevelt Road, Berwyn; 708–788–2118) has provided countrified Chicagoans with a steady stream of shows by many of the current crop of Texan singer-songwriters, including Butch Hancock and Jimmie Dale Gilmore. The club's eclectic booking policy embraces jazz and some rock, too, so check on who's booked during your stay. Tickets are in the $10–$15 range and often are available in advance. Fitzgerald's *is* a bar, though, so if you want to sit right up front, you should arrive early.

Prefer to stay in the city limits? There are plenty of places to hear a twangy guitar not far from the Near North Side steak houses mentioned earlier. One is the remarkable **Cubby Bear** (1059 West Addison; 773–327–1662), a bar kitty-corner from Wrigley Field that has showcased acts ranging from Johnny Cash to Jo Carol Pierce. It's crowded and can be smoky, but imagine seeing the Man in Black up close in a neighborhood bar. Tickets to that show were $30 apiece, but prices that high are rare. Like Fitzgerald's, the Cubby Bear books a wide range of acts, so you'll want to check on who's playing when you visit.

Several other clubs book a broad range of country and western, rockabilly, Tex-Mex, and similar musical styles. One great spot is **Schubas** (3159 North Southport Avenue; 773–525–2508), a friendly bar that is favored by many discerning fans of country and its relations, and where cover charges won't set you back much. Check on who's playing, and be open-minded. You may be lucky enough to catch a performer you both adore, or maybe you'll take a chance on someone you don't even recognize. Either way, it could be an experience that gives you and your country cutie a memory to treasure.

DAY THREE: MORNING/AFTERNOON

Brunch

Skip the hardtack-and-bad-coffee part of down-home livin' and start your day with a Sunday-mornin' barbecue brunch. **Brother Jimmy's BBQ** (2909 North Sheffield Avenue;

773–528–0888) opens at 11:00 A.M. on Sundays to serve geographically distinguished barbecue, Northern being sweet-sauced and Southern vinegary. There's also fried chicken and, of course, *good* coffee to wash down a pecan-pie dessert. Brother Jimmy's is sometimes crowded and can be casual to a fault, but it's a great place to get your rib fix at reasonable rates. In fact, if you want to pull up a chair and stay put, a Sunday all-you-can-eat deal covers ribs and beer for just $18 per person.

eૐ૭

Or tear yourself away from that barbecue and head out (about an hour's drive) to the western suburb of Streamwood. Here you can saddle up for real at **South Forty** (Bode Road at Route 59, Streamwood; 630-830-4895), Set near the extensive recreational holdings of the Cook County Forest Preserve, South Forty is a stable that rents horses for guided trail rides along the forest preserve's system of trails. The stable is as friendly to the tenderfoot as the experienced rider, says stable hand Jenny Eisman. "If you don't want to run or gallop, you don't have to," she says. "We'll make sure the ride is nice and easy if that's what people want."

South Forty is open from 9:00 A.M. till 5:00 P.M. daily (weather permitting; no riding in the rain), and guides usually take riders out in groups. The least busy times are weekdays, Eisman says, and early arrivals are less rushed, too. No reservations are accepted, but guides will take a couple out by themselves if a group hasn't assembled within a reasonable period after you arrive. An hour-long ride costs $16.00 per person, with an extra $2.00 fee for an annual equestrian license (similar to a fishing license).

For More Romance

If you're in the area during fall or winter, and can pull together at least thirteen other adventurous people, take 'em on a hayride or Christmas-wagon ride at South Forty. Hayrides are offered through the fall, for a minimum of fifteen people at $6.00 each. And Christmas wagons, Eisman says, are "basically a hayride, with a holiday theme." When you're in town to visit family and everyone needs to get out, remember: Dress warm, snuggle up, celebrate!

HAUNTINGLY ROMANTIC

HALLOWEEN WITH YOUR HONEY

*H*alloween makes everyone long for somebody to love—and hug when the lights get dim. When you're lucky enough to have each other, it's a fabulous time to seek out thrills and chills together. Here's a sampling of ways to do that.

Practical notes: A downtown hotel offers good transportation to the Far North Side and the Near South Side. Driving is a good way to go, too, but then you'll have parking fees downtown.

DAY ONE: MORNING/AFTERNOON

Check into a downtown hotel that may not be haunted—but who's to say? The **Palmer House Hilton** (17 South State Street; 312–726–7500) is the nation's oldest continuously operating hotel, and there just *have* to be a few skeletons rattling around there somewhere. Ghosts or no, you'll enjoy its red-velvet atmosphere of a bygone era. The Beaux Arts ceiling alone, restored by an artisan who also worked on the Sistine Chapel, is more of an eyeful than you'll find in many new hotels.

The Palmer House's recently redone rooms offer a cozy home away from home, and suites let you spread out in style. Also consider the deluxe Towers, which whisks guests skyward via private elevator to a Towers lobby and lounge. Continental breakfasts are free here, as are cocktail-hour hors d'oeuvres and the services of a concierge. And all the Palmer House guests have access to a fitness club featuring a pool, steam room, sauna, whirlpool, exercise equipment, and even computerized equipment to measure your body fat. Regular room rates start at $160 for a double, but ask about the special rate of $109 for a double, or $159 in the Towers (both are based on availability).

From the hotel you can take the Howard elevated train (which stops right under the Palmer House) to its terminus on Howard Street. Here, **A Lost Era** (1511 West Howard Street; 773–764–7400) is an absolute classic: an old-fashioned, slightly dusty jumble of antiques, clothing, and assorted stuff that would make a perfect setting for a suspense novel—maybe a *Bell, Book and Candle* romance involving witch and mortal.

If you and *your* mortal mate are planning to attend Halloween festivities that call for a costume, this is the place to look. There are old coats, capes, suits, dresses, accessories, shoes, even wigs and makeup. There is knowledgeable help and enough space to try on. You can rent or buy props as well as costumes, so even if you don't need a get-up this year, think ahead. Next year, after all, you might be throwing your own party.

Some people just know that a gorilla suit, not vintage duds, is what they really need. For them, **Broadway Costume** back downtown (954 West Washington Boulevard; 312–829–6400) is ready to help. Founded in 1886, Broadway does many shows' costumes and offers the wonderful extra of having seamstresses on hand to help fit what you want. Here, too, you can buy or rent, and it's worth a visit just to browse through the dozens of hats and accessories you'll find here.

If you're not into dress-up, here's a low-key Halloween project your inner children can enjoy together. Get some felt-tip markers (or small cans of black, white, and red paint, plus several little sponge brushes), a spray can of shellac, and a bunch of miniature pumpkins. Then settle down in the park for a jack-o'-lantern session. See which of you can create the scariest face, the funniest face, the face that looks most like your sweetheart. It's an entertaining, inexpensive way to play together.

Which park to pick? That depends mostly on the weather and where you're starting from. If it's pleasant and you're on the North Side, head for the magical realm of **Oz Park** (60–733 West Webster Avenue; 773–742–7898), where the entrance is marked by a statue of the Tin Man and there's even a yellow brick road. The park and trappings commemorate L. Frank Baum, who lived in Chicago while writing *The Wonderful Wizard of Oz*. Or, if you're downtown on a beautiful day, establish yourselves down by the river: specifically, on the north bank of the Chicago River, east of Michigan Avenue. This is where Sandra Bullock strolled with Jack Pullman in *While You Were Sleeping,* the Chicago-made romance in which the underdog guy gets the girl (yes!). Secluded, it's not . . . but there is the privacy city people allow each other in public. And how romantic to create your own little world here as you draw and giggle.

Lunch

Oz Park is conveniently near a good spot for lunch. The **Red Lion Pub** (2446 North Lincoln; 773–348–2695) is a restaurant-bar that calls itself "the next best thing to being in England." At Halloween time, the Red Lion's big draw is its reputation as the haunted home of a woman whose death upstairs is said to have left a lingering lilac scent. Order a burger and decide for yourselves if there's any smell but beer in this cozy pub's atmosphere.

Do the Halloween thing with a dignified touch by strolling together through one of the city's most interesting cemeteries—so interesting, in fact, that the Chicago Architecture Foundation offers tours. **Graceland Cemetery and Chapel** (4001 North Clark Street; 773–525–1105) is the resting place of many wealthy Chicagoans whose graves are nearly as ornate as their earthly homes were. Look for the beautifully decorated Getty Monument, which was designed by famed Chicago architect Louis Sullivan, and Lorado Taft's sculpture of a hooded figure, titled Eternal Silence. Money continues to talk at Graceland—and please, no Elvis jokes.

If you'd like to take a tour of the cemetery with the Chicago Architecture Foundation, call 312–922–3432 for information. If you want to go on your own, the cemetery is open daily.

⟡

Then head to the Near South Side neighborhood of Pilsen, where an artists' colony coexists with a predominantly Mexican population. Both influences are evident at the **Mexican Fine Arts Center Museum** (1852 West Nineteenth Street; 773–738–1503), which features an annual *Dia de los Muertos* (Day of the Dead) exhibit. This traditional Mexican version of All Souls' Day is celebrated on November 3, as families build *ofrendas*, or altars, that salute and/or evoke the spirit of a dead relative or friend. Of course, the spirit is welcome to pay survivors a visit; and some daring or humorous altars suggest a teasing invitation to death itself.

The museum's altars are created by artists, with a different theme each year. One year, for example, the theme was grandmothers, and it's no work to imagine how heartfelt and touching those *ofrendas* were. The show's popularity kept it in place until December as thousands of artists and regular folks came to see a sophisticated brand of folk art. Although some images look macabre to non-Mexicans—grinning skeletons are everywhere—it's an eye-opening look at another culture's attitude toward death. The museum is open from 10:00 A.M. to 5:00 P.M. Tuesday through Sunday, and admission is free.

DAY ONE: EVENING

Dinner

You'll probably want to spend some afternoon time exploring the Pilsen neighborhood and, when you're ready for dinner, to lighten up on the spooky stuff. A perfect choice, though at another point on the cultural spectrum, is **Schulien's Restaurant** (2100 West Irving Park Road; 773–478–2100), a wonderfully traditional German spot whose dark paneling holds countless photos of old-time politicians and citizens. Sports memorabilia and other city treasures are here, too, as are many connoisseur beers and a hearty menu of German fare. You can skip the schnitzel and go with a lighter broiled fish if you feel you must, but spaetzle are not to be missed. Anything simmered or braised is a good bet, too. Dinner for two will run about $60 total—but what's free is the special part of dining here. After you've finished your entrees, the house magician will visit for ten minutes or so of card tricks, coin tricks, disappearing tricks, and patter. Children adore it, and grown-ups can't resist, either.

The Irish say that the one thing the devil can't stand is laughter, so scare off the spooks by taking in a show at **Second City** (1616 North Wells Street; 773–337–3992). Over the years, this Chicago institution has nurtured many of the *Saturday Night Live* performers and writers, as well as actors and writers whose accomplishments run the cultural gamut, from Mike Nichols's highbrow directing career to later members' hit movies, such as *Ghostbusters, Animal House,* and *Caddyshack.*

Second City's improvisational approach to comedy gets a workout in the latter part of the show, and many people prefer the 11:00 P.M. shows on Friday and Saturday because they believe the later hour leads to greater wackiness. No matter what show you catch, the satire is wicked and the laughs are plentiful. Ticket prices range from $5.00 (on Mondays, for a live "best of" show spanning thirty years of sketches) to $10.50. This also is the place for an after-dinner drink while you chuckle.

DAY TWO: MORNING/AFTERNOON

Breakfast/Lunch

Make it a late breakfast or early lunch as you prepare for a full afternoon of thrills, chills, and "maybes." You'll begin the afternoon at **Goose Island Brewing** (1800 North Clybourn Avenue; 773–915–0071), where an early lunch might skip a brew but certainly includes one of the brewery's great sandwiches.

Finish up by noon, when you'll board the bus for the **Chicago Ghost Tour.** Skeptics may doubt "professional ghost-hunter" Richard Crowe, who has offered these tours for more than a decade, but there's no question he's got every local ghost story down. From Resurrection Mary—a ghostly girl often spotted hitchhiking along South Archer Avenue, trying to reach a long-ago dance—to sightings of Clarence Darrow's promised return to the spot near the Museum of Science and Industry where his ashes are scattered, Crowe is brimming with tales and possibilities.

The tour, which is offered from noon till 5:00 P.M. and from 7:00 P.M. till midnight daily during the Halloween season, covers a wide slice of the metropolitan area and costs $28 per person. Crowe reports at least one wedding uniting a couple who met on a ghost tour, and it's doubtless his stories will make you cuddle a little closer to your safe, secure sweetheart. The only snag is that tours fill quickly during October and November, so Crowe encourages people to sign up early. Write P.O. Box 557544, Chicago, IL 60655–7544 with the date you want, or call him at (708) 499–0300.

DAY TWO: EVENING

As you leave the tour, you're sure to have *more* than enough to talk about! Do it over a brew at Goose Island, which really is a must for any beer lover. Then have a wonderful dinner and bring your evening to a close under yet another spell—the kind a wonderful musician can cast. At **Palette's** (1030 North State Parkway; 312–440–5200), the arty atmosphere is strictly for looks; the menu is a friendly list of steaks, seafood, pastas, and trendy pizzas ranging from about $10 to about $30. (Sample the Gorgonzola cheesecake—wow!) And the entertainment is sophisticated and timeless, provided by veteran piano man Dave Green, who has been tickling the ivories around town for years. He's a charming, bowler-hatted guy who prompted *Chicago* magazine to name Palette's piano bar the best in town. And at this time of year, he probably doesn't have to be asked to do "Bewitched, Bothered and Bewildered" or "Witchcraft"!

FOR MORE ROMANCE

Give your sweetheart—or both of you!—a peek into your inner self with Chicago's favorite psychic, **Sonia Choquette.** Sonia's impeccable reputation among intelligent people rests on her way of exploring what she calls your "soul path." There's no "you'll meet a tall, dark stranger" here; rather, she'll focus on your hopes and dreams, obstacles and strengths. She works in hour-long consultations, in which her tools include I Ching, tarot cards, and astrology (no crystal balls, thank you!).

Sonia does only individual sessions and won't consult with a couple together, but you can get a gift certificate for a consultation. Call far ahead, since Sonia is booked months in advance; or call on the spur of the moment to see whether a cancellation will let you in sooner. Meanwhile, check out her writings in *The Psychic Pathway* and the forthcoming *Your Heart's Desire*. To book a consultation or arrange a gift certificate, call (773) 989–1151. Looking deeper isn't cheap—Sonia charges $250 for a consultation—but her legions of fans swear she's worth every penny. Judge for yourselves!

GENERAL INDEX

Ace Limousine, 225, 231
Active Endeavors (sports equipment), 19
Adagio, 205
Addis Abeba (restaurant), 248
Air & Water Show, 41
A La Carte, 187
Alcala Western Wear, 255–56
Al Khayam (restaurant), 246, 249
A Lost Era (antiques), 262
Alta Vista Terrace, 197
Ambassador West Hotel, 155–56, 158
Ambria (restaurant), 100, 102–3
American Hands, 8
Ancient Echoes (objets d'art), 18–19
Andersonville, 3–8, 10,
Andy's (jazz), 148, 237
Anna Held Flower Shop, 7
Ann Barzel Dance Collection, 156, 158
Annoyance Theater, 193
Ann Sather (restaurant), 4–5, 190
Argyle Street, 238–39
Arie Crown Theater, 65, 230, 231
Armitage Avenue, 14–23,
Army & Lou's (restaurant), 54
Art Institute of Chicago, 52, 133–36, 174,
    175–76, 233, 256
    Garden Restaurant, 135
    Restaurant on the Park, 135
    Thorne Rooms, 174, 175–76
Artists Cafe, 169
Arturo Express, 60
Arun's (restaurant), 236, 240–41
Au Bon Pain, 133
Auditorium Theater, 134, 137–38, 168–69

Baby Doll Polka Club, 26, 27–28
Barneys New York, 60
Beach Club Ltd. (custom swimwear), 250
Beau's Bistro, 64
Bed & Breakfast Chicago, Inc., 4, 14, 26, 82,
    100, 147, 164, 245
Ben & Jerry's Ice Cream Parlor, 22

Benkay's Sake Bar, 237
Berghoff (restaurant), 118
Best Western Inn of Chicago, 253–54
Best Western River North Hotel, 254
Betsey Johnson, 60
Beyond Words Cafe, 129
Biddy Mulligan's, 6
Big (bar), 37
Big Chicks, 6
Bigsby & Kruthers (menswear), 202
Big Shoulders Cafe, 23
Billy Goat Tavern, 41
Blackhawk Lodge, 166
Bloomingdale's, 45
Blue Chicago, 237
Blue Mesa (restaurant), 170
B.L.U.E.S., 149
B.L.U.E.S. Et Cetera, 149, 194
bookstores, list of, 125–26
Bop Shop, 63, 169
Bread with Appeal, 18
Breakfast Club, 159
Broadway Costume, 262–63
Bronzeville, 49–53
Brookfield Zoo, xi, 100, 103–5
    Indian Lake, 105
Brother Jimmy's BBQ, 254, 258–59
Bub City Crabshack & Bar BQ, 254
Buckingham Fountain, 82, 83, 94
Buckingham's (restaurant), 144–45
Buddy Guy's Legends (blues club), 134, 138
Bughouse Square, 124
Bulls, Chicago, 199, 203–5
Bulls, The, (jazz club), 205

Cafe Ba-Ba-Ree-Ba!, 174, 177
Cafe Iberico, 124
Cafe La Cave, 226
Cafe Pyrenees, 77–78
Cafe Selmarie, 132
Cafe Spiaggia, 70
Cafe Suisse, 39

Calo (restaurant), 6
Candlelight Dinner Playhouse, 164–65
Cape Cod Room, Drake Hotel, 58–59, 233
Caribbean American Baking Company, 247
Carlo's (restaurant), 182, 183
Carlucci (restaurant), 148, 224, 227
Carson Pirie Scott & Co., 65, 117
Celebrity Cafe, 239, 241
Champagne Flights (balloon rides), 76–77
Chanel Boutique, 61
Charles Ifergan (salon), 61
Charlie Trotter's (restaurant), 14, 15,
Charlie's Ale House, 93
Chatto (salon), 61
Checkerboard Lounge, 149
Cheli's Chili Bar, 211
Cheney House Bed and Breakfast, 110, 111
Chicago Architecture Foundation, 264
    River Cruise, 110, 120
Chicago Bears, 181, 186, 187
Chicago Bee Building, 51
Chicago Blackhawks, 207–8, 211
Chicago Botanic Garden, 81–82, 84–86, 235,
    236, 239–40
Chicago Bulls, 199, 200, 203–5
Chicago Children's Museum, 210
Chicago Convention and Visitors Bureau, xiv
Chicago Cubs, ix, 189, 190, 191
Chicago Cultural Center, 150, 233
Chicago Flower & Garden Show, 88
Chicago Ghost Tour, 266
Chicago Hilton and Towers, 144
Chicago Historical Society, 22–23, 52, 174,
    176
Chicagoland Canoe Base, 78–79
Chicago Opera Theater, 145–46
Chicago River, 75, 78, 89
Chicago Sportfishing Charter, 95–96
Chicago Sun-Times Building, 36
Chicago Supernatural Cruise, 90, 95
Chicago Symphony Orchestra, 147, 148, 152
Chicago Transit Authority (CTA), xii, xiii

the El, 129–30
  Regional Transportation Authority Information, xiv
Chicago White Sox, 198
Chicago Wolves, 207, 208, 211
Chinatown, 231, 243
City Suites (hotel), 191
Civic Opera House, 139–42
Claridge Hotel, 122
Coffee & Tea Exchange, 18
Cognac Bar, 103
Comiskey Park, 198
Como Inn, 200, 203
Continental Airport Express, xii–xiii
Convito Italiano, 76
Coq D'Or, 58
Corner Bakery, 97
Cotton Club (dancing), 156, 157
Court Theater, 26, 30, 167
Cousins (restaurant), 4, 10
Crab House, 93
cruise ships
  Odyssey, 34, 40, 90
  Spirit of Chicago, 90–91
  Windy, 93
Cubby Bear, 190, 193, 258
Cubs, Chicago, ix, 189, 190, 191
Cynthia Rowley (boutique), 16

Daley Bicentennial Plaza Ice Rink, 208, 210
Dance Connection (dance instruction), 161
David and Alfred Smart Gallery of Art, 26, 32
Davis Theater, 131
Deleece (restaurant), 196
Des Plaines River, 76
  Offshore Marine, 76, 77
Dick's Last Resort, 151
Dish (restaurant), 196
Division Street (nightclub), 38
Division Street Russian Baths, 247–48
Dixie Kitchen & Bait Shop, 26, 27
Documentary Films, 27
"Do-It-Yourself" *Messiah.*, 65
Donald E. Stephens Museum of Hummels, 226

Double Door, 151
Drake Hotel, 57–58, 144, 182
DuSable Museum of African-American History, 52–53

Eat Your Hearts Out (brunch), 169–70
Edgewater Beach Apartments, 7
Edgewater Beach Hotel, 7
Eighth Regiment Armory, 51
Eli's, the Place for Steak, 257
Emperor's Choice, 231, 243
Entre Nous (restaurant), 37
Ernest Hemingway Museum, 115
Escada USA, 61
ETA Creative Arts Foundation, 54–55
Evanston, 181–86
Everest (restaurant), 140, 142

F.A.O. Schwartz, 62
Faded Rose (furnishings), 17
Fine Arts Cinema, 71, 138
Findables (boutique), 20
Fireside Restaurant, 12
Fischer Flowers, 16
Fitzgerald's, 253, 258
Foodstuffs, 79
Four Seasons Hotel, 43–46, 48, 144
Fourth Presbyterian Church, 64, 201
Fourth World Artisans, 194
Frank Lloyd Wright, 109–14, 224
  by Bus, 112
  Home and Studio, 112
  Prairie School of Architecture National Historic District, 112–13
Friends of the Chicago River Cruise, 92
Frontera Grill, 254, 255

Geja's Cafe, 14, 20
Gethsemane Garden Center, 8–9
Gibsons Bar & Steak House, 38, 257
Ginger Man (bar, restaurant), 193
Giorgio Armani, 60
Gladys' Luncheonette, 51
Gold Coast Guest House, 82

Gold Star Sardine Bar, 174, 177
Goodman Studio, 170–71
Goodman Theater, 58, 63, 134, 137
Goose Island Brewing, 266, 267
Gordon (restaurant), 158
Graceland Cemetery and Chapel, 264
Grant Park, 33, 81, 87, 94
Grant Park Music Festival, 82–83
Great Lakes Spa Suites, 211
Green Dolphin Street (jazz club), 63–64
Green Mill Jazz Club, 130, 151
Griffin Theatre, 9, 11
Gucci, 61, 70

Harold Washington Library Center, 128–29, 149
  Beyond Words Cafe, 129
  Uncommon Ground (coffee shop), 129
  Wintergarden, 129
Hau Giang (restaurant), 238
Heaven on Seven (restaurant), 208, 209
Helmand, The, (restaurant), 190, 193–94
Henri Bendel, 46
Hermes of Paris, 60
Hino & Malee Boutique, 60, 61
Hong Min, 174, 175
Hotel Nikko Chicago, 236
Hot Tix, xii, 164, 166
Hubbard Street Dance Company, 156, 157
Huddle Sports Bar, 184
Hyde Park, xi, 25–32

Illinois Center, 34
Illinois Center Golf, 35, 39
Ilona of Hungary Skin Care, 61
Improv Olympic, 193
India House (restaurant), 246, 249
Inter-Continental Hotel, 116
Isis on Armitage (boutique), 20
Italian Cultural Center, 67–68
Italian Village (restaurant), 140, 143–44

Jackson Park, 29, 53, 81
  Wooded Island, 29, 31
Jazz Showcase, 153

Jeweler's Center at the Mallers Building, 208, 209
Jilly's (bar/restaurant), 38
Jimmy's (The Woodlawn Tap and Liquor Store), 26, 30
John Hancock Building, 117
Signature Room on the Ninety-Fifth Floor, 118
Joffrey Ballet, 156, 159
Julie Mai's Le Bistro, 4, 6

Kan Zaman (restaurant), 10–11
Kathy Osterman Beach, 5
Kitty O'Shea's (bar), 145
Kona Kai (restaurant), 251
Kopi, A Traveler's Cafe, 8
Korean Restaurant, 236, 243
Kuni's (restaurant), 240

La Bocca della Verita (restaurant), 132
La Donna Restaurant, 6
Lake Michigan, ix, x, 40, 41, 54, 75, 78, 80, 89–91
    Odyssey (cruise ship), 34, 40, 90
    Odyssey Jazz Brunch, 96–97
    Windy (cruise ship), 93
La Locanda (restaurant), 130
Landmark of Andersonville, 8
La Strada Ristorante, 233
Laura Ashley, 62
Le Bouchon (restaurant), 165–66
Light Opera Works, 146
Lillie Rubin, 46
Lincoln Park, xi, 5, 13, 14, 22, 60, 81, 84
    Grandmother Gardens, 84
Lincoln Park Boat Club, 78
Lincoln Park Conservatory, 84, 102
Lincoln Park Zoological Gardens, 22
Lincoln Park Zoo, 99–100
    Cafe Brauer, 101
    Farm in the Zoo, 100–1
    Lindas Margaritas, 65
Live Bait (theater), 193
Looks Like the Front Row, 200

Lord & Taylor, 62
Lounge Ax, 151
Lower Wacker Drive, 34, 35, 40–41
Lunar Cabaret, 127
Lutnia (restaurant), 79–80
Lyric Opera, 139–42, 144

Madrigal's Cafe, 6
Mango (restaurant), 126–27
Marc Benaim (salon), 61
Marilyn Miglin (salon), 60–61
Marina City, 95, 117
Marriott Suites, 224, 225
Marshall Field's, 62, 64–65, 116, 209
Mashed Potato Club, 150
Mathiessen State Park, 220
Matsuya (restaurant), 192, 236
Maud Travels (B&B), 164, 245
McCormick Place, xi, 65, 91, 229–32
    Chicago Room (restaurant), 229
McFetridge Sports Center, 212
McGuane Park, 69
Medici's Pan Pizza, 26, 31
Mei Shung (restaurant), 238–39
Merrick Park, 187
Merz Apothecary, 131
Metro, 150, 192–93
Metropole Lounge, 37
Metropolis (restaurant), 18
Mexican Fine Arts Center Museum, 262, 264–65
Mia Francesca (restaurant), 192
Michael Jordan, 199–204
Michael Jordan Golf, 200, 202
Michael Jordan's Restaurant, 200–1
Michigan Avenue, 34–36
Magnificent Mile, 57–62, 67
    Streeterville, 59
Michigan Avenue Bridge, 36, 93
Midway Airport, xiii
Midwest Buddhist Temple, xi, 241–42
Mitchell Tower, 32
Mizepah Bead Company, 16
Monadnock Building, 117

Montrose Harbor, ix
Monument to the Great Migration, 50
Morton Arboretum, 81, 82, 87–88
Morton's of Chicago, 257
Morton's—The Steakhouse, 224, 227
Mrs. Park's Tavern, 62
Museum of Broadcast Communications, 233
Museum of Contemporary Art, 166
Museum of Science and Industry, 26, 28, 66, 174
    Colleen Moore's Fairy Castle, 174–75
    Santa Fe Model Railway, 174
Music Box (movie theater), 190, 194

National Heritage Corridor Cruise, 97
Navy Pier, 34, 37, 39, 90, 91, 93, 207, 208, 210, 211
Navy Pier Skating Rink, 210
Neo-Futurarium (theater), 9, 11
Newberry Library, 122, 123–24, 156, 158
Nick's Fishmarket, 224, 227
Nike Town, 200, 201
900 North Michigan Cinemas, 70
Noble Horse (carriage rides), 59
Noodle Noodle, 242
North Beach Leather, 62
North Pier, 34
Northwestern University, 181
Northwestern University Wildcats, 181, 182, 184–85

Oak Park, xi, 109–15
Oak Street, 58, 60–61
O'Hare International Airport, xi, xii, 223–25
Ohashiatsu Chicago (massage), 236, 240
Oh Boy (objets d'art), 17
Okee-Chee's Wild Horse Gallery, 7
Old Town School of Folk Music, 19, 148–49
Omni Orrington, 182, 184
One Touch of Nature (gifts), 8
Orchestra Hall, 65
Orly's (restaurant), 30
Oz Park, 263
Paladino's (restaurant), 200, 204–5

Palette's, 267
Palm, The, (restaurant), 39
Palmer House Hilton, 261–62
Park Avenue Cafe, 64
Park Brompton (hotel), 190, 191
Park West (nightclub), 14, 21–22
Pepper Lounge, 190, 196
Petersen's Restaurant & Ice Cream Parlor, 114
Philander's Oak Park (restaurant), 115
Piccolo Mondo (restaurant), 28–29
Pizzeria Due, 68
Pizzeria Uno, 68
Pleasant Home Mansion, 114–15
Poor Phil's Shell Bar, 115
Pops for Champagne (wine bar), 233
Prairie Avenue Historic District, 230, 231
Primavera (restaurant), 119
Printer's Row (restaurant), 137
PS Bangkok, 192
Pump Room, 156–57

Rainbo Roller Rink, 10
Ramada Hotel O'Hare, 225
Ravinia Park, 86
Instant Ravinia, 86–87
Red Door Inn, 215, 220
Redfish (restaurant), 94–95
Red Lion Pub, 263
Red Tomato (restaurant), 195
Renaissance Buttons, 16
Reva's Place (diner), 4, 11
Reza's (restaurant), 10
Rigoletto (restaurant), 143
Ritz-Carlton Cafe, 233
Riva (restaurant), 39–40
Rizzoli Book Store, 62
Rogers Park, 6,
Rookery Building, 116–17
Room Service (gourmet delivery), 83, 123
Rosa's Blues Cruise, 152–53
Rosehill Cemetery, 4, 11–12
Rosemont, 223–28
Rosemont Convention Center, 226
Rosemont Horizon, 207, 211, 212, 224,

227–28
Rosemont/O'Hare Convention and Visitors
    Bureau, xiv
Rosemont Suite Hotel, 224
Rosemont Theater, 159, 224
Rush Street, 38
Russian Tea Time (restaurant), 137, 168

Saks Fifth Avenue, 61
Salon 1800, 18
Savoy Truffle, 122, 123
Schuba's (bar, music), 258
Schulien's Restaurant, 265
Sears Tower, 118
Seasons (restaurant), 44–45
Second City, 265 66
Shakespeare Garden, 82, 88
Shakespeare in the Park, 116
Shaw's Crab House, 37
Sheraton Chicago Hotel & Towers, 89–91
Sidney Marovitz Golf Course, 5
Skate on State, 208–9
Soldier Field, 181, 186, 187
Sole Mio (restaurant), 16
Song-Huong (restaurant), 238
Sonia Choquette (psychic), 267
South Forty (stable), 253, 254, 259
South Pier Restaurant, 96
South Shore Cultural Center, 53–54
Spiaggia (restaurant), 70
Spirit of Chicago (cruise ship), 90–91
Starbucks, 18
Starved Rock State Park, 215–21
Steppenwolf Studio, 170
St. Germain (picnic baskets), 83
Strega Nona (restaurant), 195–96
Studio 910 (boutique), 16–17
Sugar Magnolia (boutique), 60
Sulzer Regional Library, 131
Summer Sunset Cruise, 90, 94
Swedish American Museum, 6–7
Swedish Bakery, 6
Swissotel, 34–39
Syd Simons Cosmetics, 61

Tabula Tua (gifts), 17
Tania's (restaurant), 246–47
Taste of Chicago (event), 33–35, 38–39
Terra Museum of American Art, 256
theaters, list of, 167, 171
Think Small by Rosebud (dollhouses), 174, 177
Third Coast (cafe), 151
Tiffany & Co., 61
Toguri Gifts and Mercantile Co., 242
Tony 'n' Tina's Wedding, 44, 45
Tribune Tower, 36
Trio (restaurant), 183
Tucci Benucch (restaurant), 46
Turtle Creek Antiques, 16
Tuttaposto (restaurant), 246

Ultimo, 60
Uncle Tannous (restaurant), 103
Uncommon Ground, 129, 196
Union Station, xiii
United Center, 201, 203–4, 207, 211, 212
Unity Temple, 110, 113–14
University of Chicago, 25–27,
    Rockefeller Memorial Chapel, 26, 31
Urban Gardener, 17

Va Pensiero (restaurant), 185–86
Venetian Night (event), 41
Village Cafe, 156, 159
Village Theater, 23
Vinci (restaurant), 170

Wabash YMCA, 51
Walker Bros. Original Pancake House, 186
Walk of Fame, 50
Walnut Room, Marshall Field & Co., 208, 209
Washington Park, 51–52
Water Tower, 13,
Water Tower Place, 62–63
Welles Park, 131
Whiskey River, 254–55
White Sox, 198
Whole Foods Market, 78

Widow Newton's Tavern, 211
Wikstrom's (deli), 5
Wildflower Works Garden, 83
Wild Hare & Singing Armadillo Frog Sanctuary, 246, 249
Williams-Sonoma, 61–62
Willowbrook Ballroom, 156, 160

Windward Sports, 80
Wishbone (restaurant), 127
Wisteria (clothing), 194
Woman Wild (gallery), 7–8
Women & Children First (bookstore), 7,
Woodfield Mall, 225–26
Wright, Frank Lloyd, 109–14, 224

Wrigley Building, 36
Wrigley Field, 189, 190, 191–92, 197
Wrigleyville, 189–97

Yvette Wintergarden (restaurant), 142

ROMANTIC RESTAURANTS

Note: Restaurants in this book are categorized as inexpensive (less than $20 per person for appetizer, entree, and dessert), moderate ($20 to $40 per person), and expensive (more than $40 per person). One dollar sign indicates an inexpensive restaurant, two dollar signs indicate a moderate restaurant, and three means expensive. Remember: *Always* call first!

African/African-American
Addis Abeba ($), 3521 North Clark Street, 248
Army & Lou's ($), 422 East Seventy-Fifth Street, 50, 54
Gladys' Luncheonette ($), 4527 South Indiana Avenue, 50, 51

American
Blackhawk Lodge ($$), 41 East Superior Street, 123, 167
Blue Mesa ($$), 1729 North Halsted Street, 170
Brother Jimmy's BBQ ($$), 2909 North Sheffield Avenue, 254, 258–59
Cafe La Cave ($$$), 2777 Mannheim Road, Des Plaines, 226
Dixie Kitchen & Bait Shop ($$), 5225 South Harper Avenue, 26, 27
Fireside ($$), 5739 North Ravenswood Avenue, 12
Heaven on Seven ($), 111 North Wabash Avenue, 208, 209
Instant Ravinia ($), Ravinia Park, 86–87
Mashed Potato Club ($$), 3941 North Clark Street, 150
Michael Jordan's Restaurant ($$), 500 North La Salle Street, 200–1
Mrs. Park's Tavern ($$$), Doubletree Hotel and Suites, 62
Orly's ($$), 5498 South Hyde Park Boulevard, 30
Pump Room ($$$), 1301 North State Parkway, 156–57
Red Door Inn ($$), 1701 Water Street, Peru, 215, 220
Restaurant on the Park ($$), Art Institute, 135
Ritz-Carlton Cafe ($$), Ritz Hotel, 233
Riva ($$), Navy Pier, 39–40
Seasons ($$$), Four Seasons Hotel, 44–45

Signature Room on the Ninety-Fifth Floor, John Hancock Building ($$), 118
Walnut Room ($), Marshall Field's State Street store, 208, 209
Widow Newton's Tavern ($$), Navy Pier, 211

Asian
Arun's ($$$), 4156 North Kedzie Avenue, 236, 240–41
Benkay ($$$), Hotel Nikko, 237
Emperor's Choice ($), 2238 South Wentworth Avenue, 231, 243
Hau Giang ($), 1104-06 West Argyle Street, 238
Hong Min ($), 221 West Cermak Road, 174, 175
India House ($), 2548 West Devon Avenue, 246, 249
Julie Mai's Le Bistro ($$), 5025 North Clark Street, 4, 6
Kona Kai ($$$), Marriott O'Hare Hotel, Rosemont, 251
Korean Restaurant ($), 2659 West Lawrence Avenue, 236, 243
Kuni's ($), 511 Main Street, Evanston, 240
Matsuya ($), 3469 North Clark Street, 192, 236
Mei Shung ($), 5511 North Broadway Avenue, 238–39
Noodle Noodle ($), 3475 North Clark Street, 242
PS Bangkok ($$), 3345 North Clark Street, 192
Song-Huong ($), 5424 North Broadway Avenue, 238

For Breakfast
Ann Sather ($), 5207 North Clark Street, 4–5, 190
Beau's Bistro ($), 1300 North State Parkway, 64
Breakfast Club ($), 1381 West Hubbard Street, 159

Celebrity Cafe ($$), Hotel Nikko Chicago, 239, 241
Reva's Place ($), 1754 West Balmoral Avenue, 4, 11
Walker Bros. Original Pancake House ($), 153 Green Bay Road, Wilmette, 186

For Brunch
Dick's Last Resort ($), 435 East Illinois Street, 151
Medici's Pan Pizza ($), 1327 East Fifty-seventh Street, 26, 31
Odyssey Jazz Brunch ($$), off Navy Pier, 96–97
Park Avenue Cafe ($$), 199 East Walton, 64

Casual/Cafes
A La Carte ($), 111 Green Bay Road, Wilmette, 187
Artists Cafe ($), 412 South Michigan Avenue, 169
Arturo Express ($), 919 North Michigan Avenue, 60
Au Bon Pain ($), 122 South Michigan Avenue, 133
Beau's Bistro ($$), Ambassador West Hotel, 64
Beyond Words ($), Harold Washington Library, 129
Big Shoulders Cafe ($), Chicago Historical Society, 23
Billy Goat ($), 430 North Michigan Avenue, 41
Bread with Appeal ($), 1009 West Armitage Avenue, 18
Cafe Brauer ($), Lincoln Park Zoo, 101
Cafe Chicago (aka Chicago Room, $), McCormick Place, 229
Cafe Selmarie ($), 2327 West Giddings Street, 132
Cafe Suisse ($$), Swissotel, 39
Cheli's Chili Bar ($), 1137 West Madison Street, 211
Corner Bakery ($$), 516 North Clark Street, 97
Foodstuffs ($), 2106 Central Street, Evanston, 79
Garden Restaurant ($), Art Institute, 135
Goose Island Brewing ($$), 1800 North Clybourn Avenue, 266, 267
Kopi, a Traveler's Cafe ($), 5317 North Clark Street, 8
Metropolis ($), 924 West Armitage Avenue, 18
South Pier Restaurant ($), 6401 South Coast Guard Drive, 96
Starbucks ($), 1001 West Armitage Avenue, 18
St. Germain (picnics, $$), 1210 North State Parkway, 83
Third Coast ($), 29 East Delaware Place, 151
Uncommon Ground ($), Harold Washington Library Center, 1214 West Grace Street, 129, 196
Whole Foods Market ($), 1000 West North Avenue, 78
Wishbone ($$), 1800 West Grand Avenue and 1001 West Washington Street, 127

For Dessert
Ben & Jerry's Ice Cream Parlor ($), 338 West Armitage Avenue, 22

Finnigan's Ice Cream Parlor, Museum of Science and Industry, 28
Peterson's Restaurant & Ice Cream Parlor ($), 1100 Chicago Avenue, Oak Park, 114
Swedish Bakery ($), 5348 North Clark Street, 6

Eclectic
Charlie Trotter's ($$$), 816 West Armitage Avenue, 14, 15
Deleece ($$), 4004 North Southport Avenue, 196
Dish ($$), 3651 North Southport Avenue, 196
Eat Your Hearts Out! ($$), 1835 West North Avenue, 169–70
Geja's Cafe (fondue, $$), 340 West Armitage Avenue, 14, 20
Gordon ($$$), 500 North Clark Street, 158
Mango ($$), 712 North Clark Street, 126–27
Palette's ($$), 1030 North State Parkway, 267
Printer's Row ($$$), 550 South Dearborn Street, 137
Savoy Truffle ($$), 1466 North Ashland Avenue, 122, 123
Trio ($$$), 1625 Hinman Avenue, Evanston, 183
Tuttaposto ($$), 646 North Franklin Street, 246

French
Ambria ($$$), 2300 North Lincoln Park West, 100, 102–3
Cafe Pyrenees ($$), River Tree Court, Milwaukee Avenue at Rt. 60, Vernon Hills, 77–78
Carlos' ($$$), 429 Temple, Highland Park, 182, 183
Entre Nous ($$), Fairmont Hotel, 37
Everest ($$$), 440 South La Salle Street, 140, 142
Le Bouchon ($$), 1958 North Damen Avenue, 165–66
Seasons ($$$), Four Seasons Hotel, 44–45
Yvette ($$), 1206 North State Parkway, 144
Yvette Wintergarden ($$), 311 South Wacker Drive, 142

German/Middle European
Berghoff ($$), 105 West Adams Street, 118
Lutnia ($$), 5532 West Belmont Avenue, 79–80
Russian Tea Time ($$), 77 East Adams Street. 137, 168
Schulien's ($$), 2100 West Irving Park Road, 265

Italian
Adagio ($$), 923 West Weed Street, 205
Calo ($$), 5343 North Clark Street, 6
Carlucci ($$$), 2215 North Halsted Street, 6111 North River Road, Rosemont, 148, 224, 227
Como Inn ($), 546 North Milwaukee Avenue, 200, 203
Convito Italiano ($$), Plaza del Lago, 1515 Sheridan Road, Wilmette, 76

Italian Village ($$), 71 West Monroe Street, 140, 143–44

La Bocca della Verita ($$), 4618 North Lincoln Avenue, 132

La Donna ($$), 5142 North Clark Street, 6

La Locanda ($$), 745 North La Salle Drive, 130

La Strada ($$$), 151 North Michigan Avenue, 233

Mia Francesca ($$), 3311 North Clark Street, 192

Paladino's ($$), 832 West Randolph Street, 200, 204–5

Piccolo Mondo ($$), Windermere Hotel, 1642 East Fifty-sixth Street, 28–29

Primavera ($$$), Fairmont Hotel, 119

Red Tomato ($$), 3417 North Southport Avenue, 195

Rigoletto ($$), 2478 North Lincoln Avenue, 143

Sole Mio ($$), 917 West Armitage Avenue, 16

Spiaggia/Cafe Spiaggia ($$$/$$), 980 North Michigan Avenue, 70

Strega Nona ($$), 3747 North Southport Avenue, 195–96

Tucci Benucch ($$), 900 North Michigan Avenue, 46

Va Pensiero ($$$), Margarita Inn, Evanston, 182, 185–86

Vinci ($$), 1732 North Halsted Street, 170

Latin American/Spanish

Cafe Ba-Ba-Ree-Ba! ($$), 2024 North Halsted Street, 174, 177

Cafe Iberico ($$), 739 North La Salle Drive, 124

Frontera Grill ($$), 445 North Clark Street, 254, 255

Lindas Margaritas ($$), 47 West Polk Street, 65

Tania's ($$), 2659 North Milwaukee Avenue, 246–47

Middle Eastern

Al Khayam ($$), 2326 West Foster Avenue, 246, 249

Cousins ($$), 5203 North Clark Street, 4, 10

Helmand, The, ($$), 3201 North Halsted Street, 190, 193–94

Kan Zaman ($$), 5204 North Clark Street, 10–11

Reza's ($$), 5255 North Clark Street, 10

Uncle Tannous ($), 2626 North Clark Street, 103

For Pizza

Medici's Pan Pizza ($), 1327 East Fifty-seventh Street, 26, 31

Pizzeria Uno ($$), 29 East Ohio Street, 68

Pizzeria Due ($$), 619 North Wabash Avenue, 68

Seafood

Bub City Crabshack & Bar B Q ($$), 901 West Weed Street, 254

Cape Cod Room ($$$), Drake Hotel, 57–57, 233

Crab House ($$), 745 North Wells, 93

Nick's Fishmarket ($$$), 10275 West Higgins Road, Rosemont, 224, 227

Philander's Oak Park ($$), Carleton Hotel, Oak Park, 115

Poor Phil's Shell Bar ($$), 139 Madison Street, Oak Park, 115

Redfish ($$), 40 North State Street, 94–95

Shaw's Crab House ($$), 21 East Hubbard Street, 36–37

Steakhouses

Buckingham's ($$$), Chicago Hilton and Towers, 144–45

Eli's, the Place for Steak ($$$), 215 East Chicago Avenue, 257

Gibsons Bar & Steak House ($$$), 1028 North Rush Street, 38, 257

Morton's of Chicago ($$$), 1050 North State Street, 257

Morton's—The Steakhouse ($$$), 9525 West Bryn Mawr Avenue, Rosemont, 224, 227

Palm, The, ($$$), Swissotel, 39

ROMANTIC LODGINGS

Note: Bed & Breakfast Chicago handles bookings for many B&B homes listed here. The company's policy is to give guests the B&B's address only after a reservation is made. We've therefore listed B&B Chicago properties by neighborhood but without addresses.

Inexpensive
Bed & Breakfast Chicago: 4, 14, 26, 82, 100, 147, 164, 245
 Edgewater, 4
 Gold Coast Guest House, 82
 Hyde Park, 26
 Lincoln Park, 14, 100
 Maud Travels (Wicker Park/Bucktown), 164, 245
 Old Town, 147
Cheney House Bed and Breakfast, 520 North East Avenue, Oak Park, 110, 111

Moderate
Best Western Inn of Chicago, 162 East Ohio Street, 253–54
Best Western River North, 125 West Ohio Street, 254
City Suites, 933 West Belmont Avenue, 191
Claridge Hotel, 1244 North Dearborn Street, 122
Inter-Continental Hotel, 505 North Michigan Avenue, 116

Marriott Suites, 6155 North River Road, Rosemont, 224, 225
Omni Orrington, 1710 Orrington Avenue, Evanston, 182, 184
Park Brompton, 528 West Brompton Place, 190, 191
Ramada Hotel O'Hare, 6600 North Mannheim Road, Rosemont, 225
Rosemont Suite Hotel, 5500 North River Road, Rosemont, 224

Indulgent
Chicago Hilton and Towers, 720 South Michigan Avenue, 144
Drake Hotel, 140 East Walton Street, 57–58, 144, 182
Four Seasons Hotel, 120 East Delaware Place, 43–46, 48, 144
Hotel Nikko Chicago, 320 North Dearborn Street, 236
Palmer House Hilton, 17 South State Street, 261–62
Sheraton Chicago Hotel & Towers, 301 East North Water Street, 89–91
Swissotel, 323 East Wacker Drive, 34–39

NIGHTLIFE

Dancing
Baby Doll Polka Club, 26, 27–28, 160
Cotton Club, 156, 157
Pump Room, 156–57
Tania's, 160, 246–47
Village Cafe, 156, 159
Whiskey River, 254–55
Wild Hare & Singing Armadillo Frog Sanctuary, 246, 249
Willowbrook Ballroom, 156, 160

Dance Performance
Chicago Dance Coalition (performance hotline), 155
Hubbard Street Dance Company, 156, 157
Joffrey Ballet, 156, 159

Classical Music, Opera
Chicago Opera Theater, 145–46
Chicago Symphony Orchestra, 147, 148, 152
Do-It-Yourself *Messiah* 65
Grant Park Music Festival, 82–83
Light Opera Works, 146
Lyric Opera, 139–42, 144
Ravinia Park, 86

Jazz and Blues Clubs
Andy's (jazz), 148, 237
Biddy Mulligan's (blues), 6
Blue Chicago (blues), 237
B.L.U.E.S., 149
B.L.U.E.S. Et Cetera, 149, 194
Bop Shop (jazz), 63, 169

Buddy Guy's Legends (blues), 134, 138
Bulls, The, (jazz), 205
Checkerboard Lounge (blues), 149
Green Dolphin Street (jazz), 63–64
Green Mill Jazz Club, 130, 151
Jazz Showcase, 153
Lunar Cabaret (jazz, eclectic), 127
Rosa's (blues), 152–53

Venues for Other Popular Music
Cubby Bear (rock, pop, eclectic), 190, 193, 258
Double Door (rock, eclectic), 150–51
Fitzgerald's (country, rock), 253, 258
Lounge Ax, 151
Metro (rock), 150, 192–93

Old Town School of Folk Music (folk, eclectic), 19, 148–49
Park West (rock, pop, eclectic), 14, 21–22
Schubas (country, rock), 258
Wild Hare & Singing Armadillo Frog Sanctuary (reggae), 246, 249

Theater
Annoyance Theater, 193
Arie Crown Theater, 65, 230, 231
Auditorium Theater, 134, 137–38, 168–68
Candlelight Dinner Playhouse, 164–65
Court Theater, 26, 30, 167
ETA Creative Arts Foundation, 54–55
Goodman Studio, 170–71
Goodman Theater, 58, 63, 134, 137
Griffin Theater, 9, 11
Live Bait, 193
Neo-Futurarium, 9, 11
Shakespeare in the Park, 115
Steppenwolf/Steppenwolf Studio, 170
Tony 'n' Tina's Wedding, 70–71

Comedy Clubs
Improv Olympic, 193
Second City, 265–66

Movie Theaters
Davis Theater, 131
Documentary Films, 27
Fine Arts Cinema, 71, 138
Music Box Theater, 190, 194
900 North Michigan Cinemas, 45
Village Theater, 23

Cocktail Lounges and Bars
Benkay's Sake Bar, 237
Big, 37
Big Chicks, 6
Charlie's Ale House, 93
Ginger Man, 193
Huddle Sports Bar, 184
Jilly's, 38
Jimmy's (Woodlawn Tap and Liquor Store), 26, 30

Kitty O'Sheas, 145
Pepper Lounge, 190, 196
Pops for Champagne, 233
Red Lion Pub, 263
Whiskey River, 160

Cabaret and Piano Bars
Cognac Bar (Toulouse on the Park), 103
Coq d'Or (piano bar), 58, 59
Gold Star Sardine Bar, 177
Metropole Lounge, 37
Palette's, 267

Evening Cruises
Chicago Supernatural Cruise, 90, 95
Rosa's Blues Cruise, 152, 153
Spirit of Chicago, 90–92
Summer Sunset Cruise, 90, 94

ABOUT THE AUTHOR

Susan Figliulo is a lifelong Chicagoan whose flirtations with Paris and other European cities have only deepened her love for her hometown. A former copy editor at the *Chicago Sun-Times,* she compiled the newspaper's entertainment listings for two years, creating the "Singles" category, and has written extensively for its entertainment, fashion, food, travel, and general features sections. She is the author of three books, including a revised edition of *Chicago in Your Pocket* (Barrons), and a columnist whose pieces are distributed worldwide by the *Los Angeles Times* Syndicate. She lives near Chicago's lakefront in a charmingly dilapidated Victorian house with her family.